Noah's Ark

BARBARA TRAPIDO

BLOOMSBURY

First published in 1984 by Victor Gollancz
This paperback edition published 2007

Copyright © 1984 by Barbara Trapido
Introduction copyright © 2007 Helen Dunmore

The moral right of the author has been asserted

Bloomsbury Publishing Plc, 36 Soho Square, London W1D 3QY

A CIP catalogue record for this book is available from the British Library

ISBN 978 0 7475 9122 1

10 9 8 7 6 5 4 3 2 1

Typeset by Hewer Text UK Ltd, Edinburgh
Printed in Great Britain by Clays Ltd, St Ives plc

Bloomsbury Publishing, London, New York and Berlin

All papers used by Bloomsbury Publishing are natural, recyclable products
made from wood grown in well-managed forests. The manufacturing
processes conform to the environmental regulations of the country of origin

www.bloomsbury.com/barbaratrapido

This novel was completed with the assistance of a bursary awarded by the Southern Arts Association.

INTRODUCTION

Helen Dunmore

W HEN THE FIRST NOAH made his ark and failed to invite the neighbours in, he turned a practical ear to the voice of God. Only so many could come on board before the overloaded ark sank to the bottom of the sea, leaving no survivors at all. Barbara Trapido's brilliantly effervescent play on the Noah story conceals a profound, realistic understanding of human affairs. The whole world has never been gathered into security, and it never will be.

Trapido's Noah, Noah Glazer, arrives in Alison Bobrow's life like a knight in a fairy tale. His first act is to yank her back from the path of a speeding car, thus saving her life. The reason for Alison's near-accident will be immediately and painfully familiar to many mothers. She is in a state of caring frenzy, so frayed by a last-minute search for the right size of gym shorts and the correct name tapes that she almost orphans the child who is to wear the kit. It soon becomes clear that Alison's marriage to petty, spiteful, faux-Marxist Mervyn Bobrow has established her in a pattern of servitude which verges on the masochistic. Even for the sake of her daughter Camilla, whom she cherishes and Mervyn abuses, she can't throw her husband out. When he finally chooses to go, he leaves behind a legacy of parasitic neighbours. Mervyn, full of political righteousness and very much in favour of communal living on his wife's behalf, has encouraged these neighbours to dump both their problems and their children on Alison. Noah Glazer diagnoses the situation with immediate, brutal clarity. These neighbours must be abandoned to sink or to swim on their own account, if Alison is to survive. Just as instantly, he falls in love with her. Alison tries to warn Noah off – it's her Quakerish demeanour that makes men feel they must fall in love with her before they can sleep with her – but Noah is not to be deterred. Working 'highly competent erogenous magic upon the female folds of her groin', Noah is soon asking her about contraception in the same breath as he enquires, 'Which way now to the Friends' Meeting House?'

This combination of verbal by-play and physical directness is typical of their relationship, and of Trapido's writing. Wit is part of the pleasure of sex, rather than a way of distancing mind from body. Noah teases Alison for her 'tremulous quim introspection' while assuring her that she fucks 'like the emperor's whore'. Alison is too intelligent not to wonder at the sexual pleasure she gets from acquiescing to Noah like 'the conniving handmaid in her own subjection', but also too intelligent to throw away the best sex she has ever had.

Trapido makes Noah's force, charm, professionalism and directness immensely appealing, but it's not an uncritical view. Noah's character is comically exaggerated in his fierce, practical, strong-minded little daughter Hattie, who is 'not gorged on guilt' and 'spread the belief throughout the junior school that the vicar kept a half-jack of whisky in the folds of his cassock'. Noah himself can be 'offensively managerial' and even ruthless when he considers that ruthlessness is called for, but his ark will never founder. Noah's attitude to personal responsibility underlines one of the novel's key questions: where do we draw the line between those people and things for which we are responsible, and those for which we are not? Noah, a specialist in respiratory medicine, is an obvious, hands-on improver of this world, with no pretensions and an aversion to ideology.

Alison's views are less clear-cut. Her upbringing in apartheid South Africa and her cruel marriage to Mervyn Bobrow have left her deeply sceptical about institutions. Her generosity is always personal and her concern directed towards individuals, but she still harbours the guilts and uncertainties that made her prey to Mervyn Bobrow's certainties. Bobrow, meanwhile, espouses ideologies for their convenience as well as for the flattering reflections they cast on his own conduct.

As the action of the novel moves to South Africa, Trapido draws a sharper profile of a political activist in Thomas Adderley, Alison's first love. Thomas is a mixed-race South African, an instinctive nonconformist who becomes an inspirational playwright, using his wit, charisma and deep, weary knowledge of the system to undermine apartheid. The characterisation here is laced with wonderfully typical Trapido ambiguities. We see Thomas through a public lens, and simultaneously feel him as Alison's muddled, enchanting, frustrating first love, who remains as emotionally baffling as ever. As another of his lovers observes: 'For all his size and loveliness, he is not altogether corporeal, if you know what I mean. Thomas is too good for this life. Too good and not good enough.'

Barbara Trapido's writing is so sparklingly clear and witty that it can be a shock to realise how strong an undertow runs beneath the surface. There is real cruelty and vice in this novel. Mervyn Bobrow's sadistic abuse of his daughter Camilla is as shocking as Alison's inability to protect her child. A girl who wets the bed until the age of eleven becomes a beautiful but insecure woman, ripe for the same disasters in love as those which beset her mother. The old are just as vulnerable as the young. Alison's former neighbour Margaret is manoeuvred out of her house and into an old people's home, after 'the bloody neighbours' smell smoke from a potful of singed ox-heart, and summon the fire brigade. Her dogs are sent to a dogs' home, her possessions consigned to a house-clearing agency. 'In the old people's home, Margaret sat in the day room like a hollow-eyed boarding-school girl waiting for the dawn of an exeat weekend.'

Trapido makes no bones about harms done, and the further harms which may proliferate from them. The South African regime and the lives it wrecks and shames are described with bitter, furious intimacy. The water is rising, and no vessel can be big enough for everyone. For all her wit, funniness and charm, Trapido makes sure that we see the outstretched hands of the drowning, and hear their cries as the ark sails away without them.

For Anna Trapido

O N E

A LI GLAZER WAS STITCHING up her husband's trouser hems, but had paused to glance up at the kitchen pinboard in some fascination. The photograph of a man, bearing a disconcerting resemblance to Thomas Adderley, had been torn from a Sunday magazine advertisement and pinned there by Ali's older daughter Camilla. The girl herself had had no awareness of that resemblance which now so forcibly struck her mother and had fixed the picture there merely because she liked the man's collarless Edwardian shirt. The man – in keeping with the clichés of capitalist realism – was manoeuvring a white stallion through a dappled glade of redwood trees and was advertising cigarettes. Ali noticed that Camilla had fixed him rather high on the pinboard where he beamed out, as from a higher plane, above the two postcards pinned side by side below him. This hierarchical arrangement struck her as altogether suitable given that she had always elevated and revered Thomas, while the postcards had come from people to whom she felt predominantly antipathetic. They had come from the Bobrows and from William Lister. The first, from the Bobrows, had been there only five days and read as follows:

Mervyn and Eva Bobrow will be
At Home
on Thursday, May 9th for
Impromptu Drinks.
6.00–8.30 p.m.   RSVP

Ali had pinned it there in a spirit of gleeful irony, the more to relish the Bobrows' talent for premeditated spontaneity.

William Lister's card, on the other hand, had been there for almost two years. It got buried from time to time under gas bills and children's party invitations, but Ali's husband Noah had exposed it at that moment in the process of unpinning his statement from American Express. Noah had campaigned consistently for it to remain there because, he said, it reminded him that William Lister was not likely to come by again for quite some time. After William's last uninvited stay in the Glazers' house it had been Noah, and not Ali, who had firmly directed him to the letting agency and told him to find himself a bedsitting room. Ali had merely cringed with embarrassment during the confrontation, but she knew that as a person with no proper walls, she needed Noah to build fences for her. He was good at heaving out unwanted guests. He had not been trained, as she had been, in that salivating, female eagerness to please.

William's postcard had been written during the course of this last visit and had been left for the Glazers on the kitchen table. It said, in William's careful, microscopic handwriting, 'I think you owe me two streaky rashers.' One of poor William's more irritating habits, Ali considered, was the way in which he had always stowed his own rations in the fridge in order that he might lodge high-minded complaints if any of these got eaten in error by anyone else. But moral one-upmanship had always been William's special area of study. He was a single-minded political animal, dedicated to what he called 'The Struggle' or, more alarmingly, 'The Armed Struggle' and even his postcards were inclined to carry gratuitous political overtones. The card on the pinboard depicted a group of grey-trousered young men clustered round a machine gun and was captioned: *North Korean Working People Express Solidarity after the Fatherland Liberation War*. Noah unpinned the card and glanced wryly at the picture. He had always regarded William Lister as belonging to that

2

category of pretentious down-and-out which appended itself with so sure an instinct to his tender-hearted wife. As such, William was fair game for his gently uncharitable ironies. He wondered why he had never before noticed that the Korean Working People were all wearing wrist watches, and it caused him to glance mechanically at his own watch.

'Long live the solidarity of Working People everywhere,' he said pointedly, handing the card to his wife. 'Speaking of Working People, Al, would you get to work please and stitch up my pants? I ought to shift my ass.'

Ali had meanwhile been staring assiduously at the photograph of Thomas Adderley's double. She had neither seen nor heard from Thomas for twenty years, yet the photograph brought home to her all the force of those heroic, Bohemian looks; those looks which, for all they had caused her to fall so dramatically in love with Thomas at the unsuitable age of sixteen, had at the same time inspired such awe that they had got in the way of contact. As a result, she and Thomas had spent their three years at the university bound in a delicate friendship of true minds. They had sat side by side in lectures. They had read poetry together and had discussed the concept of evil in the plays of Bertolt Brecht. Two precocious and idealistic adolescents, trailing ribbons of merit from the sixth forms of their respective single-sex high schools. As to their induction into that gross and glorious sweating act, which had loomed at the time always so huge and imminent, they had each of them unhappily turned elsewhere. Twenty years on, and three marriages later, this still sometimes occurred to Ali as a wasteful and unnecessary misdirection of destiny. But standing squarely before her was dear Noah, addressing her with some urgency to the matter of his trouser hems.

'Al,' he said, 'move it will you? I have a schedule.'

'I will,' she said. 'Don't worry. But what are you doing with that card, Noah? How do you suppose he came to have such a card to hand, poor William? Does he keep a miscellany of

3

political uplift constantly about his person? In one of the pockets of his capacious rucksack perhaps?'

'Search me,' Noah said. 'Make me some coffee would you, while I take a quick shower?'

'All right,' she said. 'But can you please tell me something else, now, Noah. What am I going to do about the Bobrows' "Impromptu Drink"? You'll still be in America, you lucky man. Why do you think they go on asking us when we almost never accept? But think up some lovely excuses for me.' Mervyn Bobrow was the second of Ali's two ex-husbands. She had been divorced from him for over ten years, but he and his second wife Eva were the two people whom, above all others, she still loved best to hate. Even Noah was ready to admit that they were excellent material. He kissed her benignly on the forehead, amused as always by the extent to which other people could menace Ali. It was because she had always allowed people to approach her too closely, he thought. She had no distancing techniques. Noah had never got himself into such situations of one-sided exploitation. He had in turn been deeply in love with each of his two successive wives. First with Shirley and then much later with Ali, but one's woman was altogether different. One was bound by loyalty and contractual commitment; one gave a lot and one demanded a whole lot in return. As an emotional investment a marriage was rational. Shirley, to his bitter disappointment, had turned out to be not at all strong on loyalty. She had been rather stronger on novelty. The apparatus of sexual intrigue had appeared to her as the spice of life, where for Noah it had merely appeared as bad form; an unacceptable housemaid's tangle which was damaging to personal dignity. It gave him considerable satisfaction to know that Ali was monogamous; that Ali was constant. She was also more obliging about tailoring alterations. Noah's air of brisk productive competence was being lent force that morning by the fact that he had an aeroplane to catch.

'No problem,' he said. 'You tell the Bobrows no. There is no reason why you should have your time wasted by these people while I'm away. As to William –' He paused to patronise her

4

tenderly in the hour of his leave-taking. 'If William were to show up here tomorrow wanting food and shelter,' he said, 'what would you do, huh? Are you still the softest touch in town, or have I reformed you just a little?'

Ali smiled. 'I'd tell him, "Sorry, I've got to ask my husband." That's always a great turn-off with radical types. But "streaky rashers", for God's sake! What kind of creep would quibble about streaky rashers after dossing in a person's house for weeks on end? I don't understand it. And how was I to know they were *his* when they were in my fridge? He always tried to make a point of being no trouble, poor William. Like cooking up his own disgusting, economical food in my kitchen. He would not deign to share the succulent roast. No! He had needs to hover in wait for the bone – to make soup as he said. And two hours later there was the bone, left to boil dry and burned black on the cooker.'

'He's redressing the balance,' Noah said dispassionately. 'He works unpaid for higher causes. We have bedrooms to spare. QED. Forget it, baby. Life is full of jerks. Just don't let him in.'

'Curry powder in his scrambled eggs each morning,' Ali said. 'That's not easy to forget. Oh God, Noah, throw that card away. It's an obscenity.' But Noah moved to replace it on the notice-board where Ali observed him unwittingly fixing a pin through Thomas Adderley's left ankle. It made her wince.

'Sweetheart, I want it right there,' he said firmly. 'So next time William shows, you'll maybe remember what an asshole he is. You'll maybe remember to go easy on compassion.'

'He saves used matches,' Ali said morbidly. 'It's supposed to make one feel extravagant. He won't come again, don't worry, Noah. He's scared of you, I reckon.'

'Good,' Noah said. 'For a person in the vanguard of revolution he scares easy. Make that coffee Al, while I get cleaned up. And for Chrissake, *stitch up my pants!*'

Alone in the kitchen, Ali made coffee, applying to the task a habitual vagueness; not counting tablespoons and using too large a pot. During the operation she paused again to glance up at the photograph on the pinboard. It was heartwarming but also disconcerting to her to find this impertinent lookalike staring down incongruously into her comfortable English kitchen when Thomas himself had belonged so firmly to her history and to quite another age and clime. And yet it was not altogether surprising. Thomas had always been elusive and unpredictable. He had been much given to appearing suddenly round corners, seeming to shake sparks of light from his springy, dark hair. One would not have been surprised to have found his head, like the head of Mr Apollinax, rolling under a chair, or grinning over a screen. Noah, by contrast, had nothing of the Cheshire Cat about him. He was never to be encountered without his body, so to speak. It had always been clear to Ali that Noah was all solidity and weight; that where Thomas had represented light, Noah represented weight. Noah was always laudably credible, where Thomas had been all fire and ice. Noah had always brought to bear upon her, not only the weight of his thirteen-odd stone, but the weight of his natural authority and of his million-dollar medical research grants from the US government.

Ali placed the coffee pot on the table together with two mugs and settled down promptly to turn up Noah's trouser hems. Her old needlepoint workbox stood beside her on the floor, shredded before Noah's time into dereliction by a long-dead favourite cat. There had been no cats in Noah's time since he saw no need for domestic pets and, besides, the hair gave him asthma. To be without a cat was no serious deprivation for her these days since she had Noah and the children. It was only that her younger daughter Hattie wanted a kitten so badly as children sometimes did and would never take no for an answer. Of the three children, Hattie seemed to Ali the only one of determined and clear intent, like Noah. Ali was already dressed, having been into town that morning early to shop on Noah's behalf. She had bought him, as instructed, a new linen jacket and two pairs of Marks and Spencer linen trousers in size thirty-eight because size thirty-six didn't fit him any more. Ali had not known her husband as a young man but she knew from a few old photographs that he had never been a sylph-like male, even in youth. He had never been one who could have draped himself elegantly alongside a mantelpiece and looked passably like Shelley. Noah was too busy to do his own shopping and hated to shop in England anyway, because he was American. Shopping, along with loyalty and tailoring alterations, was a service he required from Ali.

There was a seductive shaft of spring sunlight which fell, not from Thomas Adderley's sunlit, redwood glade, but from the window whence it fell upon the bowl of oranges on Ali's kitchen table, stippled by shadows from the bay tree and from the buds of Noah's climbing plants beyond the casement. The oranges were very orange, she thought. Much too orange, really, even for oranges. In the place where she had grown up, oranges hadn't come that orange. They had usually been greenish yellow. She had once told this to her son Daniel, but he hadn't believed her 'They must have been lemons,' he said, with his powerful four-year-old certainties.

Ali's son had foreign parents – as Ali had had before him, so she understood. She could remember from her own childhood the oddity of looking out from a subtropical veranda on to flamboyant bougainvillaea and listening to her mother's tales of the wine cellar at *Lindenstrasse vier und achtzig* and of the laundry in the loft gone stiff in the night with frost. 'White sheets standing like ghosts,' her mother had used to say. But Ali hadn't known what cellars and lofts were, because all the houses she had ever seen had been single-storeyed and built on shallow eighteen-inch stilts to keep the termites from gnawing at the floorboards. And there was the Berlin Zoo, her mother would say, where the ice bear had paced at the railings and where Ali's uncle, Karl Heinrich, had once got his head stuck as a child. 'And muffs,' Ali's mother had said with feeling, remembering nights at the Berlin Opera House, '*Ach Gott*, I had countless muffs. *Aber* countless muffs!' Ali's mother had watched *Götterdämmerung* once in a box at the Opera House in buttoned boots and a muff. Like in Tolstoy. How life had uprooted them all, leaving one generation after another sighing always for that land where lemon trees flowered and golden oranges shone out in the dark. Having Thomas's photograph on the wall had suddenly made Ali feel like an exile.

'Oranges aren't ever not orange, Mummy,' Daniel had said reproachfully, on the occasion of this conversation.

'Yes, they are,' Ali had said, laughing, patting the backs of his inviting solid little legs. 'They get sprayed with chemicals to make them so orange.'

'They don't,' Daniel had said.

'They do,' she said, 'ask Noah.' The children loved her more, but Noah was the one they believed, because he had the resources of science to back his utterance. Instead of running for the encyclopaedia when somebody asked a question relating to tear ducts or the ozone layer, Ali would say to ask Noah. This was a great convenience she found, but odd since answering her little ones' questions was precisely the role for which she had been reared.

'You *gels*,' her headmistress had been wont to say, in order to egg her pupils on to greater application, 'You *gels* are the mothers of the future.' That's what it had all been for. All that knowledge which one had assimilated with such enthusiasm and skill. It had been for somebody else. Never for oneself. Noah, in his admittedly patriarchal way, was the only person who had ever made her feel that she could use it in her own interest. Anyway, children never asked questions in the tradition of girls' high schools. They always asked you what was a laser and which whale had the most teeth and why did smoking give you lung disease. Only occasionally a question or two requiring a little speculation. Like whether or not God had servants or was he a black man or a white man. Never, was he a man? Of course he was a man! All that rash and bold enterprise required in creating the universe; it had to be male. Daniel, if questioned, would have been quite as clear about it as he was resolute about *Lassie* on the television. Lassie was a boy dog, Daniel said, while Hattie crowed and jeered. He *was* a boy. He *was*. By the time children were at all interested in the things one knew about – like Dadaism for instance – they no longer wanted one's opinion on anything. Take Camilla. Beautiful grown-up Camilla, with Mervyn Bobrow's crazy yellow eyes. Whenever she thought about Camilla, Ali's heart beat faster with an entrenched habit of maternal anxiety.

All the while her fingers worked at the trouser hems. Ali was a practised needlewoman and Noah was pressed for time. He had, as he had said, to 'shift his ass'. Ali had always cherished this particular expression as her husband's most forceful idiomatic peculiarity.

The oranges on Ali's kitchen table were in a high glazed white china fruit bowl, latticed like basket weave. She had bought the bowl once in an auction sale and loved it dearly, as she loved a lot of the old things she had painstakingly accumulated about her in twenty years of keeping house. 'Spinster's junk,' Noah had called it some ten years before on the day he had first taken her to bed. Some of it had promptly given him asthma. All the old pillows, the dried flowers harbouring house-dust mites, and the old embroideries. Noah had steadily cut the clutter down to size. Some of the stuff had outlasted Ali's previous two husbands and he meant to make damn sure it didn't outlast him too. But he had no objection to the fruit bowl. He had called it a 'beautiful piece' when they met. 'You have some beautiful pieces,' he had said to her. The phrase had embarrassed her slightly, as some of his phrases still did. A whiff of alien cliché.

'Oh that,' she had said. 'Yes, well, I only like it I suppose, because I wasn't ever allowed to like anything that was got up to look like something else when I was a child. I wasn't allowed to like plastic tablecloths that were made to look like lace, you see, or salt cellars that looked like tortoises – not unless they were

Benvenuto Cellini of course. I grew up in a dictatorship of tasteful Bauhaus prudery –'

'You're an artist,' Noah had said promptly, who had never heard of Benvenuto Cellini and had not much idea of what Bauhaus prudery meant, but he could see that she hung her curtains from brass rings on broom handles and kept calligrapher's pens in a marmalade jar.

'I'm just a person who likes pressed flowers and old lace,' she had said, fearing that she had sounded pretentious. And then, though she had hardly known him, but had observed that his shoulders were reassuringly wide, she had suddenly told him how much she had loved the Zulu housemaid's cottage jampot as a child and had often begged her mother to buy one the same. A multi-coloured cube it was, with china roses climbing in a bas-relief around the front door and the lid made into a thatched roof and the knob on top made into a chimney. She had naturally had no foreknowledge then that Noah was soon to become the roof and cornerstone. Nor that he would bestir himself to grow flowering plants to clamber over the portals. Thanks to Noah, the jampot house had become all hers. She had not known this as a child when her mother had so adamantly refused to buy her one. Ali's mother wouldn't have been seen dead with such a tasteless hybrid in her house full of streamlined birchwood and steel. Her own father had been a Bauhaus architect, and she had always had standards to protect. Ali's mother had once sat on the knee of Walter Gropius as a small child, and had also once – this much, much more exciting – shaken the hand of Roald Amundsen on a boat in the North Sea. He was a nice old man, Ali's mother had said, but Ali knew he was really a wicked hun explorer who had beaten our own dear Captain Scott to the South Pole by the unscrupulous and un-English use of dogs. The history teacher had said so with all the zeal of an Englishwoman abroad.

Noah used animals occasionally in medical experiments, so the sacrifice of huskies was a smaller thing to him. So did his friend and protégé Arnie Weinberg. Charming Arnie who turned up to supper some Friday nights if his nocturnal experiments in the lab got truncated by an animal's death. He would stride amiably into the Glazers' kitchen spreading general joy and using code to disguise his doings from Ali's children. 'Croak,' he would say shamelessly, to denote the unredeemable condition of his research subject. And he would kiss Ali's cheek and lay his murderer's hands all over her two younger children, who would climb upon him in delight, plait ribbons into his hair and borrow his glasses. Arnie was wonderfully attractive to Ali's children, being that much younger than their father and gratifyingly willing always to collapse on all fours, or to charge to the topmost rung of the climbing frame yelling, 'Man the controls, you idiots! We're approaching the target area!' Arnie came from Connecticut. But he would occasionally treat the children to Woody Guthrie infant songs while plucking at Hattie's guitar. Their favourite was a song about skipping down to the pretzel man even though neither of them really knew what pretzels were. It was enough that Arnie sang about them. Arnie was thirty-nine like Ali but he seemed to her so much younger, being unattached and childless. He was also refreshingly unmedical in his style. He had recently had one of his ears pierced by a ward sister who was sweet on him and who had done it using a hypodermic needle and wearing sterile gloves. She had left Arnie complaining loudly in a chair with the syringe hanging in his lobe while she had removed her own left sleeper and placed it in the steriliser with tongs.

Arnie's pierced ear had caused Noah much wasted time of late, since he had been required to spend an afternoon assuring an appointments committee that a man with a pierced ear could, nonetheless, be the most able man for a job. Loyal Noah, legitimacy shining, somehow, out of his every utterance, grumbled afterwards to his wife that Arnie Weinberg could have waited to pierce his goddam ear until after the goddam committee had met, couldn't he? But perhaps it was in the nature of protégés to let one down just a little?

II

Noah splashed shaving soap off his jaw and pulled on a large towelling bathrobe before returning to his wife in the kitchen.

'Noah,' Ali said, biting off thread, 'shall I have my ears pierced while you're away?'

'Oh, Jesus Christ!' Noah said. He liked Ali the way she was. Tall, thin and unadorned. Her white body; her white un-painted face; the blue eyes fringed with pale gingery lashes. It had come initially as a great surprise to him to find himself so strongly attracted to her, but since that first departure from type he had never wavered. He liked her long bony feet and her cracked untended fingernails, which had smelled slightly of turps ever since he had sent her to the art school. It provoked in him an excess of tenderness to watch her bundle up her pale red hair, already now streaked with grey, and fix it with a single giant kirby grip. He dearly loved her long white neck.

'The point is, I could be finished with those nasty little gold stud things within days,' she said. 'Then I could wear luscious pendant rubies in my ears for you – that is, if you could brook the expense, of course.'

'Al,' Noah said firmly, 'ear piercing is mutilation, for Chris-sake. It has to do with the status of women as chattels. It mutilates not only the body. It mutilates the female character.' Ali thought only how splendidly patriarchal men could be in defence of one's female rights.

'Rubbish, Noah,' she said. 'What you mean is you think it's common. What you mean is you like classy-looking, dowdy, goy women, like me.'

'Not *like* you,' Noah said. 'You. I like *you*, Al.'

'What you mean is you think pierced ears are for low-status ethnic minorities – and for the lower class,' Ali said, 'and not for upmarket, Quakerish women like me. You're out of date, Noah.'

Noah laughed complacently. 'Oh my. Is that what I mean?'

'Arnie has a pierced ear,' Ali said. 'He isn't a mutilated female.'

'I'm not married to him,' Noah said. 'Leave your ears alone, Al.'

'You mean Arnie can do as he likes because he's a man,' she said.

'Because he's not married,' Noah said. 'He can do what he likes because he's not married.' Noah's standards with regard to mutual conduct in marriage had always been uncompromisingly high. He blamed this tiresome ear business not only on Arnie but on his twenty-year-old stepdaughter, Camilla. When Noah had met Ali, Camilla had been an extremely worried eleven-year-old with nervous tics, who peed in her bed and showed all the signs of her parents' terminal marriage. Now, deliciously full of *joie de vivre*, she had hennaed her hair, pierced her ears and won an open scholarship to Cambridge. All that appeared to remain of her former insecurity was an aura of helplessness, which caused male undergraduates to capitulate to her in large numbers.

Noah had always been terribly good for Camilla and Camilla was devoted to him, though she was given to complaining good-naturedly of late that he lectured her too much, which was true. He did. Lecturing was a form of communication, which sat well on him. He accused her most latterly of promiscuity and lectured her on venereal diseases. He reminded her pressingly that while her oral contraceptive pills would protect her from conception, they would not protect her from VD.

'Abstinence is a more dependable strategy,' Noah said. 'Or restraint. Try restraint, Camilla.' But it only made her smile.

'There's a kind of VD you can't cure,' Noah said. 'You must know that.'

'Of course,' she said. Then she asked him to renew the licence on her motorcycle.

'You've overspent on your allowance,' Noah said, doing his fatherly act which had always been so deeply gratifying to them both. To Noah because she had replaced the children he had long before left behind when he divorced his first wife, and to

Camilla because her own father had never learned to handle the role.

'That's right,' Camilla said and she waited brazenly for him to pull out his cheque book and sign. Recently Camilla had led him by the arm into a claustrophobic boutique to buy her a birthday present. She had chosen two pairs of silver earrings. One pair of sparkling three-inch drop earrings and another pair of small floral clusters. Now she wore both drop earrings in her right ear and one of the clusters in her left.

'The fashion is clearly against symmetry,' Noah said. He smiled at her because she was so much like Ali under the plumage and paint, and because she wore such absurd secondhand clothes, with padded shoulders, which reminded him of women on the subway during the last war.

'What do you plan to do with the fourth earring?' he asked her. 'You mean to save it till you pierce one of your nipples?'

'I'll give it to my boyfriend,' Camilla said. Noah's instinct was not to care too much for personal adornment in men since he himself had no feeling for it. He was the kind of man who, having been coaxed out of turn-ups just in time for the fashion to revert, could not be coaxed back again.

'Mummy wants to pierce her ears, too, you know,' Camilla said.

'Over my dead body,' Noah said. 'I will not allow it.'

Ali now poured coffee.

'What about Camilla then?' she said. 'Camilla looks gorgeous with her pierced ears.'

'Camilla looks like she ought to be selling violets in Drury Lane,' Noah said. 'Or telling fortunes. Gorgeous she may be. I don't deny it.'

'How about your secretary then?' Ali said, because Noah's research unit boasted a dark-eyed Cypriot typist, who wore silver filigree earrings halfway to her shoulders, and whose looks Ali greatly admired. All that wonderful gloss in the hospital canteen was a great antidote to disease and pestilence, she thought.

'Al,' Noah said, 'what the hell is this that I am drinking? Gravy mix?'

'Sorry,' she said. It had crossed her mind suddenly that she would like to paint the vulgar, bright oranges there in the precarious fluctuating sunlight, in their funny bowl. Oil paint simulating china, simulating basket weave. And then the view from the window beyond the kitchen was so inviting, with Noah's tangled climbers all beginning to bud and the field, beyond the out-houses, with cows. The cows so black and white that they stood on the green field as though appliquéd upon an emerald banner, carried in a church procession.

Ali had begun to paint with the advent of Noah and the paintings recorded, appropriately, a certain hard-won domestic contentment. She liked to paint food, flowers and children. A stone jug with poppies on a striped seersucker cloth; her eight-year-old daughter Hattie arranging narcissi in a jam jar or back from a party with ribbons in her curly dark hair. Like the Dutch painters of the seventeenth century glorying in hung rabbits and bundles of asparagus, in scrubbed forecourts and in dew on vine leaves, Ali liked to celebrate through these things the ending of lean times. Noah had put an end to her lean times.

'The coffee shop is right alongside where you buy your artist's materials,' Noah said. 'For Chrissake Al, why can't you go there to buy coffee? Freeze the beans. No problem.'

'Eva Bobrow sends Mervyn there,' Ali said with apparent irrationality, but wishing to register a strongly felt reaction both against Eva's managerial style and against the parade of food connoisseurs. 'She *insists* on the Colombian, she says. She does the insisting and he does the shopping. Oh my God, it's all so disgustingly advanced it makes me want to puke. Why am I so backward in these domestic matters? It's no wonder he ran out on me.'

'Okay,' Noah said. 'How about if I take over the buying of coffee? I see no reason why Mrs Bobrow should determine what coffee I drink.'

'My dear Noah,' Ali said. 'As if you were ever in one place for long enough to buy anything except in Duty Free shops. I'm sorry it's such foul coffee. I wasn't thinking when I made it, that's all. There's nothing wrong with the beans, but I'll go to that poncy shop from now on – only because it's for you. Oh Jesus, Noah, wouldn't it be nice if you weren't going today?'

Noah's expertise in the matter of human respiratory pathology had always caused him to board aeroplanes far too often – unlike Ali, who resolutely never went anywhere, except to the same place on the Cornish coast once a year. Noah went to conferences in Sardinia and in Tokyo. He had been to conferences in Czechoslovakia and in Peking, and in the northernmost part of Norway where there was nothing but fish and fishermen. Nothing to eat but fish. Fish rolled into balls and stewed. Smoked fish cold on crackerbread. And even the museum full of fish, he told Ali. Embalmed fish with eyes that lit up at the flick of a switch. Most of the time, however, he went to New York to 'liaise', as he said, with colleagues.

'Sure,' Noah said. 'To stay home right now would be great.'

Connubial gratification had come to him late in life and he liked less and less to be parted from its source. Nor did he like to leave his garden when the season had just now drawn him out of doors again after the winter. Nor did he relish the necessary tedium of a day's jet lag, which worsened with increasing age. He was intensely and romantically involved with Ali and loved to watch her – especially as she was now, with her head bent over her sewing, because while he scrupulously granted women the right to whatever roles they chose, he nonetheless found them at their most attractive when engaged in domestic labour. Like Degas he liked women's haunches bent over a mop and the look of female arms up to the elbows in soap suds. He liked the whole genre of sock-mending by lamplight. Ali's sewing reminded him unconsciously of his mother. Noah was one of those unusual people who liked his mother. Noah's mother had been that apotheosis who had always been ready with a hot breakfast before he went on his newspaper round. On the quiet Ali had always found Noah's mother a little suspect, with her aura of maternal sanctity and her benign grey-haired infallibility. Besides, she was a writer of very silly letters. But it didn't matter to her much, because the woman was safely in Florida and Noah was worth any number of mothers.

Along with Noah's regrets at having to leave was the specifically favourable state of Ali's menstrual cycle. It had not escaped his notice that Ali did not need to use her rubber diaphragm from the next day. It was a bad time to be going away when one could be enjoying the additional perk of one's wife's unguarded cunt. He knew this because he kept tabs on Ali's menstrual cycles in his pocket diary and always had. She was no good on dates and punctuality. He had found it both unbelievable and infuriating when he met her that she had not owned a watch; that she would lean out of the bathroom window far enough to catch sight of the local church clock – which was itself often far from accurate. Now he had learned to accept it more or less. The diaphragm had been introduced by himself to replace Ali's hazard-prone alternatives, but it had to be admitted that the taste of spermicidal cream on the tongue could inhibit one's pleasure in oral exploration.

'You're not fertile from tomorrow,' he said wistfully. After ten years in England he still pronounced 'fertile' to rhyme with 'myrtle'. Ali did not hear him because she had her mind once again on the oranges. If one could paint wood like Holman Hunt, she thought. And why did one like pictures through windows so much? Did they imply advance or retreat? Could one ever go forward by looking back or did it always hamper? To go backwards – did one regress or move forward? And did pictures through windows merely imply a blinkered vision; a fear of life itself? Here again the picture of Thomas's double impinged and Ali resolved at once to remove it when Noah had gone. The man was advertising cigarettes! That was surely in itself a heresy in Noah's house, when Noah had always been so uncompromising

17

in his rules against cigarette smoking. Had one always wanted reality in easy, measured doses, she wondered; boxed in and bounded in nutshells? Probably. And had that been the real reason why one had let Thomas Adderley slip like water from one's emotional grasp and had gone on to embroil oneself in two hopelessly unsuitable marriages – first with a philistine and next with an ego-maniac? Thank God for Noah!

In the National Gallery there was a small Dutch box, by Samuel van Hoochstraaten, which revealed, through a spy hole, room upon room. An illusion. A mirror trick, but Ali loved that box; wanted to get inside it. Let sea discoverers to new worlds have gone; that box would be an everywhere. Noah had always made her feel safe; had built her an ark of gopher wood and pitched it within and without.

'Sorry,' Ali said, starting out of private thoughts, 'I wasn't listening to you. I was thinking.' She laughed slightly, because he was staring at her. 'I was engaging in some "tremulous quim introspection".' The phrase was an old joke between them since Noah had used it on her once a long time ago with greater dramatic effect than he had anticipated. 'You may be full of tremulous quim introspection,' he had said to her, 'but baby, you fuck like the emperor's whore.'

'What I was thinking was, shall I paint those oranges?' she said.

'Why not?' Noah said. 'Do you know something, Al? I'm gonna lie awake in that goddamned hotel room tonight wishing I could get my hands on your ass.'

He pushed back his chair to accommodate her on his knee and swallowed hard, gulping down intensity. 'Come here sweet-heart,' he said. Ali put down her sewing and went to him chewing her index finger to hold down an impractical rush of sexual desire. She could see her little Daniel through the doorway, stumbling dozily towards the downstairs loo, pulling out his infant prick in readiness for the day's first pee. He always slept late because he went to bed late. He played on the living-room floor with his toy soldiers every evening while his parents watched the ten o'clock news. It didn't matter, because he went to the afternoon session of the local nursery school.

Noah kissed her sexily on the right of the neck, near the collar bone. He was invariably so good at finding the right spot, Ali thought admiringly, almost as if one had taken the trouble to draw rings in marker pen around one's erogenous zones.

'If I were twenty years younger, I'd have you up against the wall, Al,' he said, 'right now, my baby. I guess I wouldn't make it to stagger on to that plane if I were to try it now.'

Ali smiled. 'It would be very bad for jet lag, Noah,' she said, 'pre-prandial ejaculation. Besides, I was such a fool twenty years ago, I didn't know how to take on a good thing when it came my way. I would have passed you up, I reckon. Think of it. Me at nineteen. Oh Noah, I wish you weren't going today.'

'I want for you to paint those oranges, okay?' Noah said.

'Yes,' she said.

'And water my bedding plants, will you?' he said. Ali nodded. Noah had a small greenhouse which he loved, full of yoghurt pots with lolly sticks, all of it rather beyond her area of expertise.

'I will take the greatest care of all your children,' she said.

They listened to the sound of Daniel's urine frothing satisfactorily in the lavatory bowl, before he appeared in the kitchen. He was already in his baseball cap, which he wore to flatten his curls. These he considered unmanly. The cap had been a present from Noah's mother who wished her grandson to overcome the disadvantages of growing up in England. She wanted him to be a good mixer and a good all-rounder. Outgoing, sporty, brave, ambitious and clever. Ali would rather have had Daniel a good pianist than a good all-rounder, but she believed he had the right to be as unambitious and introverted as he liked. Noah glanced shrewdly at Ali as he began to cram the last of his stuff into a travelling bag.

'Al, I want that boy in school while I'm away,' he said with emphasis. 'Okay?' Noah said that Daniel had to go to nursery school so that Ali could be a 'mensch'. That was why he had insisted on the art school. He believed that she was absurdly soft on Daniel – softer even than on Hattie and Camilla – and that was saying something. Ali was soft on everyone, but it was perfectly true that she would have been especially happy to have had Daniel at home all the time. He crawled into bed with her when Noah wasn't there. Even now that he had turned four, he occasionally sucked at her nipples when she bent down to wash the floor, like a little goat. Noah believed that Daniel was overindulged. Ali believed, on the other hand, that Noah's mother had probably never been soft enough on him.

'Is it school?' Daniel said, suspiciously.

'Yes,' Noah said before Ali could shilly-shally on the subject. 'But you're in luck this week. Thursday's a day off. There's a local election. The school hall is used as a polling booth.' Noah couldn't vote in British elections, but he did his bit, when he could, by ensuring that his wife, who had British nationality, got to the polling station on the right day. This was especially scrupulous of him since he knew she would vote Labour.

'Is it Fursday?' Daniel said hopefully, which made Noah smile.

'It's Wednesday,' he said. 'Tomorrow's Thursday.' Daniel was dedicated to the belief that Noah went to America to hunt. He knew from the song that Davey Crockett shot a bear in America when he was only three, so why else would one go there? He clung to this fantasy though Hattie called him 'Stupid' and 'Baby' and pointed out that Noah brought home things from Zabars in his luggage, not bearskins. Daniel was a natural predator, patient, quiet and dedicated. He set bird traps in the garden with string and bacon rashers. He wanted badly to catch real live fish. He had once seen a film of *Huckleberry Finn* and now constantly lamented the regrettable absence of rafts in modern life. He had worn a dagger round his neck all last summer and had said he was Mowgli. Ali had read him the Mowgli stories, but she had left out the bits about Bagheera and the child beating because she could not bear the idea of anyone beating children, especially in the cause of moral improvement. Could not bear it. It made her shake to see a child being smacked at a bus stop. Noah said that the sadistic pages were probably the very pages that kids like best. Wasn't that why Daniel always lingered longest over the page in his Arthurian Legends where King Pellinore's stab wound gushed blood?

Ali cast an eye over Noah's remaining luggage. Last-minute sweatshirt and socks from the tumble dryer. Razor and shampoo. Airline ticket and passport. A sheaf of medical papers which he meant to read on the plane. One large jar of gritty peanut butter, which she had bought at his instruction in the health food shop. The absurdity of it now delighted her.

'Why you should be taking peanut butter to New York beats me,' she said. 'I thought Americans invented peanut butter. For a straight man, Noah, you have some wonderfully eccentric habits.'

'I promised some to Barbara,' he said. 'Her peanut butter is nothing like as good as the peanut butter we buy here in the health food store.' Ali looked surprised. Barbara was a research doctor who worked with Noah in America. She came to stay sometimes and brought presents and took the children strawberry picking. Once she coincided with a resolute spell of snow and knew immediately that a sledge was the best of all presents. Ali liked people who liked her children. It was her major criterion for judging guests.

'Al,' Noah said. 'Do we have a couple of extra orange juice cartons I could take along?'

'Yes,' Ali said, but with some surprise, 'of course. Does Barbara want you to carry the British carton to America?' Noah's dislike of the British carton appeared to ruin his breakfast some mornings. It didn't pour properly, he said. Not like the ones in the States. Ali could not bring herself to call America 'the States' though it was more accurate. It sounded too in-groupish for all but the citizenry.

'I could use it on the flight,' Noah said. 'It doesn't do one's jet lag any good to get dehydrated. Airlines don't give one enough.' Ali got the orange juice from the cupboard, thinking wistfully of Noah with his informed and disciplined eating habits. The preparation of virtuous food was often, sadly, so laborious.

'Take scissors, Noah,' she said, 'to open the cartons. Dannie and me will drive you to Heathrow.'

'Only to the train station,' he said. 'That's all I need. I don't need to waste your time.' Noah was always considerate of Ali's time, though she herself so happily squandered it. He put pen and scrap pad into her hands.

'Some small chores I have hanging over,' he said briskly. He recited a familiar list of minor 'phone calls and errands which he delegated to her, consisting of meetings to be postponed and references to be handed on to typists. And could she, please, he said, tomorrow midday, call Arnie Weinberg and tell him his curriculum vitae was sitting on the desk in the study? Arnie had applied for a job in California which, regrettably, he just might get, but after ten years of working with him, one couldn't stand in his way.

'He'll be back sometime tomorrow a.m.,' Noah said, sounding like the speaking clock. 'It's absolutely vital that you call him, Al. He'll need to get it in the mail.'

'All right,' she said. She drove him, once he was clothed, to the railway station, with Daniel in the back seat in his cap and striped pyjamas. On the platform they held hands till the train came in. Ali stepped back and looked at him objectively, as she sometimes did in public, wanting the pleasure of seeing him with public eyes. 'I like your looks,' she said. Noah was broad and stocky. Heavy in the jaw and short in the leg, which was why his trousers always needed taking up. He had a head of thick but receding grizzle hair which had used to be dark brown before Ali knew him. He had about him an air both of substance and good sense from which his wholehearted indifference to fashionable dress did nothing to detract. It contributed instead the implication that his mind was concerned with more important things.

'Good,' Noah said, 'Eat properly, Al, won't you?'

'Yes,' she said, knowing as well as he did that she would lapse into slovenly orgies of tinned ravioli in his absence. 'Love to Barbara,' she said.

'I will,' he said. Then he faced her squarely. '*And don't forget the gallery*,' he said. He pointed the words with his forefinger, jabbing with emphasis at her arm.

'I won't,' she said. 'Don't worry. Though it's more than I deserve.'

'Nonsense,' said Noah, who knew nothing at all about painting, but who, with a loyal and possibly inflated conviction about Ali's artistic talent, had placed at her disposal all the advantages of his own drive and readiness to subsidise framing and haulage costs to enhance her stature as a painter. As a result, she had exhibited locally quite frequently in the foregoing five years and was due, the following Friday, to meet with the owner of her first London gallery.

They parted with apparent ease, as the train came in, since Noah had long ago reconciled himself to the fact that Ali would not travel with him. She did not like aeroplanes and, having at last found her niche in the English countryside, she would not leave it. Once only had she left the shores of England with him when she had gone to New York and the excursion had been a decided failure. Noah loved New York and had promptly led her upon a week-long binge of ethnic eating, much of it on the Lower East Side. But in his enthusiasm he had not perhaps properly considered how much the proximity of the dispossessed would disturb her tender egalitarian soul. Like many a native New Yorker, Noah was quite accustomed to stepping over homeless junkies in the subways on his way to restaurants, but for Ali the place had been a walking psychiatric ward; an alarming vision of hell by Hieronymus Bosch. She was haunted by glimpses of people hallucinating on the subways, staring with crazy eyes or with bleeding heads cracked open; by gnarled old women bathing arthritic knees in the holy water of St Patrick's Cathedral. Once she had seen a person walk naked down Broadway, arms outstretched against the stream of traffic, like a tortured prophet.

She had found it hard to raise her eyes from the gutters towards the airy pinnacles of those aspiring cathedrals of commerce and neither had the food always served to expunge her unease. On the contrary. In the Szechuan Chinese restaurant, where – owing possibly to an error in translation – the menu had offered her 'Live Carp in Black Bean Sauce', Ali had turned noticeably grey.

'I'll eat it raw, if I have to,' she had said, 'but I will not eat it live.'

She had been very much aware that she had failed him utterly as a travelling companion, and yet all the while, even in the restaurant, Noah had been moved by a consciousness that he loved her as much with his middle-aged self as ever he had loved Shirley in his youth and that, furthermore, Ali suited him so much better. He had thought so even as the restaurant chair had drilled painfully into his lower back, as restaurant chairs often did. Shirley had been by profession a chiropractor and he had never been able to deny that the loss of her unmatchable skills in this field had been a considerable inconvenience to him.

Noah had injured his back once, working on a construction site as a medical student. He had visited a chiropractor regularly in the twenty years since his divorce, but he had never in all that time found a practitioner quite as adept as Shirley had been in the manipulation of sacroiliac joints. As to Ali – she had proved quite remarkably maladroit, even in the matter of a little interim home massage. Noah had early on tried to buy her a book on massage but, finding the field of self-help crowded out with diet and sex manuals, he had given up and had learned to accept this limitation of hers.

24

'I've taken *The Times* from home,' he said, as he planted a parting kiss on her mouth through the window of the carriage corridor. 'Is that okay?'

'Of course,' she said. 'You must know by now that I only ever read *Exchange and Mart*.'

'I love you, Al,' Noah said. 'Take care.'

TWO

Aᴸɪ ʜᴀᴅ ᴍᴇᴛ ɴᴏᴀʜ the year after Mervyn left. She had met him in circumstances consistent with her subsequent relationship with him, which took the dual form of rehabilitation and love affair. She believed that he had saved her from a violent death, while Noah would concede only that he had saved her from multiple fractures. Mervyn's departure had been good for her looks, though she would have been surprised to have had anyone tell her so at the time, because though day-to-day living had become more serene, more conducive to a smoothing of the skin, his going had left her humbled and at bedtime she still afforded herself the regular luxury of crying without being observed by Camilla.

Admittedly Mervyn had played out his departure so often over the foregoing twelve years that the apparent permanence of this last one had brought with it a certain relief – like the relief of death after wasting illness. And it came in unexpected form since previously his departures had been short-lived and had always taken place around midnight. Mervyn had slammed the front door, bawling recriminations to wake the ageing neighbour's dogs and bearing his own righteousness aloft like a parcel bound up in a spotted handkerchief on the end of a stick. He had then spent a night, sometimes even two, dossing in his sleeping bag under a bridge, in the municipal car park, or in an unbolted allotment shed. These episodes he had then incorporated into the proud mythology of his own posturing Bohemianism. Mervyn as Supertramp, passing rough nights in reckless abandon with meths drinkers, or fending off vagrancy charges by the city police. He would haul them out at dinner parties, suitably embroidered, to bolster his penchant for colourful living. What was truly remarkable was that these episodes never made him ill. Exposure never hacked at his kidneys or at his lungs, because, though he was as mad as the proverbial hatter, he was also as tough as time-honoured old boots.

It was sometimes during these distressing episodes that Ali began to discover within herself an understanding of what it was that had drawn her to Mervyn in the first place. It seemed to her at such times that, after the brief emptiness of her first marriage, it had been a certain wildness in Mervyn's temper, a certain eccentricity, which had recalled for her what in Thomas Adderley had been an easy, unconventional panache. But that flamboyance which Thomas had worn so comfortably as a part of his inner clothing Mervyn had taken on as the cloak of a vain and troubled man in search of disguises.

At any rate, Mervyn's ultimate walk-out had all been quite different from these explosive rehearsals. With a quiet, purposeful competence, he had packed his clothes, his books, his tranquillisers and all the best records into a large ticking laundry bag which Ali's mother had made for her the year she left for university and this he had placed in the back of the Mini. He had then left promptly, after an adequate breakfast, for his girlfriend's bedsitting room. The girlfriend had come as a great surprise to Ali for, although Mervyn had always been in every other respect wholly unreliable, he had never before, to her knowledge, been seriously interested in other women. There had always been those examples of ideal female type which he had flung at her occasionally so that she might show up the worse by comparison, but not one of these had actually ever turned him on. They were usually no more than a wishful compound of Hannah Arendt and his own Polish grandmother.

Having spent much of the past twelve years haranguing his wife on the subject of her inadequate domestic industry and womanly care; having caused her to labour in penance over his mother's marble-covered, handwritten Jewish cookery note-books and mess with grated raw potatoes and fish skins and minced offal until she conceived the firm opinion that no culinary tradition combined being as disgusting with being as horribly labour-intensive, he pronounced her suddenly, over his last breakfast, insufficiently liberated; too much swamped in kitchen and childcare. Then he left her for a twenty-year-old undergraduate in ethnic wrap-over skirts, who kept a blown-up photograph of Virginia Woolf Blu-tacked, facing outwards, from the dusty window of her rooming-house bedsitter along with the sign of a clenched female fist. Ali, who had subsequently got herself a cleaning job to make ends meet, passed the place on her bicycle three times a week. She was herself inclined to regard Mrs Woolf as a fragile upper-class genius, subtle, private and snobbish, with a traumatising past and an admirably supportive husband, but there it was. Mervyn was in there and loving it; growing headier every day on the rejuvenating effects of scrambling eggs in a blackened aluminium frying pan over a student's gas ring.

Once a month, like a debt collector, Mervyn would return ostensibly to collect his lingering possessions, to borrow communal ones, or to ask about letters which he suspected hadn't been sent on. He had, in the six months prior to his departure, reverted to writing – driven no doubt by his clandestine passion – and was waiting to hear from publishers. But mostly Mervyn came to parade his newfound state of bliss before her because his new woman appeared to suit him remarkably well. She was made of sterner stuff than Ali for all her tender years and, being less easy to manipulate, appeared to provoke in him none of the same destructive instability. But nevertheless he continued to enjoy an audience and Ali made him such a good one in her abject state. She had no emotional devices for slamming the door in his face; no power even to demand that he relinquish his key to the front door. Instead, she would stand in her kitchen and shakily measure out Nescafé for him with her silver-plated apostle teaspoons from the antiques market and weakly hope that he wouldn't stay long. Mervyn would enter light of step without troubling to knock and would settle himself into a chair.

On one occasion he sat with a pile of cheaply produced feminist papers in his lap – a student woman's paper which his girlfriend collated in her basement. On the cover, crudely reproduced, was Michelangelo's David, a caption stamped over his crotch. WARNING, it said, HISTORY BOMBARDS WOMEN WITH IMAGES WHICH SURROUND AND DEGRADE THEM. Mervyn was delivering them. Mervyn, who could not move a step without carrying his male equipment reverently before him, as obtrusively as that of a male ballet dancer in tights! Mervyn, to whom the very Post Office Tower sang triumphant hymns of phallic domination. Mervyn, as happened with him from time to time, had evidently been born again.

Another time he sat juggling a small plastic bag of ten-penny pieces in his lap which he had just got from the bank. His woman's gas supply worked on a coin meter, he explained. So delightful, so studentish, to have the bath water run cold on one when the ten pences ran out and to flee naked and shivering into the arms of one's mistress. The image struck home with Ali whose first memorable evening alone with Mervyn had taken place around an ancient gas fire in Belsize Park, powered by just such a coin meter, but in those days one fed them shillings. Mervyn had singed his hair that night, lighting Woodbines from the irregular blue flames which fed the gas fire's yellowing clay teeth. He had read his own poetry to her against the backdrop of its penetrating hiss. What had dazzled her then, apart from his pent-up air of impending tiger spring, was his absolute lack of humility. Having so much of it herself, she took vicarious pleasure in his lack.

'To think,' Mervyn said, that first night, clearly lost in wonder at his own precociousness, 'to think I wrote that poem when I was only twenty-three.' Ali had studied him carefully to determine how deceptively well he wore his advancing years.

'How old are you now, Mervyn?' she said.

'Twenty-four,' he said.

The following evening he had demonstrated to her delight that he could walk upstairs on stilts. She had stirred up packet chicken-noodle soup over the gas ring that evening and had made toast for them while, again, he read to her. Now he scrambled eggs and heated soup while his girlfriend read to him from articles on media sociology. It was clear that to Mervyn this admittedly radical change constituted not so much a reversal as a great leap forward. Mervyn stirred his coffee with the sugar spoon – a thing he had done almost invariably for as long as Ali had known him – and watched her as she knelt, trembling slightly, at the hearthstone to tap at kindling with an axe.

'You need a man about the place,' he said. He had never balked at hitting below the belt 'Perhaps a dating agency could fit you up with an identikit of that – what was his name? That ten-foot scholar-gypsy man you used to sigh for at a sweet distance in your youth. Adkins? Ad-man? Attaturk?'

'Adderley,' Ali said. 'Why are you so miserable to me?' She knew that it had never ceased to rankle with Mervyn that he himself had not grown in height beyond five feet four inches. He was nicely proportioned and finely turned, but Ali was half a head taller.

Ali had given up expecting money from Mervyn and was living on weekly handouts from the social security, supplemented with illicit extras earned from her cleaning job and from running up toddlers' smocks at night on an old treadle machine for a local children's boutique. Thrown upon her own resources after eight years, she quickly discovered that openings for one-time school teachers like herself had contracted into nonexistence and that cleaning up after bachelor men upon informal contractual obligation was in any case a more soothing, uncomplicated occupation than surviving either the daily assault of urban adolescents locked in classrooms against their will, or the daily backdrop of Mervyn's abuse as one picked up his discarded socks and nail parings from all over the hall floor. The only sacrifice was in status. To muck out after men who were off at work all day and who left one five pounds in an envelope at the end of the week was moderately satisfactory, especially when one considered the alternatives in the cold light of reality. These appeared to be waitressing in black crêpe at the Kardomah Café or selling ladies' underwear door to door on commission. True, the pages of *Exchange and Mart* always announced that there was money to be made in slot meters, but Ali was either insufficiently adventurous or too sceptical ever to follow them up.

Meanwhile, there was Camilla. Beautiful Camilla, the fragile eleven-year-old casualty of her parents' turbulent home life. Camilla who was conceived out of Mervyn's impatience with rubber condoms and born two months early, weighing under five pounds. That she was born at all had had to do with Ali's incompetence in running out on the abortionist. There could be no question about it – Camilla was all Ali's fault. For she had proceeded, on Mervyn's instructions, to a secret address in St John's Wood where the abortionist had materialised in a padded green smoking jacket and embroidered slippers. He had instructed her to strip and lie on the examining table. It was necessary as a preliminary, he explained, coming towards her with a clitoral vibrator, to determine the quality of her orgasm. Ali, who had vaguely imagined such an appliance to be designed for vaginal penetration and to be altogether larger – in appearance perhaps not unlike her mother's Edwardian curling-tongs – was relieved at least, by its modest size.

'Was that nice?' the abortionist said. It was only then that the unprocedural nature of the exercise dawned upon Ali, who consequently jumped in terror from the bed and ran for her clothes. The abortionist, just perceptibly, ground his teeth.

'I never cared for a skinny woman,' he said.

Mervyn had never believed her. He was, at that time, wholly

locked into the pursuit of virile but apparently unpublishable poetry while Ali went out to work. The birth of the baby brought no sign that his happy arrangement would cease. For the first four years of Camilla's life, therefore, Ali went out to work while Mervyn stayed at home, shaking ash carelessly into the child's blackcurrant juice and forgetting to change her nappies. Occasionally, when he thought about her, he tossed secondhand Ladybird books and empty plastic shampoo bottles into her playpen before returning to his fantasy life. Conversely, Ali, who was strongly maternal and had spent her childhood playing tenderly with dolls and taking neighbours' babies for walks, found herself required to claw her own shy, pitifully mother-dependent little toddler loose from the hem of her skirt each morning and catch two buses to her schoolteaching job in Bermondsey.

From this phase in their lives Mervyn had now come to perceive himself, retrospectively, as a pioneer of role flexibility, but Ali had never altogether shaken off the guilt provoked by this daily betrayal, though with that, as with so much else, Noah had helped. Eighteen years on and two children later, Ali still had her ear to Camilla's every tremulous emotion like a watchful musician with a tuning fork.

When Camilla was four years old, Mervyn underwent one of the dramatic reversals which periodically characterised his behaviour. He put by his spidery poetical notebooks and took a step sideways, via a job-retraining scheme, into community work with disadvantaged youth. With precious little to mark him out for the business beyond glaring unsuitability, Mervyn took a job as community youth worker in Oxfordshire where he promptly acquired a small terraced house chosen by Ali but bought on a mortgage made out in his own name. He began, with the advent of the job, to identify so strongly with the youth among whom he worked that he gave up his spotted artist's tie and fetching large-brimmed hat and promptly bought himself a leather jacket complete with luminous tiger on the back; took to rolling his own cigarettes and to using 'fuckin'' as his major adjective. Also to pouring scorn upon his own small daughter for her middle-class vowels, her precocious reading habits and her longing to attend dancing classes.

With the move, Ali gave up her job and set about making it up to Camilla, employing in so doing her considerable creative flair and pleasure in young children. She made playdough; she made puppet shows; she made pink and white fairytale castles for birthday cakes with mullioned windows of piped icing sugar. She read fifty picture books a day with Camilla on her knee and, in all weathers, if Camilla wished it, she pushed a swing in the park. (Or in Noah's subsequent phrase, she took on 'new excesses of servility'.) In the afternoons they took naps together with the radio tuned to *Woman's Hour* and, in between, they decorated the house. Camilla was, from the outset, endowed with quite astonishing looks. Her beauty markedly exceeded that of either of her parents whose very different features she combined in judicious measure to produce an effect of moving delicacy. But she was also stammering, timorous and given easily to tears and nightmares. Though she had taught herself to read at three from the Ladybird books which Mervyn had thrown into her cot, she had never given up peeing in her bed.

Mervyn, who watched his wife and daughter's closeness with ever-increasing resentment, took it upon himself to redress the balance, both by accusing them of lesbian involvement, and by adopting a zealously punitive stance with the child which was not pleasant to witness. With regard to the first of these responses, Mervyn would use as ammunition that Ali by her own confession had sometimes held hands in high school with her best friend Julie Horowitz, and that she had not once in the way of campus life gone to bed with Thomas Adderley. As to his small daughter, he would lock her in her bedroom with 'homework' set by himself. If she lost a jumble-sale cardigan or a lunchbox he would send her out at dusk sobbing along the gutters in futile search. 'Someday you'll end on the gallows,' he more than once yelled after her. A curious threat, Ali thought, from a man who had repeatedly professed himself unilaterally against both prison and capital punishment, and who suffered pangs of identification if ever one of his semi-delinquent protégés got done by the police for busting open a bubblegum machine. In a temporary burst of ethnic reversion he saw fit at one time to cart Camilla off to a course of Hebrew language classes. The classes just happened to coincide with the hour of her dancing class and began three days after Ali had bought the child her first treasured pair of pink Anello and Davide ballet pumps.

'You wet your bed every night as an act of aggression,' he once announced to her helpfully before an audience of adult strangers. 'You do it because you hate your mother.' Mervyn's feelings against his own mother ran so high that he was capable, quite literally, of tearing his hair upon discovering that Ali had humoured the old woman with the gift of a silk scarf on her birthday, or had sent her an annual ten-penny Passover card.

The day that Ali met Noah had begun badly for Camilla. Always a scrupulously conscientious child, anxious to cover herself on all fronts against the possible wrath of schoolteachers; always in the vanguard of homework doers and bringers of magazine pictures for school projects, Camilla seldom boobed, but on this particular day she had risen late. She had gone to bed too late the night before after some trouble over her homework. Ali had never known Camilla to hesitate over homework before, but on this occasion the teacher had set an impossible task. She had asked the class to write about a time when they had been naughty. Poor Camilla, who had never been naughty, could think of nothing to write about and had eventually, with considerable reluctance and tears, agreed to accept one of Ali's innocent childhood escapades on loan for the occasion. Even then, choosing the right one had taken its time. There was for example the episode, whose awfulness left Camilla wincing, when Ali and her friend had trimmed the fringing on her friend's mother's rug. But trimming it straight had proved so difficult that they had had to keep cutting it shorter and shorter until finally they had hacked into the weave.

'Don't tell me any more,' Camilla said, clapping her hands over her ears. 'It's too awful.' She had found rising next morning difficult, but worse was to follow. As she entered the kitchen for a hasty mouthful of breakfast, she stopped suddenly in her tracks and clutched the doorjamb.

'I need a games kit,' she said in a voice drenched with sorrow, 'I need it today for after school. I forgot to tell you.'

'Oh Jesus,' Ali said, scrambling together Camilla's busfare in haste. 'The only thing to do, I suppose, is to pretend you're having a period.' Already, poor little narrow-hipped Camilla was, as they say, a 'woman'. The week after she had turned eleven she had hobbled home from school, limping from two raw patches on the insides of her thighs caused by chafing from dried blood. She had soaked through the two Kotex pads given her by the science teacher and had spent most of the afternoon in the medical room. Monthly thereafter, and for eight days at a stretch, she passed what looked like gouts of raw liver among a copious gory ooze. Since child modesty would not permit her the use of internal tampons, she swallowed Disprin with admirable patience, used Vaseline on the raw patches and refused to see a doctor.

'I can't pretend,' Camilla said, still standing in the doorway. 'I'm hopeless at lies.' And she burst into tears. 'She'll know it's not true. I'll get detention.'

'I'll get you the kit,' Ali said quickly, appeasingly. 'I'll buy it this afternoon. I'll be at the school gate by hometime. Promise.' Camilla wiped her strange alluring yellow eyes on the last of the kitchen paper as she cast about for a new source of anxiety.

'*Please* don't be late, Mummy,' she said. 'Please, or I'll get detention.'

'Promise,' Ali said. 'What do you need?'

35

'White plimsolls,' Camilla said, snatching up her school bag. 'And navy shorts. And a white T-shirt. Thanks, Mummy.'

'Run along,' Ali said. 'Don't worry.'

'It's all got to be labelled,' Camilla said over her shoulder 'And in a bag, or we get detention. Please, Mummy.'

'Labelled,' Ali said. 'Right. Don't worry.'

'The bag's got to be labelled too,' Camilla said, as she took her leave. 'If it isn't I'll get detention.'

Ali, after the daily rinsing of Camilla's sheets, took her bicycle to her cleaning job, noticing on the way that Virginia Woolf had lost the Blu-tack on her upper-left-hand corner and was sagging inwards in neck-arching indignity. She spent her two hours among soapsuds and alien crockery, drawing coffee cups and ashtrays and crumpled underwear out from under the sofas where her bachelor men habitually hid these things in consideration of her feelings. Then she pedalled home intending to make a sandwich and some coffee before going on to the shops. She dug out an old cushion cover and converted it into a kitbag, manufacturing a hem and drawstring and stitching on a name-tape. She put aside two more name-tapes with a view to stitching these on to the shorts and shirt in the Ladies loo in the town just as she heard the sound of Mervyn fitting his key into the lock.

'I came for the paint roller,' he said jauntily. Defensiveness caught Ali by the throat, for she had been discovered plying her needle, while Mervyn's girlfriend, Eva, would in all likehood be in the Social Sciences library working on her bibliography.

'It's under the sink,' Ali said with the belligerence of shame. 'But if Eva wants to indulge in a little home decorating, paint rollers are available in every branch of Woolworths, you know – or does she believe that property is theft?' Mervyn came towards her with his brilliant treacherous smile, his teeth, like Camilla's, small, white and strong.

'*I'm* doing the painting,' he said. He had never painted walls before in his life. 'Eva is too busy. Are you planning to make an issue over a paint roller then? Why do women of your sort always pick quarrels which centre round utensils and domestic territory?' He smiled upon her indulgently as upon some poor, dishclout scullery maid.

'Listen, Mervyn, I'm in a hurry,' Ali said. 'Take the bloody thing and with pleasure. As I said, it's under the sink. Only if you're planning to do the place over in "Nigger Brown", just rinse it through before you return it to me. That's all.'

'Racist!' Mervyn said. He had positioned himself suddenly too close for comfort and had picked up the makeshift kitbag which he was turning over and over in his hands.

'It's Camilla's gym bag,' Ali said nervously. 'I have to take it to her right now. She needs it now.'

'So do you,' he said, snatching eagerly at double entendre. 'That's going by the way you're acting with me today. You're a handsome lady aren't you?'

'Marquess of Queensbury rules, okay?' Ali said, swallowing quickly and wishing tears wouldn't start so easily from her eyes these days. 'The paint roller is all yours. Please. Take it and go away. Please, Mervyn.'

Mervyn put down the kitbag to enjoy his rising power. 'I'm off wives and daughters as you know,' he said, 'but a part-time mistress or two is something else, not so? Anytime you're interested, I'm open to offers, duckie.' He took a step towards the mantelpiece where he began to fondle a recent school photograph of Camilla which Ali had inserted into a small shell-collage frame. 'Her too,' he said, for the pleasure of breaking the bounds of good taste. 'If she doesn't baulk at incest, that is.'

'Are you on drugs, Mervyn?' Ali asked, recovering spirit under the influence of his offensiveness.

'Tell her I'd expect her to menstruate first,' he said. 'No representation without menstruation. Not in my bed.'

'I'm sorry, Mervyn, I'm off,' Ali said as she felt telling red blotches form upon the skin around her collar bone. She snatched up the kitbag and made for the door. A mild wave of nausea passed over her as she mounted her bicycle, caused only partly by the absence of lunch.

Acquiring the games kit was not an easy thing. Shorts were unseasonal by early September and the few satiny ones left in the sports shops were all beyond Ali's means. White T-shirts came with saucy messages across the chest and Camilla needed a plain one. Furthermore, Camilla's feet, being unusually narrow and elegant, fell out of regular gym shoes and required the high-lacing Dunlop kind which two out of three sports shops did not carry in her size.

Some hours had elapsed before Ali finally found suitable shorts in a charity shop, a little frayed and rumpled, and smelling slightly of body odour. The T-shirt was solved by a kindly shop assistant who advised her to ask in the men's underwear department for a small cotton vest. The problem had been one not of scarcity, but of terminology. With some agitation Ali returned to her bicycle only to remember the name-tapes. Mervyn had caused her to leave them at home. Bent on acquiring a marking pen, she stepped hurriedly off the kerb into the street only to feel the hot wind of a passing car and – at the same moment – a hand gripping her arm to pull her back. That was when she fell shaking against Noah's remarkable forty-four-inch chest.

'Don't do that again, lady,' he said. 'Not while I'm watching. It sure scares the hell out of me.' He supported her a few paces till she could lean against a wall. Then he checked her pulse, registering as he did so a half-dozen dubious lesions on the back of her right hand which she had dismissed as glorified freckles.

'So stupid of me,' she said in some embarrassment, but Noah's companion stepped forth heatedly.

'The guy was driving like a cowboy!' he said. Arnie Weinberg, in contrast to the sobriety of Noah's appearance, wore his bushy, mouse-coloured hair carelessly overgrown and its tendency was to grow not down but sideways. He had on, over a sleeveless T-shirt, a small goatskin jerkin which he wore hairy side in. A large mole was manifest in the vicinity of his left bicep and a copious protrusion of yellowish underarm hair emerged from the arm-holes of the T-shirt. He wore, besides thick steel-framed glasses, denim jeans and some highly pneumatic running shoes. Both men were staring at her the way she remembered the dentist doing once, just before she had passed out in the chair. Arnie was holding out to her a Mars Bar which he had drawn from his back pocket.

'Eat,' he said. Noah threw the car keys into Arnie's hands.

'Go get the car,' he said. 'I guess we'll take her home.' Ali was already tearing paper from the sugary goo.

'No really,' she said, backing further into the wall. 'I'm all right.' But Arnie had already left them.

'Believe me,' Noah said, 'you are very shaken.'

'I can't go home,' Ali said. 'That's the problem.' She held the kitbag aloft in a shaking hand. 'I've got these to deliver to my daughter's school. She needs them.'

'No problem,' Noah said. He used the expression frequently and to good effect. Problems of the kind which beset Ali vanished before him as chaff before the wind. 'I'm Noah Glazer. I am, as it happens, a doctor.'

'Thanks,' Ali said. 'I'm Alison Bobrow. I have to deliver these for three-thirty.'

Noah glanced at his watch and said promptly, with his peculiar and slightly compulsive moral gravity, 'If you have children, Mrs Bobrow, you owe it to them to take better care of yourself.'

'Yes,' Ali said. She was taken both by his unusual kindness and by the puzzling awfulness of his pale yellow drip-dry shirt which he wore with cuff-links. Why cuff-links on a shirt like that? Ali wore thirdhand silk shirts from jumble sales with real shell buttons and threadbare cuffs. She laundered them by hand and ironed them with love. Nothing would have induced her to be seen dead in primrose drip-dry.

'I should think you saved me from the jaws of death just then,' she said, managing a smile. 'We are standing appropriately, do you see, on the very spot where the poor Protestant bishops were burned to death.'

'Oh my,' Noah said, observing the plaque in the college wall. He considered her remark to be eccentric and examined her curiously. 'Isn't that something?' he said.

When she smiled it began to occur to him that, for those who liked this kind of woman, she was certainly good to look at even through pallor and exhaustion. She was much too thin and wore rather butch sandals, but with her white pointed face and long white neck and curiously variegated pale hair, her head and shoulders took some beating. He found himself remembering the twelve dancing princesses who had worn out their shoes at the enchanted lake. The memory startled him since the story had been read to him as a young child by his mother, only once and long ago. Noah was a person who had put by childish things early in life and, besides, his tastes in women had always run along more robust lines towards ruby lips and ample haunches in tight skirts like Shirley's. He had never been a man for pale, underslept enchantresses.

As Arnie honked from the opposite kerb they crossed the street to the car, where Noah handed her into the front passenger seat while Arnie stepped into the back.

'I got the bastard's car!' he said excitedly. 'Parked just there down the street. Can you believe it? The guy drives like a psychopath and then he parks half a block down the street. Boy, is he going places fast!'

'D'you take his number?' Noah said. Arnie slapped his forehead in self-reproach.

'Shit!' he said, 'I forgot. I was too busy. I kicked a good-size dent in the rear mudguard, see. Real British ticky tacky that car. Put your toe to the metal and it crumples just like a Coke can.'

'You what?' Noah said caustically, registering controlled paternal annoyance. Arnie was the best research student he had ever had but had already caused him displeasure that day by having driven Noah's car to a party the previous night which had extended into the morning and having then come to the hospital research unit at noon to return it direct from the party, dressed – as Noah said – like Robinson Crusoe in jogging shoes. Hurriedly Noah checked his mirror and began to manoeuvre into the stream of traffic.

'Let's get out of here,' he said. Ali was beginning to enjoy herself in spite of her shock and her anxiety over Camilla's clothing. Both men had begun to intrigue her. She wondered whether they were father and son. Or were they sexually involved with each other? For what reasons would a rigorously straight man in grey flannels keep company with a bent man in goatskin? She took them for American tourists.

'Where do you come from?' she said.

'From the hospital, ma'am,' Arnie said. 'You're okay with us. We're just harmless doctors.'

'Go on,' Ali said. 'I don't believe you. Leastways, I believed him, but not you. Are you telling me you do ward rounds in a white coat?'

Arnie laughed. 'Well, not exactly. Not right now. I work for him in medical research. You think I don't look like a doctor?'

'You look distinctly alternative to me if you'll pardon the liberty,' Ali said. 'Frankly, you look like a person who buys prayer postcards ten pence off in the Whole Earth Bookshop.' Arnie laughed again, but Noah, for whom flippant conversation, like eccentric dress, had its proper times and places, merely glanced down gravely at her seat-belt fitting.

'Fasten the seat belt, Mrs Bobrow. Like so,' he said after watching her wrestle with the clasp. Click.

Suddenly a police car was drawn up beside them, forcing Noah to pull in. There were two policemen in the front and, in the back, black hair parted dead centre, moustached and red with fury, was the driver of the fast car which had almost collided with Ali.

'That's the one!' he yelled, as plummy British as they come in his period piece, Battle of Britain voice. 'The one in the back with long hair like a girl.'

'I *am* a girl,' Arnie said to Ali's immediate delight and to Noah's dismay. Arnie leaned on the window ledge. 'What's going on around here?' He damned himself instantly, not only with his general lack of deference but with the combination of his transatlantic accent and his studenty dress.

'Oh Christ,' Noah said gloomily, under his breath.

'Arrest him officer!' yelled the fast-car man. 'Go on! Do your duty as a servant of the Crown. By God I'll see that the law has your balls, you damned Yankee trouble-maker. I'm warning you, I have the power to do it.' He fumed at some considerable length about his uncle the judge and his brother in the Black Watch.

'Jesus, Noah, is this guy for real?' Arnie said incredulously, employing a regrettably audible aside. He had been in the country for only four weeks and could not believe his unattuned ears.

'Bloody vandal!' blustered the fast-car man. One of the policemen got out and ordered Arnie rather abruptly to do the same.

'Pardon me, officer,' Noah said, intervening with calculated sobriety, 'but I have a woman here suffering from shock. Your passenger almost knocked her down as a matter of fact. May we get under way, please?'

'Is this your vehicle, sir?' said the policeman. Noah sighed.

'Sure it's my vehicle,' he said.

'Licence, sir?' said the policeman. Ali began to twitch inwardly in consideration of the time and to steal glances at Noah's watch as he reached into the glove pocket for his licence. Camilla needed her games togs by three-thirty did she not? She needed them though the heavens fell. Yet here was a pair of gallant strangers being impounded as they rose in her defence. Noah's watch, being annoyingly digital, was difficult to read upside down, but his licence – international and valid for one year – was mercifully without fault. The policeman after some scrutiny returned it with an approving nod.

'We shall need a statement from your friend, sir, that's all,' he said. 'Never to worry. We'll have him down the station for you if you'd like to call by later.' Noah looked from Ali to Arnie, weighing their respective needs with care.

'I'll call by the police station in a half-hour,' he said to Arnie. Ali watched with growing awkwardness as Arnie stepped undaunted into the police car alongside his expostulating accuser.

'Whatever are we going to do?' she said.

'Nothing,' Noah said. 'I guess nobody ever got into real trouble for kicking a car in sneakers. Not that I heard of.'

'It's all my fault,' Ali said. 'It's dreadful. I'm so sorry.'

'Don't talk nonsense, Mrs Bobrow,' Noah said abruptly. 'Who was it kicked the car? Just tell me now where we are heading. Your daughter's school, right?'

'Oh yes,' Ali said, uneasily, who hated to give traffic directions for the reason that left and right had never become second nature to her. To know right from left required a quick translation from treble clef through to one's right thumb on Middle C. A process which she feared would not be quick enough for a person who gave out an impression of decidedly practical competence.

They were late, of course. Not very late, but late enough. Camilla was immediately visible to Ali, seated woefully upon the low brick wall of the school. For Camilla, the relief of seeing her mother brought on instant hysteria. She flew at Ali, breathing misery and hurling wild reproaches.

'You're late!' she snivelled. 'You *promised*. Now I've missed the kit inspection and I've got detention tomorrow and it's your fault. You *promised* me, Mummy. You promised!'

'I'm sorry,' Ali said repeatedly. 'Please Camilla, I'm sorry. I couldn't help it.' Noah tried at first not to watch but he couldn't prevent his ears being a party to the protracted exchange. It was all most extraordinary, he thought. An eleven-year-old child who needed parents to run to and fro with sports equipment? Eleven-year-olds, as he recalled from his own sons, were people who earned their own pocket money and went back-packing all summer without writing home. Furthermore, he liked respect for mothers. Who was Mr Bobrow that he allowed this kind of misconduct to go on? *Was* there a Mr Bobrow? Here was a woman, weak with shock from a narrowly averted automobile accident, humbling herself before a hysterical child over a sports bag. He leaned over and opened the back door.

'Jump in little lady,' he said, with pointed severity. 'Your mother almost got knocked down.'

'I'm sorry,' Ali said to him. 'She's upset.' She looked furtively over her shoulder at Camilla hiccuping in the back seat and biting her lip between spasms of mucus.

'That's okay,' Noah said with level restraint. 'I've had kids myself. Fasten the seat belt, Mrs Bobrow.'

'Sorry,' Ali said, making a flustered rush upon the object in the hopes of catching it unawares.

'How about if I make a charge for every time you say you're sorry?' Noah said.

'Sorry,' Ali said and blushed. Noah shifted into gear with a stifled smile.

'Where to now?' he said. 'Right? Left? Mrs Bobrow, please, do I make a right?'

'Sorry,' Ali said.

They lived in the same street, though they had never seen each other before. Engrossed bachelor men, car-borne and coming home late, don't often notice local mothers and housewives, nor do housewives notice absentee householders. Added to that, Noah lived in a modern architect-designed infill house with almost no windows to the street side and great shop-window panes to the back. That being the way with modern glazing procedures, the windows were either all or nothing. Further-more, he lived on the first floor, because at ground level his house boasted the only garage in the street. He was, in short, by geography and inclination cut off from the life of the street. He had bought the house nine months before for its proximity to the hospital, its trouble-free plastic drainpipes and its adequate central heating system. He had lived in England for no more than a month when an agent had come up with the house and, since nobody had ever occupied the place before, the transfer had been satisfactorily uncomplicated and speedy. Ali lived, by contrast, in a prettily got-up terraced workman's cottage with a slightly crumbling stone lintel over a sanded front door, window frames which rattled loudly in a high wind and a structural crack running the length of the back. From her position within it she constituted a magnet for almost every social problem in the neighbourhood.

'Take care, now,' Noah said as he delivered her to her door with her dejected little daughter. 'I'll come by this evening,' he said. 'I'll let you know what happened.'

THREE

W HEN NOAH RETURNED with Arnie that evening, as he had
   promised, the door was opened to him by Camilla who,
having recovered herself, was modelling her hard-earned running shorts.

'Mother at home?' he said. Glancing with sideways eyes
because the memory of her emotional display that afternoon
now embarrassed her, she nodded and turned to show them
in. The inviting half-moons of her pre-teen female buttocks
protruding from the tacky but well-fitting shorts was not a
sight to pass Arnie by and he whistled through his teeth.
Camilla's delicate but undeniable beauty was already proving
to be an embarrassment to her on the school bus, where
clumsy schoolboys jostled as they passed her and cleared their
throats pointedly in the hope of catching her attention. Arnie
was in another league, of course. Bathed and shaven, he was
now dressed in a snowy-white Indian shirt with a small
collarless neckband and immaculate canvas jeans. He presented a less bizarre appearance than that which Ali had
encountered earlier. He wore his hair neatly combed though it
flounced thickly at the temples like Mark Twain's. The toe-
nails protruding from his leather sandals were manicured and
scrupulously clean.

'Call me when you're sixteen, kid,' he said.

'Eighteen,' Noah said firmly. 'Aren't you in enough trouble

with the law already?' He stepped into the living room from the tiny hall.

'Mrs Bobrow?' he said. 'Mrs Bobrow?' Because Ali, although the hour was almost eight, was giving her whole attention to four small girls who were clearly not her own. They appeared to be engaged in amateur theatricals and were at that moment playing dead upon the creamy Spanish rug, breaking out of stiffness into brief giggles occasionally, and scuffing at the rug with their sharp little patent shoes. One of them, a rosy blonde, had taken off her pants and was uninhibitedly airing her pudgy, six-year-old pubes. Noah stood and waited, watching the story unfold. Ali was narrator and also, intermittently, villain and stepmother.

'Please,' she said, looking up for a moment, 'sit down.'

'Get on with it,' said the blonde child rudely. Noah sat down warily in one of Ali's fragile basket chairs which tilted gently leftwards under his weight. He hit his head lightly upon an appliquéd lampshade which hung – for aesthetic reasons – too low over the chair and he steadied it politely with his hand.

'Hi,' Arnie said affably, as he stepped with a wide stride over the four recumbent girls.

'Shut up,' said the vocal blonde. 'We're acting. We're the Snow Whites and we're dead.'

'What, all of you?' Arnie said, in lively disbelief. 'You're all Snow Whites? Isn't there only one?'

'We all wanted to be her, so there's four,' said the child conclusively. 'Now shut up.' Noah observed meanwhile that Ali had about her a trance-like serenity which came sometimes from growing beyond despair. It gave her a touching, frail nobility.

'And the prince?' Arnie said, needling persistently. 'He gets all of you? He gets the four dead girls?' A small sullen Prince Charming, brutalised by a recent haircut, was lurking in a corner quietly fiddling with his genitals as he straddled Ali's broomhandle – his makeshift horse – awaiting his cue.

'Belt up,' said the blonde. 'Or bugger off.' What Noah and

Arnie were witnessing was the vestige of an open-house policy established by Mervyn who had declared himself in favour of communal living and neighbourhood support. The nuclear family was an evil, he said, and privacy a bourgeois luxury. The problem for Ali was not that Mervyn had now gone. It had always been that where the nuclear family still held as the norm – and the normal, by definition, stubbornly adhered to such norms – the people who invaded Ali's life to consume her Nescafé in great quantities and to unload their burdens, or their offspring, were on the whole in no emotional or material position ever to support Ali in their turn. They left her their children to care for while they listened in pubs to songs of protest and left her their marijuana plants to water while they set off in the summer to doss on Greek beaches.

They were the kind of people whom Noah within days had summed up without qualm or conscience as unworthy, leeching drop-outs. The idea that one might be soft enough in the head to run an emotional soup-kitchen from one's own home was for him beyond belief. He was content to have the state touch him for taxes to support the casualties of urban dislocation. But one's own living room – that was something else. Social workers and psychiatrists operated from behind the protective barriers of office desks, as was only right and proper.

The house, as it struck Noah, was small, cluttered and distinctly arty. It was furnished in a style which was painstakingly labour-intensive and revealed itself as a pretty, living collage of its occupant's life's collectings. She had, against the pale pink-glazed walls, a glass-fronted bureau which she had stripped years before, inch by inch, with a kitchen knife and a deadly chlorinated solvent which Noah later banished from the store cupboard as a substance whose use resulted in lung damage. The bureau back Ali had papered with pastel, hand-blocked wallpaper and she had filled its shelves, not with books, but with scalloped pink and white crockery, which sported a pattern of smocked rustics rolling hoops along winding cart tracks. Large areas of wall were covered with child art presumed to be Camilla's – in mirror-clip and plexiglass mounts, and with antique silk embroideries. These last were enclosed within old stucco frames whose moulded Grecian acanthus leaves were here and there quietly returning to plaster dust. Ali's chairs were almost all of latticed cane like the one in which he sat and padded with homemade unbleached calico cushions. In the midst of this cloyingly female house, this tastefully prettified dolls' house full of china and cane, were five ravaging and ill-mannered children who ought, he believed firmly, to have been at home and in bed.

The story wound to its close. Prince Charming dragged the broom across the rug, and stumbled, descending with sudden viciousness upon the pelvis of the blonde girl.

'Easy!' Arnie said, wishing to intercede, but the blonde required no defence.

'Leave off, Darren!' she said, getting her knee up. 'This ain't the effing Sleeping Beauty. You're supposed to get our effing apples out.' One by one he rolled them over and thumped them roughly between the shoulder blades with his stockinged right foot, slamming their ribs into the floorboards.

'There's yer apples out,' he said, waiting for praise. Then he led them, all astride the broomstick, into their own prematurely jaded little once upon a time beyond the Spanish rug. At the far end of the room, which was long and narrow, having once been two, Camilla, who had shut herself off from the scene, was quietly bent over her maths homework, biting her lip with concentration and counting on her fingers.

'Now then,' Ali said to her visitors. 'Please. Tell me what happened.' More in relish than in sorrow Arnie produced a flamboyant and spirited tale of miscarried justice. He had been held in a police cell for two hours where nobody would take a statement from him, he said, and where the police gave every sign of having been bought off by the driver of the fast car. This had staggered Arnie who had all along considered his extravagantly moustached accuser in the light of a caricatured joke. He was to be charged with wilful damage to property and would appear before a magistrate in due course. Ali was speechless, but neither Noah nor Arnie seemed unduly perturbed.

'He'll get his hair cut before the hearing,' Noah said, 'He'll wear a shirt and tie, don't worry. But whose are all these children, Mrs Bobrow?' He asked, because Ali had already begun to back away from him towards the kitchen in response to Prince Charming's brisk demands for food.

'Neighbours' children,' she said. Noah got up, carefully avoiding the lampshade this time, and followed her into the kitchen.

'Are you a childminder?' he said.

Ali laughed. 'Unofficial. Unregistered and unpaid. I suppose I am for quite a lot of the time. They have to be somewhere don't they?'

Noah looked at his watch – a thing he did often – and once again disapproved of the hour. 'Where are the parents?' he said.

Ali shrugged. 'I don't ask.'

'My Mum said to come here so she could have a bit of peace,' Prince Charming said, with artless candour. He had paused in the act of drinking the contents of her undiluted orange squash from a plastic bottle. 'Can we have them frozen chips again?' he said. 'Just chips. Not them horrible beefburger things. I didn't like them things.' Ali took a large bag of frozen chips from her refrigerator.

'These?' she said.

'Yeah. Them,' said Prince Charming. 'And lots of ketchup.'

Ali laid five brightly coloured enamelled child plates upon the marble washstand where she and Camilla usually ate their meals and followed these with five little matching mugs. Noah cast his eyes over the little plates and the mugs, and the flowered Victorian tiles in the washstand which reminded him of ageing public lavatories.

'Mr Bobrow is evidently as tolerant as you are,' he said.

'Mr Bobrow doesn't live here any more,' Ali said.

'Ah,' he said, 'and no prizes for guessing who the real Snow

White is around here. Mrs Bobrow what services do your neighbours render you in return?'

'Services?' Ali said. 'Nobody renders me services. Why should they?'

'Pardon me,' Noah said doggedly, 'but if you make both the agenda and the menu so attractive, don't you ensure that your neighbours' children will never go home?'

Feigning gaiety, and with chip bag in hand, Ali stared at him with grudging admiration. 'You get it in one,' she said, 'but you're making me feel uncomfortable.' She tried smiling at him, but merely came up against his habitually muted facial response. It disconcerted her that he did not readily smile.

'Mrs Bobrow,' he said, 'what I mean is, when I was a child, it was thought to be bad manners to be around someone else's place at meal times.'

'Me too,' she said. 'But wasn't that long ago? And what are the alternatives then? Hateful little maxims? Charity begins at home?'

'Hateful, but workable,' Noah said. 'When do you look after yourself?' Ali poured cooking oil into a pan and watched it heat in silence.

'Is there any chance of you getting rid of all these kids so the four of us can eat out someplace?' he said. 'Is that a possibility?'

'It's an attractive idea,' Ali said who hadn't eaten out in donkey's years, and only partly on account of Mervyn's habit of quarrelling with waiters. 'I have to tell you that I don't have any money.' Patiently Noah spelled out what he had imagined to be obvious, but she was in some ways so curiously humble.

'I meant of course to treat you,' he said. 'Be my guest.'

'Gosh,' Ali said, who wasn't used to treats. 'There's Camilla's homework of course.'

'Okay. So we wait,' Noah said. 'We are none of us starving.'

'No,' Ali said. She threw the chips into the oil and called to the children. 'How about take-away chips?' she said, embarrassed by the false enticement in her own voice. 'You can take them home in paper bags tonight. Wouldn't that be nice?'

'Bleeding hell!' said Prince Charming, grudgingly, who liked the more liberal regime of Ali's house better than that of his own.

'Look,' Ali said, wheedling, trying bribery while Noah looked on in disbelief. 'You can take the whole frozen bag home as well. Your mother can cook the rest for you tomorrow.'

'She don't like to fry stuff,' said Prince Charming. 'She don't like the smell, see.' Conscious of Noah watching her, Ali drained the chips on kitchen paper with as much resolution as she could sustain and sought out five brown paper bags saved from the greengrocer.

'I'm going out,' she said with unprecedented strength. 'I don't terribly like the smell either.' Prince Charming departed in stockinged feet, sullenly clutching his football shoes along with his chips. The girls picked their anoraks off the living-room floor, displaying neither resentment nor gratitude. Not one of them bestirred herself to shut the front door. Arnie handed the blonde her knickers. 'You left your underpants,' he said. Ali closed the door behind them. Then she straightened the rug. She watched Noah, at the table where Camilla sat, fastidiously checking a stool for child crumbs before he sat down. His eyes were drawn to Camilla's notepad where she undertook her preliminary working. She had drawn six buns and one third, and had divided each of the six whole buns laboriously in three. Then she counted the sections.

'Nineteen thirds,' she said, wanting confirmation. 'That's what six wholes and one third makes.'

'Right,' Noah said. 'But what happens to your method when you get two hundred thirds? Or two thousand, maybe?'

Camilla giggled candidly.

'I'd draw lots more buns I suppose,' she said. When Noah laughed, Camilla laughed too. Camilla laughed so seldom these days that Ali stood still to watch her, as if waiting for the glass to crack in the window panes.

FOUR

SOME HOURS AFTER his evening out with Ali, Noah sat in his rationally appointed town house downing his charcoal filtered bourbon whisky and listening to Maxine Silver through the headphones. He was hoping to induce sleep. His lower back was aching slightly from the restaurant chair but the major impediment to sleep was Ali. Sexual desire had come upon him clear and sudden when she had smiled at him unexpectedly over a cheap cut-glass table lantern in the local Indian restaurant. When, on parting, she had stretched out her right arm to thank him and had lingered gratefully as she touched his sleeve with that long white hand with the lesions, an inundation of tenderness had in a moment turned that desire to something close to love.

He had felt strongly tempted to draw her aside and proposition her but had thought it impolitic. Right now it ruffled him to the point of irritability, almost, to find himself precipitously in love with a woman so damned other-worldly that a sexual proposition would in all likelihood constitute an emotional assault. The thing was unreal, just as the woman was unreal; a selfless good fairy endowed with an incongruously sexy, curving mouth, living among flowering teacups and creaking chairs. For all he knew she kept a pack of Tarot cards in the bureau drawer. Furthermore, she smoked. And when he had first suggested that they eat out she had looked so startled, almost as though, had he suggested instead that she spend the evening at home turning the collars of all his old shirts, she might have considered it more appropriate.

Once again he discovered a piece of his childhood returning to him as he thought about her. 'Piano fingers' was what his mother had called people with hands like hers. Her daughter's too. He had been moved by an impractical excess of maternal devotion in her. She and the child were so alike in spirit that they appeared to breathe in unison. He had watched them closely as painful small waves of apprehensiveness had crossed and recrossed between them during the evening. The woman was in a state of anxiety over that pretty, highly strung child, whose existence was tapping her emotional energy. This was plainly not necessary. He needed to make her see that it was not necessary. He was resolved.

Procrastination had never featured among Noah's personal baggage. He rose at eight the following morning, as he always did, in spite of his late night, drank coffee as he ran his eye over the home and foreign news, and was at Ali's front door by nine-thirty, sluiced and shaven, cuff-links already in position and bearing a small gift of sweetpeas. He had not meant to give her sweetpeas, but flowerstalls, he found, were not well represented in the city and sweetpeas were all he had been able to find. He had bought them reluctantly from outside a greengrocer's shop where they had sat in a zinc bucket between lettuces and cauliflowers, but they hit the mark with Ali. The gift struck her as tender and spontaneous.

Having been laundering Camilla's sheets, she first removed her rubber household gloves to receive them and, pulling her wrap-over dressing gown closer against her chest, asked him to come in. She turned her calligrapher's pens out of the marmalade jar and replaced it on the bureau filled with water for the sweetpeas whose varying shades of pink and blue fused in flowering profusion with the bureau's papered backdrop like a heady Matisse.

'There,' she said with elation, 'I love them! Don't you just love them?' Noah merely said, rather stiffly, that he had wanted to thank her for 'a beautiful evening' and that he hoped he was not intruding coming, like this, so early, but that he was on his way to 'the unit' as he called it, and had wanted to come by before the routine of the day took him over. On the marble-topped washstand, he saw, with a curious, inexplicable pleasure, that there lay now the crumbs of her breakfast toast and the shell of her boiled egg. Ali was amused by what struck her as an excess of propriety. She smiled at him warmly.

'I'm very glad to see you,' she said. 'And I don't mind at all about it being so early, because what difference should it make to me? I've never slept in curlers.' Her hair, he saw, had been bundled up and fixed hurriedly with a child's ornamental plastic clasp, presumably her daughter's. For Noah her head and neck were thereby endowed with the distinctly provocative look of a woman surprised in the bath tub.

'Have some coffee with me,' she said.

He watched her with a critical fascination, undimmed by love, as she prepared some ominously insipid-looking instant coffee, casting one meagre concave teaspoonful into each of two pink and white cups. The kettle gave her some trouble, he noted, as she struggled to wedge it in under the tap because the sink was bulging with steeping bedsheets. These she wrung out, as the kettle boiled, into tight twisted coils like a peasant washer-woman.

'Isn't that a little laborious?' Noah said, being a compulsive time-and-motion man. 'What's wrong with the laundromat?' Ali, knowing something of why he had come, felt reluctantly that she ought to deter him. Such a long time had passed since a thinkable man had courted her affections that the experience was wholly refreshing – especially when one remembered that the last such occasion had been over a year before when a reeking, drunken tramp had singled her out from the congregation of waiting mothers at the school gate one afternoon and had

55

serenaded her with beery arias from Puccini. Yet one could not decently trifle with so imposing a person's time, especially if that person had the air of one whose time was worth some twenty guineas an hour in consultation fees.

'Camilla pees in her bed every night,' she said, unambiguously declaring liability. 'I can't be carting sheets to the launderette every day.'

They moved on into the living room and sat down at the table where Ali reached for her cigarettes and lit up.

'People are free to pee in their own beds,' Noah said. 'Just so long as they launder their own bedlinen.' The observation, along with its gloriously unfrightened tone, earned Noah Ali's sudden undying regard.

'I think that could well be the nicest thing anyone has said to me in ten years,' she said. 'Thank you for it.'

'Why do you smoke?' Noah said in reply. 'You must be aware that it will almost certainly ruin your health.' Ali laughed with a jerky, nervous gaiety.

'I smoke to protect my lungs from lead in petrol fumes,' she said, turning to flick ash into the grate.

'Don't get smart with me,' Noah said, rather rudely, she thought, in the circumstances. 'Lungs are a part of my job.'

'Sorry,' she said. 'I smoke because I'm a nervous wreck I expect. Or what do you think? And I worry about my darling daughter rather a lot, as must be perfectly obvious to a person such as yourself. Perhaps you know something of what it feels like to be worried about your children.'

'Sure,' Noah said. His two sons, from whom he had effectively been estranged for close on sixteen years, were now twenty-two and twenty. After the early phase of weekending with them – teddy bears and toothbrushes in carrier bags from FAO Schwartz – he had put them almost completely out of mind. They were called Frederick and Shane. Frederick after an enthusiasm of Shirley's for the writings of Engels and Shane after the movie. Noah had insisted upon the latter. He had liked the movie. Moreover, the name had pleased his mother as meaning 'beautiful' in Yiddish. Ali would have been considerably deterred at this time both by the ideological labelling of Noah's firstborn son or by his naming the second after a western, but she did not know. By the time she found out she was already too much disposed in his favour to mind.

'Your daughter is like you,' Noah was saying. 'She's sensitive, she's artistic; right now she's a little on edge. Those are not bad things to be.'

'You're kind to me,' Ali said, 'but I can't say I find it a great comfort – the idea that she's like me.'

'Why not?' Noah said sharply. 'What's wrong with you?'

Ali shrugged, attempting to cast off that curiously prevalent surfacing of tears. 'I must admit that I live with the constant feeling that Camilla, who is the best and most beautiful thing about me, has been botched up. By me. Well, by Mervyn and me. Both of us. Do parents need to be so destructive?'

Noah made a comfortably sceptical face. 'Among conscientious parents that fantasy is common enough,' he said, sounding a little textbookish. 'To imagine that one has power to fashion the product. But no child is clay in the hands, Mrs Bobrow. You are not that omnipotent.'

'Gosh,' Ali said. 'Omnipotent. Me?'

'You're overprotective,' Noah said, jumping in to dispense advice where he had come to pay court. 'If you protect a child as much as you do, you necessarily imply that the world is a pretty scary place.'

'And so it is!' Ali said. 'For Camilla it is. She's had a difficult life.'

'Not so it couldn't have been a whole lot more difficult without a caring mother,' Noah said.

Ali was touched by the tribute since, for all that it struck her as uninhibitedly homespun, it was also both sensible and kind. 'I protect her,' she said. 'But who's to say I overprotect her? That is merely your opinion.'

'Like you almost threw yourself under a car for her yesterday?' Noah said. 'Is that in the line of parental obligation?'

'No,' Ali conceded with a good grace. 'One could not honestly say that it was.' She took surprisingly little exception to his preachiness and know-how. As the youngest in a family of three daughters she had always accepted the management of others as the natural order. It came to her still as a great release to have others take charge of her busfare and of her raincoat. The presence of a man who dispensed advice on child-rearing or took over when the neighbours' children encroached was to her as reassuring as to have one's father about, to whom one had been able to carry one's broken dolls. 'It's nice of you to concern yourself about me,' she said. 'It's nice of you to care.'

'But I do care,' Noah said, with a gravity which she found suddenly embarrassing. 'Mrs Bobrow, I believe that I may already be a little in love with you.' Ali got up in agitation here, scraping her chair noisily on the floor as she did so. She fidgeted restlessly, attempting to fit her feet this way and that into the sections of pine floorboard, as she sought for words.

'Now look,' she said. 'Now listen to me. I know why you say this to me. It's because I look so much like a Quaker. It's happened to me before. It means that men can't fancy me without being in love with me first. But the way a person looks is just an accident, don't you see? It's the accident of that person's physiognomy. I inherited this bleached, pulpit look from my mother. It can be a terrific disadvantage with men. If you don't believe me I beg you to try watching men approach me in the street. You will be able to bet your life on it they are all coming to ask me the way to the Friends' Meeting House.'

Noah, watching her, was suddenly beaming unguarded amusement and delight. 'Come here,' he said. Ali was very much aware during that unexpected and unscheduled kissing that Noah had begun to work some highly competent erogenous magic upon the female folds of her groin, like a practised gourmet unleaving an artichoke. His accomplishment there excited her just as once – comparably but less directly – Mervyn had excited her by walking the floor on stilts.

'Which way now to the Friends' Meeting House?' Noah said. 'Would it be altogether gross of me to enquire whether you are adequately protected against conception?'

'I've got a coil,' she said. He followed her up the stairs to her bedroom where he selected the largest from among the dense scatter of cushions upon her bed and wedged it purposefully under her rump. Then he locked her ankles around his neck in a manner which, for all that it provoked a memorable effusion of erotic delight, made alarming demands upon her gymnastic agility.

'I want you to know that I can't stay like this much longer,' she said. 'Not that it isn't very good news to me of course. It's just that I've never done yoga.' Noah let down her legs with a nice lack of masculine touchiness.

'Okay,' he said, 'straddle me.'

Afterwards Ali found it always a little compromising to remember that when – while relishing that reassuring amphibian crouch – she had said to him, 'I'm frog,' and Noah had responded unexpectedly with a coolly sadistic male wisecrack having to do with dissection, she had promptly been startled into so violent and uncheckable a sexual climax that it had made her appear unambiguously as the conniving handmaid in her own subjection. She wondered occasionally whether this pleasurable quiescence was not highly suspect. Was it a dark secret worm in the female soul, planted by ages of incessant and subtle conquest? Was there a despicable but necessary Sambo lurking in the female psyche? That boat responding always gaily 'to the hand expert at sail and oar'; the heart beating always to controlling hands. Why were these the fragments to shore against one's ruin?

'Frog spawn,' Ali said happily as she took from him a timely wodge of Kleenex to mop the dribble from her thighs. 'I like you. Mister, you've got style.'

It was moments later that Noah got asthma. Having turned

over to relax face down in Ali's pile of geriatric feather cushions, he coughed twice and almost ceased to breathe. Ali, who had never seen a person get asthma before, concluded that he was expiring from post-coital heart attack.

'Oh my God,' she said in great distress that a person – such a nice person too – should have cast away his life in the cause of giving her pleasure. But Noah right then sat up, looking a little blue around the mouth and said, in curious staccato rushes between gasps, 'Bronchial spasm. No need to call on God. Just get rid of all these goddam lethal cushions. All these hairy drapes.'

Ali's pretty, cluttered bedroom was one which could have been devised in an asthmatic's nightmare, but then there was no reason why she should have been expected to maintain an anti-allergic interior in the expectation of Noah's coming, whose bronchial tubes were frankly at their most comfortable in air-conditioned airport lounges. For him the down cushions on the bed were a gravely bad thing, but they were by no means the end of the matter. Pale grey velvet curtains, thickly lined and never dry-cleaned, hung to the floor, emanating dust which danced in shafts of sunlight (one of which fell now on to Ali's pale, creamy breasts). A quiet breeze stirred in the grate, gently mingling old soot, brick dust and pigeon feathers with the crumbling particles of dried flowers which had stood for years upon the hearthstone. Among a tumble of woollen blankets which had fallen from the bed lay a handwoven bedcover in tones and textures like an Orkney ram, still sparsely embedded with cat hairs from the last of Ali's line of marmalade tom cats.

'All this spinster's junk!' Noah said rudely, as he got up and made for the door. 'I'd like to take a bath.'

In Ali's bathroom the Ascot water system leaped into action for him with the lighting up of two rows of ancient burners. Water flowed into the tub along its time-worn, lime-stained channel and filled the room with soothing clouds of steam. Crouching in deep waters, Noah breathed as a grateful archaeologist among archaic plumbing. He coughed with a grim regularity as the bronchial spasm began to ease. It was then he noticed on the wall alongside the bath, somewhat pocky with condensation marks, a small aqua-tinted drawing of a woman bathing. It was Ali's own drawing from Ingres. A woman white-skinned as Ali, he thought, but rather more amply fleshed.

'Alison,' he called with modestly gathering strength through the half-open door. 'I want you to do me a favour.'

'Yes,' Ali said. She got to her feet all too readily, for the sounds of Noah's throat-clearing were beginning to grind her down.

'Get my inhaler,' he said. He employed an economical, inventory style of speech to save on breath. 'Brown bathroom. Top shelf. A plastic device with metal canister fitted in the top. Four inches high. Keys in my pants.'

For just one stupid moment a vision rose in Ali's mind of those voluminous regulation bloomers one had worn in the junior school with a pocket to the right of the gusset for one's hanky and one's spending money but Noah had meant, of course, his trousers.

His front door, she found, had three locks topped by a sturdy Chubb which had been recommended to him by the local constabulary as the most effectively burglar-proof. Once inside, a succession of unbecoming veneered flush doors opened to her without a creak over gleaming chevron wood-blocks. Light, which usually emanated from boxy theatrical spots high on the wall, was now almost nonexistent. Ali made her way wide-eyed past two sizeable brown leather armchairs, one of which revolved at the touch upon a shiny chrome swivel and the other – a recliner – reminded her of dentists' surgeries. She sucked quietly at her teeth as she passed.

The three locks evidently existed to protect Noah's recording and sound-transmitting equipment which intruded assertively from an outsize wallhung shelf and looked like an electronically inclined burglar's delight. His houseplants appeared distinctly carnivorous to her and somewhat overlarge. The inhaler was not in the hemp-coloured bathroom, though the colour allowed for confusion. The brown bathroom, unambiguously brown and dark as a cave, led off Noah's equally brown bedroom. It had no access at all to natural light. A light switch activated not only light, but electrically ducted air, and the consequent whirring gave the place an aeronautical aura which caused Ali to reach uncomfortably for the inhaler and make off with it in haste to Noah's front door. Once back in her own little house, she mounted the stairs to the bathroom where Noah smiled at her so benignly, though heaving still through clouds of steam, that her antipathy to his house receded.

'You're great,' he said. 'You're terrific, Mrs Bobrow. Do you know that? Another time I'd like for us to use my bed, that's all.' Ali laughed with relief.

'Don't call me Mrs Bobrow,' she said. 'I'm Ali. Isn't "Mrs Bobrow" my mother-in-law? I'm really sorry about what happened to your chest.'

'How so?' Noah said graciously who had so recently been apportioning blame to her. 'Do you make yourself responsible for my body chemistry?'

'No,' Ali said. 'But for my hairy clutter, I suppose I do. I'll wait for you outside, shall I? I'm squeamish about medications.'

In the early September sunshine she passed the time coaxing seeds from last year's honesty pods, exposing the flat, silvery discs within until Noah's ample shadow crossed her lap. He brought her his shirt-cuffs to fix, dropping his cuff-links into her hands and holding out his wrists to her like a husband of established standing. The gesture, which passed him by, both startled and amused her.

'Are you better?' she said, pushing the studs into the cuffs which had already lost some of their ugliness.

'Much better,' he said. 'And now, regrettably, I must leave you. I have work to do.'

Ali smiled at him a little sceptically, because the church clock had just struck eleven. 'You'll get there in time for the morning coffee break,' she said.

'Alison, understand that I work,' Noah said primly. 'I don't clock in and out, but baby I work.'

'I know,' Ali said. 'But I wonder, will you tell me something before you go? Am I really so much like a spinster as you meant to imply?'

'Pardon me?' Noah said.

'You said I was like a spinster,' Ali said. 'You meant that I was a person to keep mothballs in my linen press. Lavender bags in my underwear drawers, not so?' Rising within him, Noah found, was a determination, clear and chivalrous, to keep her in fine Swiss underwear as soon as this became decently appropriate. Nothing vulgar, of course; nothing grossly titillating; nothing of the see-through, split-crotch variety. He would keep her, most suitably, in pale satin and lace. Once one had paid for a person's undergarments then one had earned the greater right and pleasure in removing them. But she had asked him a predictably crackpot question and he was standing unwittingly close to the fence as he made his reply.

'You may be full of tremulous quim introspection,' he said, 'but baby, you fuck like the emperor's whore.'

Unbeknown to him, Ali's elderly female neighbour was at that moment airing her half-dozen ageing pugs and suffered not at all from impaired hearing. Relations between this person and the Bobrows had never progressed beyond indirect, tactical warfare, for Mervyn had always excluded the elderly from his schemes of neighbourly interdependence and support. Indeed, he had reported old Margaret within days of his moving in for keeping unlicensed dogs and had subsequently always shied away from her in high-minded loathing. He had even on occasion been known to make time-honoured smutty wisecracks along the lines of unmarried old women and their dubious closeness with male dogs but that was, naturally, before his recent conversion to the causes of the sisterhood. As Ali perceived her neighbour's crimes, they were the familiar crimes of the contemporary urban pariah: she was conspicuously old, poor, lonely and female. In addition, she walked her dogs in the winter months in little tattered plaid coats which was enough to make her, in Mervyn's eyes, a legitimate figure of scorn.

At the sound of Noah's voice issuing forth that unequivocal statement of sexual commitment, the pugs began to bark as if on cue, working themselves to a fever pitch of bronchitic indignation, rooting and scratching at the palings as beasts possessed. Feeling his ankles at risk, Noah jumped. The neighbour's voice, as she addressed her dogs, quavered feebly over the din with pointed dignity.

'Don't bark at him, my darlings,' she said. 'I assure you *he's not worth it.*' Poor Noah, to be not worth the barking of a half-dozen toothless pugs! Afterwards he always denied that he had straightened his tie in response, but that was exactly what he did. He certainly never got round to finding the utterance funny, but in Ali's experience men did not readily laugh at things which were undermining to their dignity. This did not surprise her since she had always appreciated the awesome responsibility of being male as a hugely sobering burden. And she saw right from the beginning that Noah carried it well. Better than most. Better than anyone. Only one man in Ali's past had ever really laughed at himself and that was Thomas Adderley, who was somehow incomparable.

FIVE

THREE DAYS LATER ALI raised her voice from the comfortable orthopaedic bed where she lay unclothed in Noah's bedroom and addressed him over the sound of running water. He stood fully clothed at the hand basin of his brown bathroom-ensuite, still slightly wet around the hair from a recent shower. Ali had never known a person shower as much as Noah; had certainly never known one who did so with the assistance of pilfered plastic canisters of hospital-issue liquid soap. The soap delighted her as a reassuring blemish upon an otherwise over-scrupulous character. She had noticed that he had a tendency to turn taps off with his elbows.

'I said that I can't come tomorrow,' she said. 'It's Saturday.'

'So what's wrong with Saturday?' Noah said. 'You always practise abstinence on Saturday?'

'Camilla is at home on Saturday,' Ali said. 'I can't leave my daughter to watch the television half the morning while I totter down the road to my fancy man's bed. I could come again this evening. She has her piano lesson this evening. I could place my body at your disposal for one hour.'

Noah reentered the bedroom where he rested a hand upon his desk which stood alongside the bed. Upon it was a small, portable electric typewriter – the first Ali had seen – and an old wire-backed typing manual, sent on by Noah's mother and open at lesson one. Noah, oddly enough, had never learned to type and was now, undaunted in his fiftieth year, attempting to make good this lack, but it did not come to him easily. He raised his eyes from the manual to enjoy the wholeness of Ali's nudity. Then, taking up a narrow belt from her jeans on the floor, he fastened it around her waist. It pleased him to watch the small brass buckle lie coldly across her warm umbilicus.

'Making love twice in one day is for younger men than I am,' he said, but entirely without apology. 'Come tomorrow. Send Camilla out with a girl friend on a shopping trip. They can spend the morning checking out boutiques. That's what girls like to do, isn't it?'

'What boutiques?' Ali said. 'You're not in Manhattan you know. Anyway, Camilla hasn't really got girl friends. She prefers to spend her spare time with me.'

'I see,' Noah said, with dearly contrived restraint. 'In that case we won't discuss it.' He bent and kissed her cheek. 'I'm off. You're a great lady, Al. Lock up when you leave and return me the keys at the unit. You'll come by the hospital lunchtime, right?'

'Yes,' Ali said, because it had been very pleasant these last days to eat a late lunch with him in the canteen on her way back from her cleaning job. Yesterday it had fortified her against the unavoidable encounter with Virginia Woolf whose Blu-tack had been reactivated. But it made her smile to think of his keys; that in this life there were those like Noah who held with constant and rigorous locking and those, like herself, who used locks only intermittently and then usually to lock themselves out in error.

'You carry more keys than a jailer,' she said gaily, because her gaiety was fast returning to her, perhaps as a foil to his sobriety. 'My God, I have gone to bed for three consecutive days with a hard-core lock zealot. What's more, you're a medic, Noah. I don't care at all for medical persons as a category. I have to tell you that.'

Noah shrugged and looked quite pleased. 'I guess that way I

don't get to share you with my colleagues,' he said. 'You have no other complaints against me, I trust?'

'There is a great deal I could hold against you,' Ali said, for no other reason, really, than to delay him a little. 'There is your house for a start. You live in a house that looks as if Habitat Contract International flew in and set it up for you within twenty minutes. Houses ought to grow, Noah. I fear that no love has gone into your set-up here. Have you always lived like this?' But Noah was not responsive to questions about his history. He found them irrelevant.

'So tomorrow I'll stay home and weave rugs and drapes for you,' he said. Ali laughed to think of it.

'And by your own confession you have just had those shoes handmade for you by Duckers of the Turl.' She pointed accusingly to his feet. 'I consider that an unforgiveable extravagance even for a man with unusually high insteps. You wear ugly shirts. Furthermore, you pilfer soap from the National Health Service.'

'*Pilfer soap?*' Noah said. 'If you call that pilfering, baby, it's because you never lived through the war.'

'I did in a peripheral sort of way,' Ali said. 'I remember my mother wrapping food parcels in Irish linen for what she called "the Eastern Sector". You had to oversew the edges with buttonhole thread and write the addresses in marking ink. I don't know what happened about the stamps. I was too young to know about stamps. Perhaps you fixed them on with blanket stitching? I suppose the postmen in East Berlin ate well at any rate. Or their masters did.'

'Sure,' Noah said, whose own somewhat remote European relations had not needed food parcels since they had early on in the war been herded into synagogues and burned to death, while Ali's mother's relations had had the better fortune to end up in meagre tenement houses, nursing pre-war memories of stables, cooks and holiday houses in the Rhineland.

'We'll let the soap pass,' she said. 'But you perform experiments on live animals which is a thing I always sign petitions against in the local organic food shop.'

'Bring up your knees a moment would you?' Noah said suddenly. Ali drew up her knees. 'Just let your thighs fall open,' he said. 'I'd like to check your IUD.'

Ali continued to talk with splayed legs. 'So you see there is little to recommend you but that you steal soap and that you can't type. You are the only American I have ever met who can't type, by the way. I grant that you're dead good at feeling up women but that is to do with your great age and experience. Did you say you were fifty?'

'When did you last get this thing checked?' Noah said.

'Checked?' Ali said. 'What do you mean checked? I had it fitted didn't I? About two years ago some miserable sadist medic at the Family Planning Clinic jammed a speculum up me and shoved the thing in. It hurt like hell. A woman doctor she was, but women doctors are often even bossier than the men. They're collaborators really, aren't they? They behave like the men only more so. This particular one said that since the NHS was doing me such a favour and providing the thing, could I please try not to look so much like a "dying duck in a thunderstorm" during the insertion. Say, oughtn't you to go to work, Noah? This is no time for the laying on of hands.'

'The device is not in position,' Noah said, employing his usual deadpan manner.

Ali stiffened and drew in her breath.

'Most probably you ejected it almost immediately if the insertion was unusually uncomfortable,' he said. 'I guess you flushed it down the toilet without noticing. It's easily done.'

'Are you serious?' Ali said. He was already back at the hand basin, laundering his hands with quite unnecessary vigour.

'Sure,' he said. 'Don't forget that your system has a powerful capacity for rejecting foreign bodies. D'you ever get any abdominal discomfort?'

Ali brushed aside the question. 'You're saying I'm pregnant,' she said.

'Not necessarily,' Noah said. 'Just tell me what's with your menstrual cycle. Like when do you expect your period?' Ali searched her mind for landmarks to assist recall but it was not a thing of which she had recently had much cause to take note.

'It'll come back to me,' she said after a pause, more with hope than with conviction. 'I'm sorry, Noah, but I don't keep records.'

'Oh for Chrissake,' Noah said impatiently. 'Come on, Al. When?'

'Being sexually inactive, I had no need to remember it till now,' Ali said. 'I mean there are people in the world who don't know when they were born. The point is that people only remember what it's necessary to remember. Anyway, I thought I had a coil. Now you tell me I've flushed it down the loo.'

'If you're lucky,' Noah said, sniping nastily, though his own peasant grandmother had not known her date of birth.

'And what's that supposed to mean?' Ali said.

'The device could be in your uterus,' Noah said, rising to the subject. 'It could be Christ knows where. How the hell should I know if you don't? It's your body, Al, not mine. Why don't you take proper care of it?'

'You're saying I could have a baby with bits of copper entangled in its brain,' Ali said, morbidly.

'Listen, Al,' Noah said, 'whatever you have or haven't got in there, it ain't no baby. Not after three days. Not unless you also sign petitions in support of foetal rights in that lentil-bread and seaweed cookie store of yours.'

'I don't, actually,' Ali said trying hard by now to fight back tears. 'It may surprise you but that isn't one of my causes. Neither is astrology, nor do I shake my tambourine for the Hare Krishnas. I don't even have a dog called The Hobbit. In short, I'm no bloody fool because I don't tick the way you do.'

'I'm sorry,' Noah said, feeling justly rebuked; feeling suddenly for her battered, female self-esteem; feeling her violation at the hands of a half-baked technology which in truth he despised as much as she did and somehow had not said so, but had leaped instead into the classic response and blamed its victim; feeling profoundly that to watch Ali nursing a child would be a better thing than to be setting up abdominal X-rays for her, and pregnancy tests. He sat down on the bed.

'I love you,' he said. 'You flushed it down the toilet, don't worry. It happens all the time.'

Ali's mind made a felicitous connection. 'I'm not pregnant,' she said abruptly. He noticed that she wiped her nose peremptorily on his adjacent pyjama sleeve, but he let it pass. 'I remember now, because I had the gruelling job of finding Kotex pads for Camilla on the August Bank Holiday. She won't use my Tampax, you see.'

'Hold it, Al,' Noah said. He allowed to escape the merest hint of impatience in the expiration of his breath. 'Where does Camilla come into this?'

'Well, she comes in because we always bleed together,' Ali said. 'Always. To the day. I'm sorry Noah. I do see that menstrual telepathy isn't up your street, but there you have it. My period is due any day now. I reckon we're all right.' Noah picked up his jacket with considerable relief.

'You're crazy, Al,' he said, with infinite pleasure. 'Do you know that? I love a crazy woman. God knows why I love you.'

'It does seem a little odd to me,' Ali said. 'Not to say precipitous. I mean, after four days, Noah. For a rational man like you.'

'Call your doctor,' Noah said sharply in reply. 'Call him now while I'm watching. Tell him I want you properly checked out for any abdominal tenderness. Tell him I want an X-ray.' Ali started to laugh but tried to suppress it. 'And while you're on to him,' Noah said, 'tell him I want those lesions on your hand checked out. What the hell's so funny?'

'Nothing,' Ali said, thinking how he had just said it was her body wasn't it, not his. 'What are lesions? If you mean these geriatric blotches, they probably go away if you chew raw meat in a graveyard at full moon. Are you saying I've got leprosy?'

Noah picked up the telephone, planted it squarely before her and handed her the receiver.

'Call your doctor,' he said. He was not a person to procrastinate in the face of a necessary telephone call. He was not an accumulator of in-tray material, or of unpaid bills; not a hoarder of uncollected dry-cleaning tickets. Even in her preoccupied condition, Ali appreciated this as a great gift and a rare one. By the grace of God, this kind, thirteen-stone competent person had fallen in love with her because she had smiled at him over a candle-stub in a restaurant and had struck thereby at something deeper than culture and reason.

'You talk to him Noah,' she said. 'I haven't seen my GP in donkey's years. Go on. You'd be better at it. Just explain to him that you want the entire product overhauled and he'll do it. He'll listen to you. If I tell him he'll pass the buck to the Family Planning Clinic and I'll get the female sadist all over again. Anyway, what can I tell him? "My man friend says I've got leprosy and a fucked-up crotch"?'

'You'll cope,' Noah said. 'There's no way you'll act as dumb as you try to make out. I'll see you lunchtime, Al. Like one-thirty. Don't be late.' And, with that, he promptly left the house.

It was with the intention of telephoning Noah that Ali approached the public telephone box. She was on her way back from work. Having gone at once to her doctor's surgery and only then to her bachelor's establishment, she was running late; too late to lunch with Noah. A person was hovering near the box and was peering in rather haughtily, through either impatience or curiosity. Inside the box, slumped on the floor, was Ali's next-door neighbour.

'Drunk, I reckon,' said the observer, with a shrug.

'Or dead!' Ali said in outrage. She wrenched open the door. There was no smell of alcohol from within. Only the familiar, poignant odour of dry rot and wet dog which hangs about the clothing of the aged, dog-loving poor.

'Can you hear me?' Ali said, crouching. The neighbour half opened a glaucous blue eye and closed it again. There were small traces of recent vomit on her coat lapels. 'I'll call an ambulance,' Ali said. The mention of an ambulance induced a sudden desperate animation in the neighbour, who struggled to her knees, clawing at Ali's shins, and stumbling slightly, as she did so, in the hem of her own coat.

'Get me a taxi,' she said sharply. 'Never an ambulance.' Ali hesitated. 'Go on,' she snapped.

'A taxi,' Ali said. She rifled the Yellow Pages with a shaking hand, then dialled and spoke her needs.

'Give me a bunk up, would you?' said the neighbour. The deed accomplished, they struggled to a nearby bus stop and sat down.

'I get these turns,' she said, by way of explanation, 'but sometimes they can take me unawares. I always go prepared. I always carry plastic bags for vomit.' ('plaastic', she said. The giveaway vestige of a one-time private school gentility.) 'People think you're drunk. Can I bum a cigarette off you for now?'

'Of course,' Ali said. She groped hastily in her bag and – holding two cigarettes between her teeth – lit up with difficulty in the slight wind.

'It's bloody old age,' said the neighbour. 'It's an obscenity. *Plaastic* bags for urine; *plaastic* bags for vomit. Be warned. There's nothing prepares you for this bloody decrepitude. You live in fear of losing your teeth down a drain. I'm buggered if I'll let some bloody rat have my teeth. I've kept my turns under control for two years, now. I watch what I eat, you see. Raw egg-white,' she said as though passing on a coveted, secret recipe. 'Raw egg-white and cream crackers. That's what my stomach holds down.'

'And nicotine,' Ali said pensively. The neighbour produced an unexpected, high-spirited cackle.

'And tea,' she said. 'You could say I was a vegetarian couldn't you? Tannin and nicotine. God, but I don't half crave a bloody steak sometimes, don't you?' She had evidently been to the public library and was now shaking cigarette ash liberally into her large-print edition of GBS which lay in her shopping bag along-side an economy-size bag of bone-shaped dog biscuits. 'You can even get nostalgic for the gristle, so long as you've got your teeth. Never call me an ambulance,' she said, reverting to a former theme. 'When they get you in hospital at my age, you see, they don't bloody let you out. Then it's nothing but nurses wheeling you to the bloody lavatory along with all the other grumbling old hags till you join the coffin queue. Once a year at Christmas you get "Knees Up Mother Brown" and that's your lot till you get your bloody shroud. Paper shrouds for paupers, eh? I'd sooner be boiled up in a pot and fed to the dogs.'

'Yes,' Ali said. 'I do see your point.'

In the taxi and at the neighbour's prompting, they smoked one more cigarette apiece.

'My name's Margaret,' she said. 'You're the girl next door.'

'Yes,' Ali said, colouring slightly at the memory of the em-peror's whore.

'You've got a new boyfriend,' Margaret said, as though read-ing Ali's thoughts. 'Hope he's an improvement on the last one, but I doubt it. I never understood men. Only dogs. All that bloody male ego. All that conceit. I never had the time for it. Nor for sex either. Never came to terms with it.' The taxi driver, young, handsome, brown-skinned and sleekly moustached, en-gaged in a brief spasm like a noiseless cough and glanced furtively sideways as if to commune with a miscellany of hard porn concealed within the glove compartment. 'I accept the sex in the dogs, of course,' she said, 'but for myself I find it galling to remember that I'm here on earth as a result of it.' She tapped the driver sharply on the shoulder. 'Are you a Muslim?' she asked, pronouncing the word as though it were a bad taste on the tongue.

'Come again?' said the driver, but she turned again to Ali. 'They have no place for spinsters in their religion, you see,' she said with haughty disdain. 'Their women are all either wives, concubines or mothers. It's the same in all these bloody tinpot religions.' She described a tremulous semi-circle with her arm, to denote a regrettably infinite variety of blind heathen. 'Jews too. They can't sit next to a woman on the bus, you know, in case she's having her monthlies.'

A hint of colour had returned to the neighbour's gravel-textured cheek, as though the subject of men had excited her somehow, in spite of her protests. At the door of the house, where she strenuously insisted upon paying, the neighbour drew her week's pension money carefully from a plastic wallet giving off stray dog hairs, counted out the fare with arthritic hands and pointedly denied the driver his tip. Whether she did so on grounds of race, sex, creed or simple frugality, Ali was not to discover.

In the neighbour's kitchen where she made a pot of tea, Ali encountered a poverty and decrepitude beyond her own imaginings. It hung in the blackened cobwebs which wrapped the ceiling in oily swathes. It hung in the hot-water cylinder, rusted now into uselessness, and in the green tarnish upon the nickel-plated teaspoons. Dogs scratched at food and scraps which lurked in the patches of exposed hessian backing the ancient linoleum on the kitchen floor. A small sprouting of mushrooms was visible under the enamelled cabriole forelegs of the gas cooker where Ali boiled the water. The upper floors were a storm of plastic dustbin bags spilling a lifetime's collection of jumble-sale clothing and bric-à-brac, among which purple nylon cardigans appeared to predominate. A faded Christmas wreath and a somewhat moth-eaten velour-covered plastic bulldog adorned the mantelpiece, flanking an old West-clox alarm, now ticking its way stridently towards two-thirty. A number of small dogs twitched in dreams, or gnawed at their own balding elbow joints. Naked live wires flirted with each other in the worn electric flexes which trailed in hair-raising profusion across the floor to the only electric power socket. On the window ledge, old Margaret was growing carrot-top trees in saucers.

'We'll have another cigarette, shall we?' she said, nestling among grimy pillows. 'Have one of mine.'

Ali found her the box. 'We oughtn't to smoke,' she said, in passing deference to Noah whom she was currently standing up. 'They ruin your health, cigarettes do.'

'Don't you bloody believe it,' said the neighbour with bitter conviction. 'If these things killed you the government would be handing them out free to the elderly. Get rid of us quicker. There's more of us all the time, you see, and we're expensive to keep – even in this bloody squalor.'

'I must go,' Ali said, glancing nervously at the alarm clock. 'I have to make a 'phone call.' But the discarded elderly have ways, subtle and various, of holding on to such attention as offers itself. And, besides, Ali was charmed by her spirit.

Noah was in a meeting when Ali tried at three and when she finally got him at three-thirty he was outspokenly not pleased.

'You didn't show,' he said angrily. 'What the hell happened to you?' Ali entered upon what seemed to him a predictably extended and breast-beating circumlocution having to do with a telephone booth and a somewhat eccentric person of considerably advanced years. The rest was a macabre haze through which he gleaned resignedly that Ali's life had become entangled yet again with another neighbourhood case for the Social Services Department.

'She can't hold down her food,' Ali said in earnest tones. 'I'm quite serious. She vomits. She lives on egg-white and crackers.'

'Protein deficiency,' Noah said briskly. 'Listen, Al. Can you make it to eat Italian with me tonight? Can you organise a baby-sitter? I'd really like to eat out with you.'

'I'll try,' Ali said, 'but it won't be easy.'

'How come?' Noah said. 'What do you usually do for a sitter?'

'I don't go out,' Ali said. There was a pause following upon this altogether truthful utterance during which Ali felt fairly sure that Noah – his mind already energetically occupied with linguini and egg-plant – was counting under his breath to control impatience.

'I'll set it up for a sitter to come at seven-twenty,' Noah said. 'Leave it with me. It's no problem.' His awesome armour of competence against the adult terrors of telephones and bureaucrats appeared to her without chink. And how was it that his mind's clockface would incorporate categories such as 'seven-twenty', where her own knew only the crudities – the big hand pointing either straight up or straight down, like the clock on *Playschool*.

'Thanks,' she said. 'Will you really?'

'Listen, I'm working till late,' Noah said. 'Call for me here around seven-forty. And for Chrissake, don't be late. I didn't eat lunch, remember? Neither did you, I imagine. I want you to take care of yourself, Al.'

'I shared the old lady's crackers,' Ali said. Noah's laugh was brief, jarring and inappropriate.

'Was that with or without the egg-white?' he said.

'What?' Ali said stupidly.

'Forget it,' he said. 'Just act like I never said it. Did you get to see your doctor yet?'

'Yes,' Ali said. 'He's going to do all those things you said, like the X-rays and whatnot.'

'That's good,' Noah said. 'That's excellent.'

'Noah,' Ali said cautiously. 'You wouldn't think of looking at her, would you? The old lady. She needs to see a doctor. She really does. Much more than I do.'

'*Me?*' Noah said. 'You asking me? If she needs a doctor, call her doctor. She's got to be registered with a doctor.'

'She isn't, that's the point,' Ali said. 'She's terrified that a doctor will put her in hospital.'

'So maybe she needs a hospital,' Noah said. 'For sure she needs to be registered with a doctor. Call the District Family Practitioners Committee if necessary. Hold it. I'll get you the number.'

'No thanks,' Ali said. 'It wouldn't be ethical.'

'Al,' Noah said, with effort, 'she isn't my patient, you understand. Visiting sick old ladies isn't my job.'

'I know that,' Ali said. 'Lungs are your job. You told me.'

'Jesus Christ!' Noah said. He had only recently emerged from a ninety-minute meeting: ninety minutes spent hustling for funds on an empty stomach. 'When you cling with such ridiculous and high-minded tenacity to the values of childhood, what is that supposed to do for me? Is that supposed to make me feel guilty?'

'I'm sorry,' Ali said.

'Me too,' Noah said, clearing his throat. 'I'm sorry too. I'm sorry to upset you. I want for you to do what's reasonable, that's all. Don't do too much. Don't take on the sins of the world, Al. To play Jesus Christ as you do: isn't that a kind of arrogance, wrapped up as humility?'

'Well,' Ali said, 'possibly.'

It was five minutes later, during a brisk perusal of the Yellow Pages, that Noah discovered the absence of a single locally based babysitting agency in the city.

'Oh shit!' he said. Arnie, who encountered him at that moment, laughed.

'Don't look at me,' he said. 'I'm busy this evening. I'll call up a couple of women I know if you like.' Noah, who had just spent a measure of his committee time exerting himself, successfully, in the business of extending Arnie's research grant, looked up irritably.

'The relevant question is whether any of the women you know would make suitable candidates for the job,' he said. 'This is a decent, overprotected, middle-class kid I have in mind.'

'Ali's kid?' Arnie said. 'Sure. I don't make it an absolute rule to consort with women of dubious repute. Did your dear lady ever turn up by the way?'

Noah raised his eyes to heaven. 'She got entangled with some goddam comatose geriatric in a 'phone booth,' he said. 'She just called me to explain.'

Arnie laughed again, feeling quite correctly that the misfortunes of others were the proper stuff of comedy.

'*Gesundheid*,' he said.

SIX

Aʟɪ's sᴋɪɴ ᴄᴀɴᴄᴇʀ ʟᴇsɪᴏɴs first diminished, then obligingly
disappeared in response to regular applications of a Swiss
pharmaceutical cream prescribed by the epidemiology department. The wandering IUD was, unhappily, less amenable to
persuasion. A series of abdominal X-rays revealed it lurking,
half-embedded, behind Ali's large intestine and – having perfor-
ated her uterus – it was removable only by surgical incision under
general anaesthetic which required a week-long stay in hospital.
While Noah gnashed his teeth on Ali's behalf, Ali herself was
occupied with hand-wringing on behalf of her daughter, because
Camilla would need to survive a week without her.

'No problem,' Noah said. 'She'll be my guest.'

For Noah to stay in her own house with Camilla was, Ali knew,
unthinkable. The bedding gave him asthma. Furthermore, Mervyn might turn up at any time and discover him there. But how
would Camilla cope away from her mother in a boxy house with
whirring light switches? And didn't Noah's work keep him in the
hospital until much too late? And what was to be done about her
piano practice or her daily packed lunches or, above all, her
habitual bedwetting? Urine stains on Noah's brand-new beds!

Noah, for whom the prospect of daily sandwich-making and
nightly child incontinence beckoned with no undue menace,
waved these anxieties aside as minor inconveniences and proposed that Camilla take the bus from school to the hospital each

afternoon to do her homework in the secretary's office. He concentrated his attention upon Ali's anxiety that Mervyn would appear and cause trouble. In preparation for this eventuality he overrode Ali's qualms and saw to the changing of her front and back door locks. Then he recommended that Camilla abandon her piano playing for the week to avoid a possible encounter with her father. One thing only, Noah hazarded, might cause Mervyn to claim rights of guardianship over his daughter and that would be the discovery of another man assuming the role in his place.

Noah had met Mervyn just the previous week and had not been favourably impressed. He had called on Ali one evening after work as he did with regularity and had found Ali sitting tensely upright upon one of her creaking wicker chairs, the colour oddly high in her cheeks. Mervyn was at the ironing board at the far end of the room rigorously ironing his pyjamas. Eva didn't own an iron, he said. She was above such things. Perched beside him on the asbestos ironing mat was a glass of Noah's own bourbon whisky which Mervyn had found in Ali's cupboard. The bottle was near him on the table.

'Have a drink,' Mervyn said, playing genial host to the newcomer. He held the bottle to the light to examine its contents.

'Bourbon is a woman's drink,' he said, smiling at Noah man-to-man. 'My wife drinks while I'm away.'

Noah, who had no intention of embarking upon a public competition for the ownership of Mervyn's wife, politely downed a glass of his own whisky and talked noncommittal generalities for twenty minutes. Then – gauging that Mervyn was bent upon outstaying him and that to have the man there ironing his nightwear all evening would be of no particular benefit to Ali – Noah left. No person of sense ironed pyjamas, he reflected, especially not in another person's house. Not unless he wished to convey messages. Mervyn was hurling messages at Ali's conscience which were absolutely clear: that he had unconditional rights in her household and her person; that as a person stooping there to woman's work, he deserved at once pity for his reduced situation and praise for his advanced habits. The knowledge that this person of malevolent, fickle intensity had ever had the power to dazzle Ali – his Ali – or possibly had it still, stuck all evening like a bone in his throat. Her course was crystal clear, god-dammit! Ali was to make an application without delay for a court order barring Mervyn from access. He proposed the course next morning but Ali wouldn't agree to it. Mervyn paid the mortgage, she said. The house was in his name. How could she? And how could people who had once cared for each other be reduced to behaving like that?

'Bullshit,' Noah said, but for the time it got him nowhere.

For Camilla, that week with Noah was recalled as a golden time and as quite memorably glamorous, first of all because on the Sunday evening, after she and Noah had settled Ali into her hospital bed in a new, tucked-cotton nightdress and had taken their leave of her, Arnie had joined them for a lovely supper in the walled garden of a city pub where – while the men praised English beer, and ate quiche and talked shop – Camilla drank two whole glasses of fizzy lemonade and ate cold sausages with lashings of delicious mustard pickle and played with the pub-lican's cat. The mustard pickle was nothing short of heaven and the publican had given her such a nice lot of it.

'A little piccalilli, Miss?' he had asked and had spooned it on to her plate as though it were a French salad. Then afterwards, when they had passed by the house to collect her bags, an impromptu and delightful comedy had set in because Arnie had lit upon two old carnival masks in her toy cupboard, of a dog and an old man, and had minced about with such rheumy, crackpot conviction in the second of these that she had been persuaded to put on the first and play the old man's dog. Liberated from her own shyness behind the mask, she had yapped and snapped with manic canine glee, now ahead, now behind, all down the street like a wild puppy, while Noah silently carried her bags and Arnie – bawling gruff, octogenarian comments – mimed to untangle a leash from lamp-posts. At his own front door, Noah drew his keys from his pocket, undid the three locks, and announced, categorically, that composure would be reestablished and the masks removed as a condition of entry.

'I mean to drink my coffee in peace and quiet,' he said.

'Wuff,' Camilla said, pushing her luck, but Arnie took off the masks, hers and his own, and said in his ordinary voice, 'Cool it, Bonzo. I need his coffee, okay? Besides, he's my boss.'

Once they were inside, and while the grown-ups' coffee filtered, Noah made her a little pot of hot chocolate which he served in one of his heavy, dark green French railway cups – his only remaining wedding gift salvage which Camilla had previously admired. Camilla admired all Noah's things without reservation. She loved their opulence and glossy, shop-floor newness. She loved his dark-coloured bathrooms with their mixer taps and bidets, his dark green and gold crockery, his shiny black-stained dining table on its chrome trestles.

Understanding that Noah was not the man to be wheedled into indulging night-time television viewing, she made her hot chocolate last as long as she could before she went to bed. Even going to bed was an adventure, because the bed was like an armchair that concertinaed out into a proper single bed. Camilla put her teddy in the bed and slid her large rubber undersheet carefully into position as Ali had said she should. She hadn't really wanted her mother to tell Noah about her bedwetting, but she could see now that it was better that he knew and anyway it hadn't made him treat her as if she had three heads. And it would have been jolly difficult to have kept on hiding the sheets from him. There was a lovely bedside lamp on a bendy stem by whose light she read some more of *Girl of the Limberlost*, which was her favourite book. She had read it twice before already, but it was so beautiful and so sad, especially when the children finally found the red-headed orphan boy's little, precious handsewn baby clothes which proved that his mother had really loved him after all. It made her cry every time, all over again. It would be horrible beyond imagining to be an orphan, Camilla thought. Even worse than having parents who quarrelled all the time. But Ali had promised her that she would not die in hospital. Camilla shuddered, as a moment's terror intruded to spoil the pleasure she took in the guest bedroom and in the bendy light. If Ali died, she reflected, she would have to go and live with her father and his horrid, bossy girlfriend, who most probably wouldn't even let her wear pink, or play with Sindy dolls. Eva would probably make Mervyn send her to boarding school, like in *David Copperfield*.

The daylight, however, brought renewed contemplation of pleasures in store. For Noah, instead of making sandwiches for what he called her 'bag lunch', had sent her off to the grocer's the previous day with two pounds in her purse and had told her to buy herself five days' supply of anything she liked to eat, so long as it wasn't candy or carbonated drinks. Camilla had chosen five pots of fruit-flavoured yoghurt with a different flavour for each day and five bags of Salt and Vinegar potato crisps. Then she had bought some vacuum-packed ham and a bag of six chelsea buns because she could eat the extra one on the way home from the shop. Going to the hospital after school turned out to be a treat for her too: to take the unfamiliar bus and make one's way down the grey, gloss-painted corridors and through three sets of smoky plastic doors to Noah's research unit where one shared a desk with the secretary who let one take telephone messages and gave one photocopy paper to draw on. It made one feel grown up.

Occasionally Arnie would come in, looking strangely purposeful, bending over the secretary with tables and graphs, or pulling files from grey filing cabinets. It was a little disappointing for her that he never appeared in his hairy goatskin which Ali had told her about, but was always quite properly dressed in decent roll-neck sweaters and laundered corduroys and loafers; even more disappointing was that he was always so wholly preoccupied: a little puzzling too, because she had not yet discovered that Arnie was a person who addressed himself both to work and to leisure with an equally ruthless commitment.

'How you doing?' he would say rather automatically and he would look right past her to the secretary or to the filing cabinets. Before she learned that the question was rhetorical with him, she would try, mistakenly, to answer. 'I'm doing very badly,' she said once, hoping to interest him in her maths homework. 'It says here that if a record accomplishes forty-five revolutions in one minute, how many revolutions does it accomplish in four seconds? What are you supposed to do?'

Arnie laughed, a little callously, she thought, because he must have known that she really *did* need help, and he answered her without even bothering to take his ballpoint pen out from between his teeth. 'With that many revolutions, I guess it's got to be Bolivia.'

'I beg your pardon?' Camilla said.

'Or someplace else,' he said carelessly, even as he moved to leave. 'West Africa, maybe. I'd say three, Cam. Think about it.' But that was no good, even if three was the right answer, Camilla thought to herself in some confusion, because you had to show your working or else Miss Hartley wouldn't believe that you had really understood. Noah never called her 'Cam', but he could always be relied upon to help if ever he came in, which, unhappily, was not often. He never implied, either by word or gesture, that three minutes taken out of his afternoon would alter the course of medical history. He would draw up a typing chair and sit down. Then he would very soon show her that there was excellent sense in dividing forty-five by sixty (which was difficult enough, Camilla assured him, unless one had a grown-up over one's shoulder). The rest would be plain sailing. You multiplied the revolutions in one second by four.

'The answer's three,' Camilla said, but she wondered how Arnie had managed to work it out so quickly.

'Great!' Noah said. 'You're doing great!' He was really very nice, Camilla thought. The only awkward thing about Noah at work was that he didn't like waste paper, which was a curious foible. She was not, repeat *not*, he said, to use expensive photo-copy paper to take telephone messages or for her drawings, and he ticked off the secretary for giving it to her. He offered her a drawer full of multi-coloured oddments.

'Use the scratch paper,' he said. But the 'scratch' paper, as he called it, was usually roneo paper that had already been used on one side, and there was something distinctly less pleasurable to her in using the not quite pristine sheets. They did not glow with the same seductive promise and infinite possibility. But none-theless, Noah was kind, even if he didn't understand this obvious truth. Perhaps it was because he wasn't 'artistic', Camilla thought. People always said that she and her mother were 'artistic'.

Every evening that week Noah worked until six when they would go in the car to see Ali and take her a *Vogue* magazine, or grapes, or a paperback novel. Ali had a gory, terrifying gash held together with horrible black tailor's tacking which went all the way from her navel right into where the nurses had shaved her pubic hair. Camilla had made the mistake of asking to see it and Ali had shown it to her. It had made her feel sick. Nonetheless, Ali looked very pretty, and calm and rested, Camilla thought. It came of having nothing to do except comb one's hair and read and do embroidery. And to wait for meals which nurses brought on trays. Only poor Ali missed her cigarettes. Noah wouldn't bring her any and had made her promise not to buy any from the trolley. Camilla wondered about the ethics of this, because it seemed bossy to her and none of his business, but he meant it for the best. He made Ali chew sugarless chewing gum instead, which left her mouth full of spittle. If she didn't smoke at all for a whole week, Noah said, he would buy her recordings of all the song cycles of Schubert, even though he hated them so much himself he would have to plug his ears or go out when she played them. Ali said they were 'lyrical' in the most pure and beautiful way and Camilla knew that some of them made her cry almost as much as *Girl of the Limberlost* made Camilla cry – especially the one about the land where lemon trees flowered and oranges grew. She heard her mother say that Noah ought to be moved by the songs just as she was, because his family must once have been German like hers, if his name was anything to go by. Noah just laughed and said that his family wasn't German at all, but East European Jewish and that his father had changed his name to Glazer when he first went to the USA to make himself sound more up-market.

'You're probably related to Mervyn,' Ali said. 'Who knows? Perhaps you share a Polish grandmother?'

Camilla could tell that Noah was very fond of her mother. He always began his visits by kissing her on the mouth in that sloppy, wet way that grown-ups had, which seemed to go on for ever. Noah was 'in love' with her mother. Camilla knew this without any doubt because there was a big new glossy book on the piano at home, of Matisse paintings, which must have cost absolutely pounds, she guessed, and inside it said 'For Al, because I love her'. Noah had given the book to her mother and had signed it with his name. Matisse was her mother's favourite painter, but Matisse didn't make Ali cry. Not like Schubert.

Camilla had observed that Noah was very good at buying Ali the right presents and concluded that this was the result of his being 'in love' with her. She knew that her mother had once been 'in love', a very long time ago, with a man called Thomas Adderley, who had been tall and dark and arty, and some people had used to whisper about him that he was half-coloured. If you were at all coloured where Ali came from, you were mostly not allowed to go to the same schools or universities as white people, but Ali had told her that certain people did – if their families were old enough or crafty enough to have got classified as white in the first place. Camilla presumed that Thomas Adderley's family had been either old, or crafty, or both. Anyway, Thomas hadn't minded, even when people had said to his face that he was a half-caste, partly because he had not been racially prejudiced, which was extremely unusual, Ali had explained, and partly because he had been so brainy and so handsome that he had had the edge over the name-callers. Also he had followed his mother's advice and had taken boxing lessons. Thomas's mother hadn't been like other people's mothers who had worn high heels, and played tennis and complained about the servants, Ali said. She had worn men's lace-ups, and had given sculpture classes at the technical college and had refused to have domestic help.

Ali hadn't married Thomas. She had married somebody else whom she never talked about, other than once to say he had been a 'brief irrelevance', and that his family had been French and had sided with Hitler during the occupation. Camilla knew that it was a terrible thing to have sided with Hitler and when her father had been in one of his shouting moods he had once called Ali a 'collaborator' because her mother's family had been German, and he said that Hitler had tried to kill him, which was puzzling, Camilla thought, because Hitler hadn't ever gone to Southend, but Ali said afterwards that it was 'poetic licence' and, broadly speaking, true. Her father wrote poetry sometimes, but it wasn't lovely, magic poetry like *Goblin Market* that you could understand. It was all fangs and blood. He had also recently written a book which she had heard her mother say was 'purple'. It wasn't that he couldn't be a good writer, Ali had said to Noah. It was just that he hadn't yet learned to read through his own stuff twelve times in a Sarcastic Bystander voice. It had made Noah laugh. Her mother was good at making Noah laugh. If her parents had ever been 'in love', then the idea merely suggested itself to Camilla that people didn't always stay in love, which was horrible to believe, but perhaps sensible people like Noah always did?

It was strange to think of Noah being 'in love' at all, really, because he was quite old and he didn't look anything like the pictures of men in *Real Life Photo-Love Stories* which one of the girls had brought to school. In fact, he looked a bit like her father's Uncle Morrie who had used to run a men's outfitters in Southend and who used to wear those spiralled wire elasticky things like bicycle clips around his upper arms to hitch up his shirt sleeves. Noah didn't wear those, of course, and he looked more important, but he *did* have short arms and he *did* wear dowdy, old-fashioned white underpants with Y-fronts that looked huge and embarrassing on the washing line over the bath. Camilla knew it was silly and childish to react that way but the Y-fronts bothered her. There was something about them that made her squeamish – like jock straps – because they were so exclusively for men. She was not sure if Y-fronts were so that men could pee without having the bother of undoing their trousers, or whether they had to do with that other strange and dreadful thing she knew men did with that disconcerting appendage which afflicted their nether parts. Did Y-fronts mean they could do it without even taking their underpants off? Ugh!

Mervyn's underpants hadn't had Y-fronts. They had been small black bikini pants and not very different from her mother's pants really, except that the cloth had been thicker. In fact Ali had used to borrow them sometimes in cold weather which had made Mervyn furious, but then he had always been blowing up about something or other in that scary way. Camilla's own feelings of relief about her father's departure caused her frequent nightly sessions of fear and guilt, but these had suddenly abated in Noah's house. Her father was a lot younger than Noah and he was more slim and natty-looking but for years now he had made her flinch and shrink. Camilla didn't understand about people getting married and then making each other so miserable, because in story books they got married and they lived happily and had lots of children who went on picnics and came home from boarding school – that was unless they died first. It would be lovely to get married in a long dress and have confetti and lots of children, she thought, so long as you could adopt the children and not have to do that dreadful thing together in bed every time you wanted to have another baby. But Noah wouldn't make anybody unhappy if he were married to them because he was so sensible and quiet and fair. Only on that first morning before school she recalled that he hadn't been altogether fair to her when she had needed his help with the sheets. At the time she had thought he was being really piggy and she had nearly cried, but she had soon forgiven him because the breakfast had been so good.

'Excuse me,' Camilla had said politely, a little puffed with effort. 'I think I need help. I don't think I can lift my sheets out of the bath.' She was standing in the doorway with the sleeves of her school shirt pushed up and her knuckles red from hot water. Ali had told her to wash her own sheets in the mornings while she was at Noah's and to ask him for help if lifting them wet was difficult. And Noah, it had seemed to her, was doing nothing: just drinking coffee and reading his newspaper.

'I'm busy,' he said. Shy as she was, Camilla fixed her wonderful eyes on him with a scepticism which was lost upon him because he didn't look up.

'You're just reading the bloody newspaper!' she said.

'Watch your language,' Noah said. 'I happen to be busy with the news right now.' '*Nooz*', he said. 'Busy with the *nooz*.' Camilla suppressed an urge to pull tongues – an instinct towards lively defiance which was as unusual in her as blasphemous adjectives.

'Listen, Pumpkin,' Noah said. 'You have a choice here, as I see it. In my house you either wash those sheets yourself or you do without sheets. I don't mind. If it saves on labour, go ahead and pee right on the mattress next time.'

'I *have* washed them,' Camilla said. 'But they're heavy. And what will I do if I miss my bus?'

'You'll get up a half-hour earlier tomorrow,' Noah said. 'Clothes pins are on the line. Try not to drip water over my floors, okay?' At this point, all unbeknown to him, she had nearly cried. 'Don't worry about the bus,' he said. 'I'm planning to take you in the car.'

In all honesty the sheets were not all that difficult to lift once she really tried, because they were polycotton, form-fitted sheets and lighter than her mother's, which were flannel and were also as old as the hills and nearly all with the sides stitched to the middles, leaving an uncomfortable seam down the centre.

For breakfast Noah made her toast and a soft-boiled egg which he gave her, not in an eggcup, but whole and shelled in a coddling dish. She supposed this to be because he was American. He himself ate what looked to her like raw porridge with yoghurt. Or was it buttermilk? It was not that nice, sugary yoghurt such as she had chosen for school, but the kind that was like sour milk with lumps in it. The relief of having the sheets under her belt and the knowledge that she was to have a lift to school in the car brought on such a feeling of wellbeing in Camilla that it induced a burst of bold cultural insularity which warmed Noah's heart and made them firm friends. She glanced with yellow-eyed unease at his bowl of mixed grains daubed with clods of milk ferment, and said:

'Do you eat that raw porridge stuff because you're American?' Noah laughed.

'Go brush your teeth,' he said, 'and get your school bag.' By the afternoon he had bought her a tiny microchip alarm clock to help her wake up on time, but although she hardly *touched* the buttons something must have gone very wrong with it, because next morning when Noah woke her, he said it had played the 'Yellow Rose of Texas' twice over in the small hours.

'You messed about with it,' he said. Camilla bit her lip.

'I didn't mean to,' she said. 'Honestly Noah, and it wouldn't have woken me anyway. I used to have one with brass bells on top that I could stand on a tin plate.'

'Jesus!' Noah said. 'You know something? You're a whole lot like your mother.' Camilla giggled, because, although she knew he was criticising her, she was aware that, since he liked her mother so much, it could only mean that he liked her too. Admittedly Ali had never used to pee in her bed as a girl.

Camilla felt oddly warm then, under the night's covers, and realised that this was because her bed was dry. She drew her knees up in surprise and knocked the clock from Noah's hands.

'Noah,' she said. 'Excuse me, but I haven't wet my bed. I don't seem to have peed in my bed, Noah.'

'Congratulations,' Noah said, deadpan, wishing to hide his own surprise.

'Why not, do you think?' she said.

'Search me,' Noah said, who had not much idea. But ten years later he still had the fold-up bed in his study with its single, very large urine stain. The rubber sheet had proved altogether inadequate on what had turned out to be the last night Camilla ever wet her bed. The size of the stain was not surprising since Noah, absent-mindedly, had let her drink two glasses of Seven-Up in the pub and had made her the hot chocolate too. But he hadn't given it a thought, since he had had things to talk over with Arnie and, besides, he had been inwardly worried sick about Ali.

There was only one curious incident relating to Mervyn, which took place on the Friday before Ali's discharge from hospital. She had asked for the book on Matisse, and Noah and Camilla had entered the house to get it for her.

'It's on the piano,' Camilla said, but it wasn't.

'She's put it someplace else,' Noah said, but then Camilla saw his eyes fix on the broken catch of the back sash window and she saw him tense with annoyance.

'It's always been like that,' she said, thinking to reassure him. 'It's been broken like that for donkey's years.'

'Holy shit!' Noah said angrily. Nothing else was gone except the iron.

Camilla didn't come into the ward next visiting time, because she was busy outside in the hospital grounds with Arnie. Having laid her a bet, Arnie was now timing her with a stop watch as she ran the perimeter of the hospital fence at a creditable sprint, on those wonderful, long child legs which from the first he had so much admired.

'Use your toes!' Arnie was calling after her with gusto. 'Toes, Cam! Run on your toes, kid!'

'File a divorce petition against the sonofabitch,' Noah was saying within. 'Do it, Al. Anything you care to pin on him: desertion, adultery, unreasonable behaviour. It's a pushover. Do it now. That way you'll hang on to the house.'

'You shouldn't have changed the locks, Noah,' Ali said. 'Dearest Noah, I do wish that you hadn't. That's why he's taken my book. It's tit for tat, that's all. He won't do it again. Oh hell, but I loved that book.'

'And the iron?' Noah said angrily. 'How about the iron? You love that too. And how about me? Where do I stand in your affections? Somewhere between Matisse and the iron?'

'Oh Noah,' Ali said. 'Please.'

'You're behaving like a door mat, Al,' Noah said. 'It's small wonder that he craps all over you.'

SEVEN

NOAH PROPOSED MARRIAGE to her after a quarrel precipitated by her neighbours and an episode over a rabbit. 'For a nicely brought up, hardworking lady,' he said one evening, 'you sure have some seriously scrambled friends.'

'Have I?' Ali said. It gave her a small jolt to have her neighbourhood callers defined as 'friends'. 'Friends' were a feature of one's girlhood; a thing one had put away upon marriage. 'Friends' were the people like Julie Horowitz with whom one had shared one's homework, shared one's aspirations, even at times shared one's precious black stovepipe trousers. 'Friends' were the people with whom one had giggled in the ranks of the Saturday school of ballroom dancing, wearing one's rustling starched petticoats tacked up at the back with makeshift green thread. The rite of marriage demoted female friends, at a stroke, to the status of a music hall joke. They became 'the gaggle' and the 'hen-party'. Two or more of them gathered together could command a dubious institutional legitimacy in the baby shower and the coffee morning, but it was never again the same.

'Perhaps I'm scrambled too,' Ali said flippantly, in the hope of deflecting attention from her neighbours who clearly bothered him. 'Could it be a case of like finding like?'

'You have cleaner fingernails,' he said. Then he turned aside to confront the doorway. 'Goodbye,' he said firmly, addressing this deterrent greeting not to Ali, but to a threesome of uninvited children who had appeared at her door in the hope of gaining entry. Noah had by this time appointed himself expeller of unwelcome children who intruded upon his own and Ali's evenings together. In this role he would plant his wide shoulders squarely in the doorway and pronounce the single word 'good-bye' with a wondrously intimidating effect. He had not yet got round to expelling the adults. Not yet. Not until the night of the rabbit, which was soon to come.

'You're a pearl cast among swine,' Noah said. 'Make no mistake, sweetheart.'

'Aren't you merely saying that I'm a more socially presentable egg-flip than some others of my sex around here?' she said. 'Aren't you being elitist, Noah?'

'Oh bullshit,' Noah said. 'You're a lady, Al. It shines out a mile. You may be a little eccentric, but you're a real lady.' Ali laughed at this tautological shamelessness.

'Well, exactly,' she said. For Noah, no amount of handwring-ing 'quim introspection' on Ali's part would alter the obvious fact that among the 'alternative' people who came to her door – bringing toddlers whom they licensed to pee on her rugs, to break Camilla's dolls, to grind fish fingers into her floors, or to drag bedding all over her house, while they confided to her patient ear their drug addiction, their multiple orgasms, their childhood rapes – among these there were for sure no ladies. Some were unwashed and others took drugs. All were endlessly obsessed with themselves.

Had he not recently spent an entire evening in Ali's house in the company of a demented female who had asserted repeatedly that her eardrums would haemorrhage if she ate any bread but German linseed bread? Had he not been obliged to hear another expand – without respect either for brevity or discretion – upon the subject of her 'dry cunt' syndrome? Noah was confirmed in a belief that Mervyn Bobrow had dumped upon his weary, danc-ing princess the role of unpaid neighbourhood psychiatric counsellor and that the job had worn her out until she had been obliged to hang up her dancing shoes.

'Some people are always unlucky,' Ali said, countering with a belief in the Evil Eye. 'Bad luck seeks them out.'

One of Ali's callers was injudicious enough to proposition him during the weeks of Ali's convalescence, and so shocked him with the quality of her disloyalty that he made a point of turning her down in Ali's hearing by saying that he feared 'the clap'. This frankly brutal response had resulted in a prompt and admirable reduction in the numbers who came through Ali's door in the evenings but in the short run it had been counterproductive. It had made Ali both furious and hostile.

'What sort of unspeakable bloody bastard are you that you go undermining people like that?' she said, almost before the door had closed behind the intruder. 'Isn't it fairly obvious she's vulnerable as all hell? I hope you're proud of yourself.'

'Al,' Noah said. 'I was doing you a favour.'

'Some favour!' she said. 'I don't need your favours.' This last, given her recent history of dependence upon him, perhaps justly he considered to be untrue, but he let it pass. 'I thought that you were kind,' she said, 'but you're kind only to people you like. That's cheap; that's easy. All manner of miserable bastards can be kind to children and lap dogs. Even to certain hand-picked respectable women.'

'Al,' Noah said. 'Let's not even discuss it. Just get it straight that I do not propose to lease out compassion like a goddam community centre. I don't have the time. I also don't intend that you and I should quarrel over an expendable, goddam unwashed tramp. Understood?'

In response to this final unchecked heresy, Ali almost choked. Her voice cracked as she spoke.

'Go away,' she said. 'You are a cosy medic in handmade shoes and I hate you.'

'Me!' Noah said. 'You're asking me to leave? You harbour all these dubious cranks and it's *me* you're asking to leave?'

'Go!' Ali said. 'Oh please, for God's sake, go.'

Noah wrenched angrily at the catch which he had recently had fitted to her front door.

'You're gonna be sorry,' he said. 'I have a whole lot more to give.'

On both counts he was of course right. She was sorry, but then so was he. Noah was not in general readily forthcoming with apologies – a habit born perhaps of his profession where to apologise is often to admit liability. It was not surprising then that Ali was the one to say sorry first. She came to his door two days later in a state of underslept conciliation.

'I'm sorry,' she said. 'I think you were wrong in what you did but I was extreme. I do see that you were defending me.'

'Come in,' Noah said. 'I'm very glad to see you.' Having closed the door behind her he blew into the palms of her hands which were cold since the autumn had been showing signs of giving way early to winter. 'You ought to wear gloves.'

'I was not only unfair to you, I was probably also uncouth,' she said.

'Unfair, maybe, but not uncouth,' he said. 'I believe you to be quite unshakeably couth.'

'Please know that you are speaking to a person who has thrown clay flowerpots on to the head of Mervyn Bobrow from upstairs windows,' she said. 'I don't want you to be deluded about me.'

Noah laughed. 'There's only one thing to be said against such basically laudable conduct,' he said, 'and that is the possibility of having to explain a fractured skull to the coroner.' Ali sat down, on the foot end of the reclining dentist's chair which was really quite remarkably comfortable.

'I wanted to tell you that I once had the clap.' she said. 'Once when I was sixteen.'

'Pardon me?' he said.

'I said that I once had the clap,' she said. 'Gonorrhoea. I wanted to tell you that.'

'There is no disgrace in contracting a sexually transmitted

disease,' Noah said. 'The disgrace lies in knowingly passing it on.' He paused suddenly as if hit by a blow from falling clay flower-pots. 'Excuse me, you said sixteen? *Sweet Jesus, Al, did you say sixteen?*'

'I said sixteen' she said. 'The first time I ever took my knickers off for a man. The Evil Eye as I told you. You see how grievously it afflicts my sex. I was so bloody innocent in those days that I took my itch to the family doctor, who promptly informed my nice straightlaced mother. But you will be pleased to hear that I never passed it on. I practised abstinence religiously for the next two years until I got married. I wore a kind of two-way-stretch chastity belt on all my evenings out. A fearsome Lycra item called a Tiger Grip and quite impenetrable. My first husband was so infuriated by it that he married me just to get the damn thing off.'

'So who was he?' Noah said. 'This jerk who gave you gonorrhoea.'

'He was the one that I married,' she said. 'But as to who he was, I hardly remember. We were married not much over half a year. I believe he was a fairly loutish rugger bugger. An en-gineering student. I mean no disrespect to the profession, you understand, when I say that, where I came from, engineering students were on the whole a pretty far cry from Isambard Kingdom Brunel. He drank beer with the boys and screwed everything in skirts under the floats on Rag night. He was a fairly stereotypical yahoo but with pretensions to nobility. He wore a Gallic signet ring and said that his great-grandfather had been a "vassal" of the Duke of Normandy. He was, as you see, not high in the hierarchy of defrocked Gaulish aristocrats, but for a colonial green-girl like me he had a certain kudos. I met him when the young man I had fallen in love with – a fellow student called Thomas Adderley – hit him in the face and broke a blood vessel in his nose. His blood drenched my shirt. After someone has drowned you in blood, what can you do but marry them?'

Noah watched her, his mind aswim with images of Ali cast

adrift in the company of rogues and charlatans. Dukes and Dolphins, as in *Huckleberry Finn*.

'My personal opinion is that one could have called it quits with the gonorrhoea,' he said. 'Marriage was maybe pushing it, especially if you loved somebody else. But tell me, Al, did you always hang out with crazy people?'

Ali laughed. 'Until I met you? No, not really. I had a modest penchant for "Semitic and Titled Persons" as you might say. That is, except for just the once. But neither category is made up exclusively of crazies, as you yourself bear witness.'

'This "just once"?' Noah said. 'This man you cared for, who fell into neither category. I want for you to tell me what was wrong with him. That is, since you were so clearly drawn to those whom your "nice straightlaced mother" would have regarded as deviants. Who was he?'

'He was the person who broke the engineer's nose,' Ali said. 'I can tell you more about him if your research unit will spare you till I'm through. He was a classmate of mine in the Arts Faculty. One of the few men on the course. Real men were supposed to do engineering, you see. That's the reason why we got to see each other – during poetry tutorials, while the engineering students were busy in their manly boiler suits under the heavy machinery. I fell for him immediately; at first glance, before I ever spoke to him. I said to myself, "That's him." But it didn't work out that way. The blood determined it otherwise. Does this sound like Wagner?'

'Carry on,' Noah said.

'I had a dear friend all this time called Julie Horowitz,' Ali said. 'She had been with me right through high school. It is perhaps because of her that I always found the more secular aspects of Judaic culture so seductive, though I have to confess that Mervyn and his mother just about cured me of it. Mervyn's mother once sent me a breakdown, village by village, of Polish dead from Nazi genocide. She'd transcribed it from a slab somewhere in what she called "the Holy Land". But I digress. Where was I?'

'Your girl friend,' Noah said. 'Julie Horowitz.'

'Yes,' Ali said. 'I fell head over heels for the way her father used to crumble his matzo during the Passover and announce "Tenks Gott next veek is bread." He'd stepped off a boat from Eastern Europe at the age of ten but he'd never stopped talking like the Fiddler on the Roof. I loved being in her parents' house. My parents were both high school teachers with modest but secure incomes. Julie's parents were the first people I knew who combined affluence and precariousness in the way people do who buy and sell things with flair. They had so much more stuff than we ever had but a lot of it was a kind of insurance. It was the kind of stuff you could pick up and run with like rubies and Chinese silk rugs. Her mother practised strange, obsessional economies like saving motley scraps of toilet soap and wedging them into a tablet when she'd collected enough. These were people with their own tennis courts, Noah. She wouldn't let Julie wear flat shoes to lectures because no decent man would look at her in "flatties" she said. She was obsessed with marrying her daughter off to a man with qualifications which would be as transportable as the Chinese rugs – an accountant, or a lawyer, or a medic. She would have gone for you in a big way, Noah. Poor Mrs Horowitz. Men looked at Julie all of the time, of course, flat shoes or no, because she was so luscious. I thought all Julie's man-catching clothes were quite wonderful, but Julie hated them. We used to swap clothes in the ladies' loo until her hips got too big. She once stole a book for me from her father. She said he had never opened it and never would. A Byron it was, bound in red vellum. Inside it said "For your Barmitzvah with love from Uncle Sam and Auntie Ida". I've still got it. She meant it to imply that our friendship would endure beyond cultural boundaries but in the end it didn't. It divided us. My Frenchman was predictably anti-Semitic and Julie's men began to terrify me with their white teeth and their sports cars. I used to see her on the beach sometimes, all tan and lip-gloss, lounging with these Sabra-type wondermen. Gold stars of David tangled in the curls of their chest hair.'

'In a word, you had deviant tastes,' Noah said. 'You thought that her men were sexy and it scared the hell out of you. But what about this poetic young man of yours? Like what was wrong with him?'

'Nothing,' Ali said. 'Why should anything have been wrong with him?'

'Something had to be wrong with him,' Noah said. 'Come on, Al.'

'He was all kings and princes,' Ali said extravagantly. 'He was without fault. The others were but dross and dung beside him.'

'He was black,' Noah hazarded sarcastically.

'Not *exactly*,' Ali said. 'But you are very close, Noah. Very shrewd. I do admire you, you know. He was actually light brown, but he "passed for white" as they say in that country. He was tall, brown, wild, left-wing and highly literate; he was everything a golden man ought to be.'

Sober, cautious, middle-aged and firmly antipathetic to radical chic, Noah found himself overtaken by a brief tremor of retrospective envy.

'What was his name did you say?' he said. 'Apollo?'

Ali laughed. 'Thomas,' she said. 'He was a half-caste leftie with a fancy name. His family was British from India. That's where the brown had come from I expect. They'd boozed their way downwards till they'd ended up in a corrugated-iron house in South Africa. I am told that an iron house is quite the thing now, but in our day it was very low. Very low indeed. Also rather hot. And noisy during hailstorms.'

'Thomas who?' Noah said.

'Thomas Adderley,' she said. 'Thomas Claude Adderley. But often known as Mot. He'd spelled his name backwards as a child, you see, and it had stuck. When I first knew him he had already left the iron house. He lived by himself in a garage.'

'I see,' Noah said. 'I always thought a garage was for automobiles.' Depicting the scene for Noah, Ali had recognised a degree of unreviewed childishness in it which had made her defensive.

'We were kids, Noah,' she said. 'He was seventeen. I was, as I told you, sixteen.'

'How come you were so young?' Noah said, suspiciously. 'You were a pre-pubertal college grad?'

'I was precocious,' she said. 'Well – I was precocious at passing examinations. At everything else I was, on the whole, retarded but my sixth-form blazer was as decorated with ribbons as a maypole. It's not always the best training for life. I had no street wisdom you see. We were too young or perhaps too frightened to take on passion direct, so we read Keats together in the student caff, when the engineer wasn't wrestling with my Tiger Grip. And we sat together during lectures. But I will tell you about the day we met, shall I? It was, in its way, decisive.'

'Okay,' Noah said.

'Julie and I had spent weeks together leafing through *Elle* magazine and plotting the appropriate highbrow look for our move to campus life,' she said. 'We had no sooner turned up looking like collegiate cover girls, however, than we ran into an unexpected backlash; an initiation rite known as "Freshers' Reception" of which my engineer was one of the ruling trium-virate. It required new students to hang sandwich-boards on their chests stating name, gender and age, and to appear on the lawns in congregation to sing back-up choruses for rugger matches. A whole ragbag of racist, sexist and vaguely porno rubbish with which I won't sully your ears. During the weeks of this thoroughly down-market and, I may say, disillusioning rite, us new girls were required to answer instantly to the command of senior male students. If one of them bawled, "Freshette, come here!" you were expected to step forth and display your sandwich-board with eager alacrity. The greater obscenity, I have to say, was to watch the giggly relish with which most of the girlies played along with the system.

'Julie and I were snooty girls. We'd walk on pretending not to hear when they bawled at us, but the result of this temporarily gratifying one-upmanship was, of course, that one was singled out during the sing-along sessions for exhibitions of male sadism. We kept being chosen as demonstration models for the songs which required female mime artistes. The most compromising of these required the victim to lie on her back on the grass and mime the sex act with a first-year male victim, usually chosen for conspicuous gormlessness. Julie came in for most of the flak being bolder and more gorgeous, while I on the whole only caught the spill-over on account of the aforementioned Quaker syndrome. They called her "the Horror Witch" because she had botched the graphics on her sandwich-board and had been obliged to break up her surname on to separate lines. It read "Julie Horo" new line "witz". But on the occasion of the bleeding nose the triumvirate had for some reason chosen me. "You there next to the Horror Witch. The haughty one," bawls my engineer, "Come out here and lie down! Open your legs," he says, bantering amiably. "You know how to open your legs I hope, girlie, because if you don't, one of us here will be happy to show you."

'Lots of ho-ho and rah-rah from the back-up on the reception panel. They selected a person who was at that time the most wide-open male first year of the bunch to mime the act with me. A person called William Lister. The poor boy was sweating in terror and steaming up his glasses. He was so loath to lie on me that you could have wedged a stack of bricks between us. "Bugger off you pimply virgin!" bawls my engineer charmingly. "You couldn't get it up for Jayne bloody Mansfield. Hey you," he says, beckoning to Thomas Adderley. "Let's have you out here. Show us how you'd like to treat a lady." Well, that's it really. Mot Adderley strode up to the front and, without any warning, hit my engineer in the face. The blow broke a blood vessel in his nose. Within seconds he looked like a butcher. So did I. The new *Elle* shirt and the sandwich-board were impressively blotched with gore. Mot Adderley walked off the field unchecked on his eight-foot legs while I and the engineer beat a dual retreat to the nearest washroom where he was very solicitous with me.

Very stoical about his nose and all concern for me and my clothing. We repaired to the mens' hall of residence where he got me one of his shirts to put on. He even turned his back all proper like while I put it on. Then he brought me a Coke in the Students' Union caff and laughed the whole thing off. He had already appointed himself my protector. "You mustn't let one cheeky white Hottentot get you down," he said. "It's no skin off your nose." He was actually very handsome, even with the bashed face, only too strutting to see that it was his nose not mine which the cheeky Hottentot had put out of joint.

'That was it. Somehow, by that union of blood, I became the engineer's woman. He had lots of temporary women over the next three years who were better versed in opening their legs, but I was the one whom he had fixed upon to take home to mother.'

'So you married him,' Noah said. 'Having first handed over your virginity in protection payment. You cared for the one guy and you married the other. That figures. But you sound as if you're still sorry. What I mean is you still sound a little infatuated with this dyslexic black person.'

'Not really,' Ali said. 'Not in my more rational moments.'

'There's nothing rational about passion,' Noah said. 'If there were, I guess I wouldn't be sitting here right now, despising your Mr Adderley for his fancy name and his slovenly, poetical habits.' Ali laughed.

'And how was the marriage?' Noah said.

'Brief,' Ali said. 'We shook the confetti from our hair and found ourselves incarcerated together in a small, urban flat. He listened to commercial radio in the evenings and took me to the drive-in cinema at weekends to watch Grace Kelly and to eat hot-dogs which were clipped to the car window on trays.'

'Meanwhile you ate your heart out over the hot-dogs for the other man,' Noah said. 'Isn't that so?'

'Oh absolutely,' Ali said. 'I loved him more than my life. I used to shut my eyes in bed and think of him.'

'And with Mervyn?' Noah asked.

'Sometimes,' Ali said

'And with me?' Noah said, fixing her intently with an unblinking gaze. Ali laughed self-consciously.

'Not with you,' she said. 'I couldn't sustain the illusion, even if
I wanted to. You're much too square, Noah.'

'I want the truth, Al,' Noah said. 'If you please.'

'The truth is what I have just told you,' Ali said. 'You are the
best lover I've ever had.'

'Taking my predecessors into account, I'm not surprised,'
Noah said dryly, though he found the observation mollifying.
'And what brought you to Britain?'

'Some eight months after I'd got married I made my way, in a
moment of truth, to the passport office without even telling my
poor engineer,' Ali said. 'When I'd got the documents, I bought
me a one-way ticket to Southampton harbour with all the money
I'd traded for my years of thrift with the government loan
certificates. Then I jumped the country. I wrote to him from
the quayside and I never went back. He later married again and
did rather well in business, so I heard.'

'You never went home?' Noah said. 'But that's ridiculous.
What about your mother?'

'She died,' Ali said. 'About six years ago. I never saw her
again, but we exchanged some loving letters.'

'Jesus!' Noah said. 'This is all perfectly absurd. I never heard
such a tale of gross mismanagement.'

'A week after I'd got to England I heard that Mot Adderley had
been arrested for suspected running of a politically compromised
person over the border in the boot of a car,' Ali said. 'The person
was William Lister, who had by then become a sort of would-be
political dangerman. I still see him from time to time. He came to
England. He was English anyway. He writes pamphlets and plots
great changes from various bedsitting rooms around London SE9.
I believe that he's entirely freelance, but I may be wrong.'

'And the black?' Noah said. Ali laughed. 'He was light brown,
remember,' she said. 'The Special Branch held him for a month,

as I was told. They released him without pressing a charge. I never heard from him directly. Then I met Mervyn Bobrow in a pub, some three weeks later, reading ferocious poetry. Sort of neo-Ted Hughes. I made the mistake of falling for him on the rebound.'

'Take your shoes off,' Noah said suddenly. 'And stop talking. I've heard as much as I can take.'

'My shoes?' Ali said. 'What for?'

'Just to make a start,' Noah said. 'I can't make love to you while you have your clothes on.' Ali smiled, but rather absently, because even once he had drawn willing adult kisses from her mouth, her mind was turning on the past. In the red vellum Byron Ali remembered that Julie Horowitz had written – in black Quink and in her boldest schoolgirl hand – a most un-Byronic verse of the autograph book genre, which filled her with a sweet sadness and longing.

> Friendship is like china
> Precious, frail and rare.
> When broken it can be mended,
> But the break is always there.

Sensing Ali's wandering attention, Noah irritably broke off his kisses.

'God help any dubious poetical rads who try shacking up in my garage,' he said. 'I'll have them evicted. No problem.'

This bizarre ultimatum was followed within days by the affair of the rabbit and the proposal of marriage.

EIGHT

T HE AGEING LOP-EARED rabbit belonged to Camilla's school classroom, but was for a week during the autumn half-term holiday an honoured guest in Ali's house. It was Camilla's privilege to play host to the rabbit during which time he experienced an unaccustomed surfeit of freedom. His hutch was kept indoors in case of rain and stood on a spread of borrowed newspapers, taking up a good part of Ali's living-room floor. Meanwhile the rabbit hopped unhampered about the house spilling his small caper-like droppings into the vegetable rack, where he lurked to nibble at cabbage leaves. Or he fed on dandelions in the garden protected from the neighbour's dogs by Camilla, who loved to watch him at his endless herbivorous chompings.

In the evenings Noah would sometimes find Ali in the act of changing the rabbit's straw which she kept in a bale in the cupboard under her stairs, or – having just finished – crouching on the floor to run her eyes over items of outdated news on the spread news sheets. It puzzled him how avidly she was drawn towards last month's news, once it could claim the handicap of being spread under a rabbit hutch and strewn with bits of straw. She who had the scantiest interest in current affairs and who took no daily newspaper. She who was always the last to find out if the gas workers were on strike or if the price of postage had gone up. She had recently astonished him by revealing that she had never known the difference between Franklin and Theodore Roosevelt. Yet it pleased her to prostrate herself in the cause of last season's cricket scores or last month's furniture sales.

The newspapers had been donated by old Margaret who had revealed herself as a reader of the *Daily Telegraph* for the sound reason, she said, that it was cheaper than the *Guardian*, and for the more perplexing reason that it 'did her good' she said to find out what 'those right-wing sods' who wrote for it were saying about the underdog and the aged poor. Noah threw an envelope file on to her sofa, along with his jacket and his keys. 'Those newspapers smell,' he said, as he came to kiss her.

'Do they?' Ali said, 'Do they really? If I ever noticed, I don't any more. I must tell you, Noah, that for a person with respiratory disabilities you have a nose like a bloodhound.' Noah could always tell when she had been smoking; he could always tell when Margaret had been boiling up offal for the dogs next door.

'For Chrissake, Al,' he said, 'the stench is appalling in here. Your place is taking on an odour of mildew and boiled ox-liver. Throw them out. It's offensive. Have my old papers, baby.'

'All right,' she said. 'With pleasure.' She was not unaware that Noah was increasingly colonising every trivial area of her life these days, bringing in his wake straight roads, benign jurisprudence and general advance. Noah meanwhile, though in general adamantly against domestic pets, enjoyed the rabbit's temporary sojourn in Ali's house as further proof of her charmingly indulgent nature which clearly cried out for his care and protection. He was amused by her strenuous and often futile efforts to catch the creature at the end of the day and her tolerance of endless bent plant stems.

'Keep the animal in the hutch, Al,' he said. 'It's a rabbit.'

'Your name will be mud if you say that once more in this house,' she said. 'If I tell Camilla you'll be finished.' Noah laughed because between himself and Ali's daughter had sprung up a scion of understanding which no mere rabbit could wither.

It was at eleven the next evening that Angie, one of Ali's neighbourhood dependants, called on her with her small son,

Matt. Ali had left her attendance upon the rabbit rather late on that occasion. Camilla had gone to bed hours before. Noah had telephoned earlier in the evening to tell her he planned to stay at the hospital to work with Arnie, probably until midnight. Booze fumes wafted on Angie's breath in the hallway as she stepped noisily over the threshold. In the grip of one hand she held an unstoppered gin bottle, while in the other, manic with nocturnal exhaustion, Matt twitched and strained.

'Join me in a drink, Angel,' she said heartily, attempting to rise above drunken self-pity; her voice aspired towards a chic Belgravian abandon. 'God, I've been so fucking depressed this evening I almost tore old Matt's hair out.' She stumbled over the rabbit and let go of Matt. 'Oh my shitting Christ!' she said, holding the bottle carefully erect. 'Is it an ickle bunny rabbit or have I got the DTs?' Brainy, deserted, saddled with a child of the alien sex, Angie drank. Increasingly now, she drank to escape the wreckage which drink was making of her life.

'It's a rabbit,' Ali said wearily. 'It's Camilla's school rabbit. Look, Matt, would you like to hold him? He's a real old dear. He's like a cuddly toy.' The rabbit hopped obligingly, lippity-lop, towards the toes of Matt's shoes, but Matt, having no familiarity with domestic animals, shrank away with phobic terror.

'Get away from me, you effing rabbit!' he said. He aimed a wild kick at the rabbit's head. 'Don't you bite me you effing rabbit, or I'll effing kill you!' Ali snatched up the creature and stroked its ears.

'He doesn't bite, Matt. Really,' she said. 'He's gentle as anything.'

'Put him in his cage!' screamed Matt hysterically. 'I hate him. He scratches; he's got fleas; he shouldn't have ears like that. Why do his ears hang down like that?'

'Oh my Christ!' Angie drawled contemptuously. 'The silly chicken-shit bugger is scared! Scared of a rabbit. What bloody next? Jesus, Ali, you know how I prayed for a girl when he was born; how I longed for it. But since he's a boy, can't he *be* a bloody boy?' She came forward and wept indulgently on Ali's shoulder. 'You're so lucky, Ali, to have Camilla. Oh Christ, can't he behave like a boy, Ali? Is he a fucking transvestite? I want a man for my son, not a mouse.'

'He's young,' Ali said. 'Leave him. Matt, would you like a biscuit?'

'Do you know what he asked for last birthday?' Angie persisted. 'A Sindy doll. A bloody ballerina Sindy doll, no less. One of those plastic post-pubertal jobs with boobs and peroxide hair. Oh Jesus, Ali, it isn't as though he hasn't got enough Action Man to last him a bloody lifetime, is it? What the fuck does he need Sindy for?' She laughed with a vicious, frightening ambivalence. 'God, Mattie,' she said. 'Perhaps Camilla will let Action Man have a spree with her Sindies, eh? Not that they'd get much joy of him, poor little tarts. He's got no prick. Posturing sod has got no prick! No bloody balls either under all that fancy battledress. But then no more has our Matt. Christ, Ali, one of his testicles hasn't dropped. *It hasn't dropped!* I'm so bloody worried about it, it's driving me to drink. It's because of him that I drink, do you know?'

'You told me,' Ali said. 'Matt? Wouldn't you like to lie down? You can have my bed if you like.' But Matt wasn't listening to her. Inattention had become his only armour of defence against persistent verbal assault. Having procured himself two cake tins from Ali's kitchen he was now planning an ambush upon the lop-eared enemy. The cake tins crashed suddenly, like cymbals, against the wire mesh of the hutch, making the two women jump. Angie reached for a bunch of Matt's hair and tugged it brutally.

'Dummy!' she said.

'*Stop it, Angie!*' Ali yelled, in distress. Matt dashed for Ali's knees, where he clung for a moment dampening her jeans with his tears. 'Please, Angie,' she said. 'Let him sleep. Let him stay with me tonight. You'll hate yourself for all this in the morning. It's his first term at school, isn't it? How can he cope? How could anyone cope?' Angie began to snivel, obscenely, like a rival child, her face a mess of swollen eyes and snot.

'You want to take my child,' she said. 'Everyone wants to take my child. Even the fucking social workers want to take my child. Matt's teacher has called in a social worker. Help me, Ali. If you don't help me to dry out, those buggers will take my child.' She followed the plea with a good long swig from the bottle, just as Noah let himself in. Having seen Ali's lights on, he had parked his car and walked round. He shut the front door behind him with a quiet but pointed click. Ali saw him before her visitor did, standing in the hallway with that look, which broadchested men get in cutaway jacket lapels, of being about to expand and burst from their clothes like the Incredible Hulk. Angie turned her attention to him, politely, the recovery of her poise sudden, remarkable and apparently complete.

'Come in, Herr Doktor,' she said, assuming a jovial Senior Common Room voice. 'Or is it Herr Professor? Have a drink. I've heard everything about you.' Noah stepped forward, tired and deadpan. He took the bottle from Angie's hand. Then he checked it to comfirm that its contents were nine-tenths gone and planted it on the bureau.

'Ma'am, it's late,' he said. 'Your child needs his bed and Al needs hers. Goodnight to you.' Angie, choc-full of drunken gregariousness, was at first rendered speechless with indignation. When she spoke her face was red with annoyance.

'Ali, tell this pompous shithole your boyfriend that when I offer him a drink, he'll bloody well drink,' she said. 'Drink, damn you.'

'Get out,' Noah said. 'Get out and make it quick.'

'Are you by any chance addressing me, you stinking jumped-up quack?' she said. 'Whose house is this anyway?'

'Get out,' Noah said. His hand was on the telephone. 'Get out or I call the police.'

Ali stood white and trembling in the aftermath. Angie had left, rousing Matt from the rug where he had at last dropped into sleep, against Ali's protestations.

'She's different when she isn't drunk,' she said. 'She's very decent to that little Matt. She spoils him to make it up to him. He has more Scalectrix cars than Hamley's toyshop. Oh God, one could weep for both of them.' Noah took up the bottle, walked slowly to the kitchen and poured its dregs into the sink. Then he dropped it into the rubbish bin.

'Weep all you like,' he said. 'Weep and let it fester.'

'Don't put glass in the bin,' she said, absurdly. 'I always take it to the bottle bank.' Noah washed his hands at the sink.

'Forget it,' he said. He left the bottle where it lay. 'Just put it all behind you. Step over it. Broken glass; running sores. It's all you can do.' It was curious advice coming from a professional healer. He moved slowly towards her. 'I'm too old to be called your boyfriend. Marry me.'

'I'm married already,' Ali said with her heart pounding. Noah, to her surprise, suddenly banged on the table with a fist. The pepper mill jumped.

'You'll divorce this wretched man and you'll marry me,' he said. 'You'll do something sensible for once in your whole goddam life.' Ali stood still wondering at the clenched fist on the table and listening to the bumping of her heart against her ribs.

'Yes,' she said. 'All right.'

'Then we'll get out of this overpopulated bear garden and buy a nice quiet house someplace with large rooms and a decent garden – preferably surrounded by an electrified ten-foot-high fence,' Noah said.

'Yes,' Ali said, feeling profound relief as the burden of decision-making fell from her; the Rock of Ages cleft and she would hide in it. Camilla would be overjoyed that she was taking this sensible and also rather palatable course. What was sensible was often also palatable, though in her past this connection might have shocked her.

'I'll marry you,' she said. 'I'd be honoured. That's if you're really sure you want me.' Noah kissed her promptly with such a strong, grateful intensity that the action caused the newly knit seam of her abdomen to stretch alarmingly and then to shrink again.

'I've wanted you all my life,' he said, meaning something more metaphysical than that which usually characterised his thought. 'You have a gorgeous ass. My wife has a gorgeous ass.' Noah rejoiced in the terminology of marriage. Husband. Wife. These were words he liked to use, while the same words had always given Ali trouble, but whether for their explicit sexuality or their institutional implication, it was difficult to determine.

'Thanks,' she said.

'You're welcome,' he said, taking a section of her haunch in his grasp. 'Tell me, did a man ever fuck your ass?'

Ali was no longer unaccustomed to the eclectic adventurism of Noah's sexual style, but occasionally the exploratory dynamism behind it was at odds with her own nature. For Noah – though he had strong traditional notions of filial loyalty – the art of life in other respects was change. It meant five years here and ten years there. It meant working through the Linguaphone course in French. It meant sabbaticals at Princeton, a constant seeking in consumer magazines after microwave ovens and home calculators. Life was the application of myriad problem-solving methodologies, where for Ali it was a primitive art of survival; a matter of clinging like a limpet to the known rocks until some battering wave prised one loose. Noah had that gift of personal sobriety, moreover, which made the innovative appear always consistent with the status quo – a gift which had proved useful in his professional life. Ali by contrast could often not purchase a toothbrush without making the act appear eccentric.

'I thought it gave people piles,' she said. 'I have to warn you that I have always regarded it as a form of perversion.'

'I guess if it doesn't suit you, you pack it in,' Noah said. He was nothing if not tolerant. 'But are you trying to tell me that your decadent French nobleman never got up your ass?'

'He was just like any other bourgeois Protestant in bed I suppose,' Ali said. 'Come to think of it, I've never actually been in bed with a bourgeois Protestant. And I only mentioned the nobleman to shock you.'

'You succeeded,' Noah said. 'He shocked me. Almost as much as this Bobrow shocks me. Almost as much as the crazy black in the garage shocks me.' Ali laughed.

'The Nigger in the Woodpile,' she said. 'He wasn't black, Noah. I keep trying to tell you that.'

'If we could move on,' Noah said suddenly, as though he were ticking off matters on a committee's agenda and, having exhausted the business of rectal defloration, was eager to push on to the next item without wasting time upon the subject of Thomas Adderley. 'When we marry, how do you plan to occupy yourself, Mrs Glazer?'

'*Occupy* myself?' Ali said. 'You mean I have to be productive? I can't just cook for you and keep the place nice? I wouldn't open the door to anyone selling poisoned combs and red apples, Noah. Isn't that enough?'

'You're artistic,' Noah said. 'I want for you to draw. You dissipate your time and energy. If I were to pick you a career, I'd say you'd do a whole lot better at drawing than at all this unpaid social work.'

'Drawing?' Ali said.

'Sure,' Noah said. 'Drawing, painting. All that stuff.'

'Camilla draws well,' Ali said. 'Have you noticed? I haven't done much drawing since I left school.'

'So go back to school,' Noah said. 'Marry me and go back to school.' It struck Ali then that to marry Noah would be very much like going back to school, but she had always done so swimmingly well at school, so much better there than anywhere else, that it gave her a sanguine conviction about her imminent union. It also made her giggle. Ribbons of merit/Adorning the blazer/of the estimable/Mrs Glazer. It was not uncommon for Ali to behave childishly with him, since he was adult enough for both of them.

'What's so funny?' Noah said.

In his hutch, planted squarely on the foregoing Saturday's *Times*, the ageing lop-eared rabbit was lying dead. The sudden battery of cake tins, following hard upon Matt's blow to his temple, had been too much for his heart.

It rankled a little with both of them that Mervyn beat her to it. With fortuitous timing he had submitted a divorce petition and soon afterwards married his girlfriend, who was pregnant and whose father materialised as a legal counsellor of some consequence. The basement bedsitter had been a misleading piece of undergrad slumming. The divorce was easy given the lapse of time, and Mervyn gave notice of his intention to reoccupy the house within six months when the baby would need a room of its own. He made a systematic inventory of the house contents and decided – upon the advice of a valuer – to keep the piano, the sanded bureau, Camilla's wooden cradle, and the silver shell spoons. The rest he donated to Ali. Camilla was not part of the bargain beyond the usual visiting rights, which were seldom exercised. It was Eva's opinion, where Camilla was concerned, that there was not much that even she or Mervyn could do and she had expressed herself in an audible aside on the subject during the one and only visit Ali had made to the basement in the course of these painful negotiations.

'Frankly,' she had said to Mervyn, over Ali's head – and she had risen to activate Virginia's sagging Blu-tack for the fourth time that month, since the condensation in the basement was terrific – 'the child has been so damaged by female inferiority feelings transmitted by her mother, that I'd rather we gave her up and started again with our own. That way we'll be in *control* from the start.'

Ali's relief upon hearing this was such that it left her surprisingly philosophical about the loss of her house and her things. She had already agreed to marry Noah who had no time for either. Both houses were too small for their needs as he perceived them, and the neighbours made unreasonable demands upon Ali which he would not tolerate indefinitely. Moreover, from what Ali had let slip with regard to the electrical arrangements in Margaret's adjoining interior, he had begun to fear for the entire block as a potential tinderbox.

NINE

NOAH WAS IN NEW YORK when Ali received her first letter from Mervyn's solicitor informing her of the divorce petition. Having tried repeatedly to get in touch with Noah by telephone and having come up, each time, against the answering machine in Barbara's apartment, she lunched instead with Arnie Weinberg who told her funny stories against himself, to divert her from the business. He had himself only recently returned from a trip to New York and Michigan. Both Noah and he were never without Pan Am tickets protruding from their breast pockets. Ali, who had made her one long journey to England on the last of a glorious line of Union Castle mail boats which had docked darkly one cold January morning in Southampton harbour, had never been on an aeroplane in all her life, and her reluctance to do so had by now become entrenched.

This frequent and apparently voluntary mobility in the men seemed to her a flagellating addiction. There was clearly no 'lonely impulse of delight' in this committing of oneself over and over to the departure lounge or to the airborne charabanc with its plastic food on trays. They grumbled about it stoically as a necessary evil – an evil upon which Noah at least spent very little of his own money, since his trips got funded by various research committees, but upon which Arnie appeared to spend almost all of his earnings. After paying his travel costs he was left with enough money to cover the cost of running his newly acquired sports car, to paying the rent on various ever-changing bedsitting rooms in the Abingdon Road, and to funding a degree of sexually gratifying high-life in London at weekends. He had recently terminated a brief affair with the girlfriend of a Soho flick-knife king which had been rash, to say the least, and with its risky consequences he now lavishly entertained Ali. He never discussed these things with Noah but Ali invited intimacy. It was clear to Ali that Arnie's encounter with the Oxford police was part of a pattern of minor hazards which, as a disaster-prone person herself, drew her into a feeling of kindred warmth with him. During his recent trip to the States, he said, he had borrowed a friend's car and had driven from Michigan to New York City where he had been stopped in a police road block. The car had been extensively searched and, in the process, vandalised.

'So I'm watching these cops rip up the carpeting and slash the seats, right?' Arnie said, causing various restaurant crockeries to totter slightly as his narrative proceeded.

'I don't believe you,' Ali said.

'As true as God, Al,' Arnie said. 'They're looking for stolen bank notes, see. Someone just robbed a bank and made a getaway in a Michigan car, just like what I'm driving. Finally they get word that the thief has been caught, so they wave me off with my friend's car looking like it's been worked over by Glaswegian football hooligans and one of the policemen says to me, all friendly and nice – wait for it Al – he says to me, "Welcome to the Big Apple".' Ali gargled accidentally on the house red, which promptly made a brief, reckless detour through her nasal passages and out again in agitated sputterings.

She asked him about his family who were the last word in peri-urban respectability he said and from whom he had been – for the two years after he left high school – completely estranged. Arnie had spent this time selling food stamps to the unemployed, he said. He had then, for a while, taken off on a Norwegian fishing trawler and had spent time being penniless in Paris, after which – for entirely instrumental reasons – he had affected a

116

reconciliation with his family. He had needed his father to pay his tuition fees and his living expenses through college and then through medical school. Just as he was toying with the idea of ditching medicine for a course in mime at a Parisian clown school, he had met Noah, whose work had commanded his attention.

'You'll like my parents' address,' Arnie said, with an engaging, un-English emphasis on 'ad'. 'My parents' address is Country Club Road, Middletown, Connecticut.'

'I don't believe you,' Ali said again. 'There's no such place and even if there were, your family wouldn't be living in it. Jews in Country Club Road? Since when?'

'It's the truth,' Arnie said. 'They got two lawns, Al. They got a "looking lawn" and a "walking lawn".'

'All right,' Ali said. 'I believe you.'

'So that's maybe why I'm living in England, see,' Arnie said. 'Suffering in the Abingdon Road. Al, can you tell me how it is the draughts get to blow through the walls in those houses?' Ali laughed.

'It'll be down draught from windows,' she said. 'Or from the flue. You want to plug the flue with newspaper. Or it could be cracks in the floorboards of course. Underlay the carpeting with newspaper. It's useful stuff, newspaper.'

'I'm telling you, it comes through the walls,' Arnie said. Ali lent him a hot-water bottle – which leaked and woke him in the small hours. 'Did you ever wake up to find yourself in bed with a dead alligator?' Arnie said, with feeling.

'No,' Ali said. The analogy made her comfortably aware that, once the issue of legal separation was over, she would wake up to find herself in bed not with cold crocodiles, but with Noah, whose square, heavy body gave off heat like an electric generator.

Arnie appeared around breakfast on the wedding day bearing, as gifts, two careful studies in tastelessness. The first – calculated to quash Ali's dormant homesickness – was the ugliest household object he had been able to find in all of the West End: a monstrous copper wallclock shaped like a map of Africa and dotted about with raised cut-outs of African wildlife in beaten brass. The second, for Noah, he had bought in a Soho novelty shop. It came in a black plastic bag labelled *La Chaîne Haute Fidélité* and comprised a length of sturdy-looking plastic chain with handcuffs at either end.

'Thanks, Arnie,' Noah said. 'It's just what I always wanted.'

'What is it?' Camilla said.

'Joke,' Ali said. 'It's a handy accessory to bondage. Have you had breakfast, Arnie? Noah is making breakfast.'

The wedding ceremony in the local registry office – cheek by jowl with the Friends' Meeting House – was followed by a small party in Noah's house where old Margaret, on her fourth glass of bubbly, and in a hat resembling a crushed meringue in collision with a brace of woodpigeon, was observed by Ali to be heatedly interrogating a Muslim Egyptian cardiac man on the subject of vaginal stitching customs. The cardiac man made repeated small bows to her and nibbled apprehensively upon Twiglets. He attempted now and again, without success, to introduce his wife who was talking to Camilla. Camilla looked more lovely than ever in her pastel blue, bell-like dress and pale matching tights.

'Oh boy!' Arnie said, coming up to Ali. 'To watch that kid of yours walk. It's like poetry. Mobile poetry.'

'*Poetry?*' Ali said. 'Arnie, are you drunk?'

'Noah!' Arnie said, raising his voice quite deliberately in the hope that Camilla would hear him and make those unwittingly provoking, sideways eyes at him. 'Hey, Noah?' he said. 'Would you check that kid of Al's? The way she moves – it's dynamite! The whole damn kid is dynamite! You're gonna have to lock her up.' Noah was working hard, filling his guests' glasses.

'Against whom?' he said. Arnie laughed. He was wearing his hair newly cut and had put on a neat, dark suit for the second time in five days for he had finally appeared in court, where he had been found guilty, fined thirty pounds and bound over to keep the peace. It gave him immeasurable satisfaction thus to have acquired a criminal record.

Noah had already sold his house and had bought another, jointly with Ali. The house was more rural than either of them had expected or intended, while being only three miles from the city centre, and had been quite irresistible. It had belonged to an ageing farmer who had sold both house and land to a company which, having no use for the farmhouse, had soon offered it for sale along with a half-acre of garden. To have a house set among fields which were tended by the labour of others was the best of all possible worlds. The undergraduates who had inhabited the house in the interim between owners had already departed for Christmas, leaving behind them a shed full of empty lager bottles. Camilla's piggy-bank soon weighed heavy from the deposits on reclaimed empties. Noah was indefatigable in the matter of telephoning plumbers. In particular, the sewage disposal arrangements did not meet with his approval and neither were his reservations quelled by a helpful notice tacked by the undergraduates to the door of the upstairs loo. 'WARNING,' it said. 'DODDERY BOG. FLUSH ONLY FOR SHITTING AND BURN ALL USED PAPER IN THE GRATE.'

Some of the grates went too, in the wake of an oil-fired central heating system.

Noah moved his black leather swivel chair and his dentist's recliner into a sizeable attic study. Ali began to prepare a portfolio of work for the local art school's admissions committee. She collected Camilla from school in Noah's motor car, occasionally drove out old Margaret for cups of coffee and illicit cigarettes when Noah wasn't there, and continued her habit of lunching with him in the hospital canteen. Noah meanwhile bought himself a small Japanese motorcycle which he used for getting in and out from work – an innovation which caused Arnie to gloat without charity.

'Where's your sense of virility, Noah?' he said. 'How can you drive a thing like that?' But Noah, indulgent from the strength of knowing his virility to be bound up with Ali and not with modes of transport, made him no reply. They were at that moment undertaking a wintry Sunday walk with Camilla. Noah was not unaware that Arnie was right then wearing a girl Scout's woollen cap. A Brownie's hat. He had borrowed it from Camilla who had never been a Brownie since Mervyn Bobrow had flown into a fury at the very idea of his daughter joining a Christian-imperialist paramilitary organisation. She had acquired it in a jumble sale for one of her teddy bears. Now, some four years later, she knew in herself that the Brownies were soppy, but remembering how much she had once wanted to belong had given her a useful reserve of strength: she knew that if you wanted something which you could not have for long enough, eventually you lived your way through it. Time could heal. It could blunt desire. Right now she laughed at Arnie who was taking liberties with her stepfather.

'You look like the wolf dressed up as Red Riding Hood's grandmother in that silly old hat,' she said to him. 'You really do. Especially with your glasses on.'

'I am the wolf,' Arnie said.

Christmas was what Camilla liked best of all that year because Mervyn had always practically had kittens if she blew *Away in a Manger* on her descant recorder at Christmas time, and he had always insisted that Ali make Irish stew for lunch on Christmas Day. He said he liked it but really it was just to stop anyone else from having roast turkey. The year before, after he had left, they had had a small tree and she and Ali had stood it on the table and decorated it with iced biscuits and little German woodcarvings. But Noah's idea of a Christmas tree was much more splashy and wonderful. Camilla had gone with him to the covered market where they had bought the biggest tree at the stall half-price because nobody else had wanted one that size. The man had helped them tie it to the roof of Noah's car because Noah's back was not so good, and they had driven home and staggered into the house with it. And while Ali was busy cooking they had decorated it *entirely* in blue. Noah had asked her what her favourite colour was and she had said 'blue', so he had bought blue everything. Blue tinsel, blue aerosol glitter-spray, blue glass baubles and some lovely twinkly blue fairy lights that you had to plug in.

'Gosh,' Ali said when she entered, 'isn't it big? It looks like what the Norwegian government sends to Trafalgar Square each year. Why is it so blue?'

'Isn't it fantastic?' Camilla said. 'Isn't it all yummy blue and sparkly?'

'It's certainly very blue,' Ali said. 'Come Twelfth Night you could recycle it as a moonlight stage prop for *Giselle*.'

'You don't like blue?' Noah said. Ali laughed.

'On a second thought, I love it,' she said. 'I mean, it's a shock, that's all, but who ever heard of a tasteful Christmas tree? It's a contradiction in terms.' Noah Glazer, guardian and guide, had saved her once again, she reflected. This time he had saved her from the snares of a Bauhaus Christmas tree.

The next day Camilla noticed that when the Egyptian cardiac man came to Christmas lunch with his wife, Noah, without any prompting, dissected the hot Christmas pudding to ensure that no taint of burning brandy would sully the Muslim half. The gesture touched her profoundly. She knew then for certain that getting married could be as good as in story books after all and that Noah and Ali would live happily together for ever after. That afternoon she went upstairs and began, in an empty notebook, to write an extended moral fable in which the institution of marriage, tried, abused and endured, was ultimately seen as most blessed.

TEN

'SCISSORS!' Ali said from the driver's seat of the Audi. The car had been Noah's choice and was heaven to drive. Having sent off her husband on the train to Heathrow, she drove away from the railway station with her son in the back.

'Dannie,' she said. 'He's forgotten to take the scissors. He'll have to open the cartons with his teeth – what a good thing he's got such nice, strong teeth.' All the men she had married had been endowed with first-rate teeth. Ali ran her tongue apprehensively along a row of capped and crowned incisors, then round to where an ominous proportion of steel and porcelain replacement molars hung on by bridges and buttresses to fragments of the original fabric. One day the whole structure would go down like a stack of dominoes. She would make it into the sear and yellow leaf with those galling, detachable teeth like old Margaret's, living the while in fear of losing them down drains or in sticky macaroons. Or perhaps one would go out gnawing defiantly on hardened, toothless gums, slurping soup in restaurants with a napkin tucked in at the chin, one's adult children hissing 'Stop it, Mummy!' in shame. But Noah would go on loving her as long as he lived. It had begun recently to alarm her, during his absences, that she would in all likelihood be required to face the dog-end of old age without him, since Noah was about to turn sixty, and the odds were that he would not make it to her eightieth birthday.

'Stop it, Mummy!' Daniel was saying, 'It's disgusting. Stop sucking your teeth like that.'

'Sorry,' Ali said. 'Hey, Dannie,' she said suddenly, 'let's go and eat something delicious in a caff.' With Noah away, Ali's frequent instinct was to propose forbidden fruit. Noah was wholly against sugar. He had no need of it. The more of it you ate, the more you needed, he said, and vice versa. Abstinence thus lent ease to abstinence. He had by this lucid persuasion managed early on in their marriage to put a stop to his wife's twice-hourly munchings upon lemon curd sandwiches, but he had never really cured her of a weakness for Christmas mince-meat. He still came upon her in the pantry from time to time, eating it straight from the jar with a pudding spoon and knew now that nothing would cure her, short of long-term psycho-analysis or more cheaply, electrified pudding spoons. Some deep-rooted sense of privation had surely motivated this pleasure in sugar. He had at first thought it a reaction to the penance-and-cabbage-stalk existence she had led with Mervyn Bobrow, but surely it went deeper? There was for example the account she had produced for him once of the time Julie Horowitz had bought fifty-six marshmallow fish, thinking to cure Ali of an addiction by overexposure. Ali had laid them nose to tail along the length of the Horowitz swimming pool and had demolished them with unabated pleasure during the course of the afternoon.

Noah planned, this year, to make his wife a fortieth birthday present of two-score jars of Christmas mincemeat. He enjoyed making an occasion of her birthday.

Kneeling on a bentwood café chair, Daniel noisily gurgled up the last drops of his chocolate milkshake through a striped plastic straw. They were a heavenly pleasure to him, these stolen treats alone with Ali, dense with a great mass of love. And that night he and his teddy bears would share her bed because Noah wouldn't be there. After the café they strolled together to a neighbouring trinket shop, hand in hand, where Daniel bought a plastic lookalike banana with money advanced to him by his mother. He intended to trick Arnie Weinberg with it, who would make such a gratifying pretence of being duped by the thing. They dawdled idly home via the horses at the north end of Port Meadow, feeding the animals on sugar lumps previously filched from the café.

'I went shopping in my pyjamas,' Daniel said suddenly, as the realisation struck home.

'It's like going to bed in your clothes,' Ali said. 'Only the other way around. That's what Hattie sometimes does, isn't it? It makes getting ready for school much quicker in the morning. Oh my God, Dannie, school!' she said. 'I forgot. It's quarter-past one.'

'Silly Mummy,' Daniel said with satisfaction.

'Silly me,' Ali said. 'I'll take you tomorrow.'

'Tomorrow's Thursday,' Daniel said. 'It's the 'lection. Noah said.'

Back in the car, Ali headed for home.

From within the gate giving access to the farm which led to the house, Ali could see an unfamiliar car in the drive. One of its wing mirrors was making a reflective sunspot which focused with nervous brilliance upon the adjacent field. Ali came to a stop at her gate where she got out and released Daniel from his child-proofed rear door. The car belonged to Mervyn Bobrow, who had never visited the house before.

He had been gazing up at her house front as if to award it marks. Noah's clematis, clambering prettily over the doorway in its May plumage, had lent its annual splendour to the small front porch. As he turned, Ali noticed that he carried in his hand a small snakeskin clutchbag for men, to which he had attached his 'Men Against Sexism' badge, in a double act of wishful avant-garde which caused her a lurch of antipathy. It was both curious and encouraging to her that this person by whom she had once been attracted now had an effect upon her akin to the scrape of chalk on blackboard.

'This house of yours,' Mervyn said, undulating towards her in his tight trousers, his teeth glinting like his wing mirrors. 'This place! What a testament it is to your upward mobility.' He revealed to her with the utterance how deeply he had caught his wife's preoccupation with upward striving during the past ten years, but whether he said it merely to needle her, or whether to highlight his own much greater material advance in the intervening decade, she could not determine.

It seemed to her that the separation had been as good for him as it had been for her. Mervyn had attained greater status and greater prosperity. The luminous tiger and roll-your-own cigarettes had become things of the past along with the whole category of disadvantaged youth. The stilts appeared to be nowhere. He was backed, not only by his wife's university salary and his wife's inheritance, but by the royalties and fees from his impressively ubiquitous writings. Mervyn was in the process of metamorphosing from person to personality. He had become a man who looked for his name in the *Sunday Times* birthday lists and felt himself slighted to find it omitted. But not all things had changed. His trousers were as tight as ever. They reminded Ali of a recent piece of Hattie's infant smut, got from her friend Rebecca. Tight trousers were like 'a cheap hotel', Hattie had said, because they had 'no ballroom'. Once, after running into them in a café, Hattie had announced that the Bobrows were 'posh'. This was a terrible insult since Hattie was strongly against all things posh. Poshness was taboo.

'You realise that your next move will be to Boar's Hill?' Mervyn was saying. The remark caused Ali a tremor of nervous embarrassment. It was somehow pitiful that, living as he did, with a sociologist, he should read social cues so badly. Ali blamed Southend. There had often been times in the past when watching Mervyn wrestle with the British class system had left her glad to be both an outsider and a woman. If you came from a society where status was to a greater degree dependent on colour or caste you had no need to jostle so feverishly with the competition. You couldn't win anyway. If you were a woman you had no need to jostle at all. For all its appalling inequalities, such a system left people easier on the nerves.

Mervyn, by contrast, had never recovered from having passed into the grammar school elite a year early. He had written the eleven-plus examination at the age of ten and had been drilled for the intelligence tests by his schoolteachers in a small group of seven infant superbrains where he had become so proficient at them he could boast that 'Intelligence' was his best subject at school. Thirty years later Ali felt that Mervyn's best subject was still Intelligence. Not humanity, maturity or good sense. He was all untempered IQ.

'Eva and I thought about buying a house near here once,' Mervyn said casually, as they walked towards the kitchen door. 'We had our doubts about the local school. We felt that Lucy needed something *better*.' The local school, which Hattie attended, was a comfortable muddle where children messed with batik in plastic aprons and went on frequent outings to dig up fragments of broken china and old clay pipes from Victorian refuse dumps. In the afternoons the children exercised 'Options'. Noah's jaundiced belief was that the 'options' lay between throwing Lego bricks in the classroom and flicking water in the toilets. While the school's good-hearted lack of academic rigour caused him periodic bursts of anger, it was defended loyally and zealously by his wife on grounds of egalitarian and progressive principle. Most of all she liked it because the other parents were all so nice. Not surprisingly the ethos of the place had driven out the parents of push and muscle and left the more relaxed among the species behind. The school had been an excellent source of female friends and had prompted a fruitful renaissance in this respect.

Mervyn and Eva, on the other hand, having given up their attempt to manipulate the state educational system to the advantage of their child, were now spending the rent which they derived from Ali's old house on paying Lucy's way through a private establishment offering twilight prep at time-worn oak desks and multiplication tables chanted daily before the morning assembly. Fencing and Diction were charged as extras. It was gall and wormwood to Ali that Lucy Bobrow in consequence now read Jane Austen at nine and knew the date in French, while her own dearest Hattie read only large-print pony books and then under duress when there was nothing to watch on the television – but she would never admit to it. On the contrary, she had turned her own unease into an added zeal with which to beat down Noah's misgivings. In this way she had always exorcised her own.

'Coffee, Mervyn?' Ali said.

In the kitchen the breakfast leavings still lay in evidence around the vibrant oranges on the table and the floor here and there was stippled with the sparse remnants of Noah's departure. The green plastic Marks and Spencer bag lay on the floor beside a discarded hold-all with broken shoulder strap and topped by the forgotten pair of scissors.

'Turn a blind eye to the heap,' she said feeling, as she said it, the irony of playing scrupulous hostess to a man whose unwashed socks she had once dragged out from under the sofa for washing. 'Noah left for New York this morning. We've only just got back from dropping him off.'

Mervyn lit a cigarette. 'I can't help envying these medics,' he said. 'There're so *marketable*, aren't they?' While Mervyn was wont to market his every thought on average once a fortnight in a catholic selection of newspaper columns and had even earned the ultimate accolade of being quoted in Pseud's Corner, it had not quieted his vigilance to the marketability of others. 'They collect five livers in a jar,' he said, 'and watch them for a week. Then they write a paper on it and presto! It earns them free airfares to conferences in Bermuda.'

Ali made him no answer. She could not in good conscience deny that Noah was a shade peripatetic in his professional habits and, since neither she nor Mervyn knew anything much about his work, they could, by discussing it, only pool their respective ignorance and bias. Besides, Daniel had just stripped off his pyjama top to reveal his protruding infant abdomen. Noah had once explained to her that this prodigious bulge was caused by the liver. The liver being so disproportionately large in young children, he said, it caused the abdomen to protrude. She did not like to think of livers in a jar. Especially not right now with Noah out of the country for a week.

'I came about the party,' Mervyn said. 'Just a small impromptu affair. Will Noah be back in time for our party? Eva tells me you people haven't yet replied. She's sent me to chase up a few tardy friends.' Ali wondered whether his presence in her house could really constitute no more than a coercive round-up of potential guests – especially guests as unlikely to attend as her and Noah. She doubted it. His motives for visiting her, she felt certain, lay elsewhere.

'I don't think he will be,' Ali said. She was entertained by speculation about what was now to follow. Would the thing be dropped outright, or would the invitation stand? Had she earned consideration as a 'woman-in-her-own-right', or was she still 'just-a-housewife?' Eva and Mervyn had always maintained a laudably high-minded stance on the matter of female self-sufficiency. Eva had early on in her career taken a strategic step sideways from the study of what Noah dismissively called Slums and Blacks into the more hopeful growth area of Women's Studies and was now so much a 'woman-in-her-own-right' that she occasionally even gave dinner parties in her house to which she did not invite her own husband.

'Come anyway,' Mervyn said, after a moment's tell-tale reflection. As an afterthought he uttered an awkward, brief laugh. 'That's if you can find a babysitter,' he said. The remark was a reference to the last occasion upon which there had been any direct contact. An invitation had come to dine, and Noah had consequently telephoned to point out that he and Ali would of necessity bring along Daniel, who was at the time a two-month-old baby. Eva Bobrow had replied to his considerable annoyance that since one went to 'rather a lot of trouble' to arrange these adult parties, one did rather expect one's guests to rise to babysitters.

'Al has a sitter for Hattie, obviously,' Noah had said tetchily, 'but the baby is breast-fed. That's the whole point.'

'I recommend that she leave a bottle with a sitter just this once,' Eva had replied. 'I did it myself as a breast-feeding mother.' Eva was in general much given to presenting her single experience of motherhood as a blueprint for other, lesser parents. 'It's a good idea once in a while,' she said. 'It liberates the mother.'

'For what?' Noah had said, with a kind of contained ferocity. 'Liberates the mother for what? For dinner parties? No thanks.' He had been more than glad to cry off in the expectation that invitations from that unwelcome quarter would finally cease and had taken Ali and the baby to the *Saraceno* restaurant instead, where the sense of reprieve had been so great that Ali had got drunk on one glass of Soave and had punctuated the meal thereafter with gems remembered from a previous Bobrow occasion.

'This is your actual scrag end,' Eva had said, as she had yanked at the dumb-waiter. 'It's more economical by far than a leg.' The college head had been there among the judiciously selected guests, with his superior Danish wife coolly raising her blonde eyebrows at the more screaming of Eva's *déclassé* give-aways. A woman of invulnerable elegance who was herself a 'woman-in-her-own-right'; a person who had once endured a protracted spell in the Third World collecting anthropological material on cultural transvestitism. Ali's fantasy fixed itself upon Eva's hectoring her way through the contents of each course until these took on the violated look of the well-gnawed bones. 'I make it an *absolute* rule never to use cornflour when preparing desserts. Always arrowroot,' she mimicked. 'And where an orange comes into it, my motto is "waste nothing". I use the juice; I use the zest; I have an excellent Israeli recipe for boiling the rind with sugar syrup to make glacé fruit. An orange will work for a knowledgeable cook in a thousand different ways. When the whole point of being an Israeli,' Ali said, interrupting her own narrative, 'the whole point is that you can afford to be as profligate as you like with an orange. It was the way in which Mervyn strained port through a specially laundered nose-rag that bugged her the most, she said. It was the way the Bobrows played at being Oxbridge when they were Oxbridge.

'I'll tell you what I love about you, shall I?' Ali had suddenly said.

'What?' Noah had replied. 'My age? My cheque book?' A hint of touchiness disguised as jest.

'I love you because you don't make me give dinner parties,' Ali had said. 'Did you used to make Shirley give dinner parties?' Noah had disregarded the question, because, while Ali's relationship with him had always been characterised by a strong element of the confessional, Noah had never revealed much about his past and nothing at all about Shirley. The past seemed not to interest him. His present was thoroughly satisfactory. The past was past. Autobiography was not his field. His field was medical research.

'And I love you because you're crazy, Al,' he had said.

Daniel Glazer was now gazing at Mervyn Bobrow with unchecked animosity. He cared not at all for babysitters. Nor for liver. Yuck! Liver and custard were his two worst things. Or was it mustard? Was it custard or mustard that he hated so much? If this sniping, measly stranger would stop holding Ali's attention in that offensive way he could have asked her which it was. A babysitter was definitely not on as far as Daniel was concerned. He would see to it. He did occasionally accept nice Mrs Gaitskell the cleaning woman as a stand-in, but then only grudgingly and only provided that his mother agreed to compensate him adequately for an evening's absence with suitably palatable treats left under his pillow for the morning. But for one Mervyn Bobrow? Never! His mother belonged to him, and not to the world. Mervyn Bobrow, whoever he might be, had no right to come here between them, making ugly red blotches appear on Ali's beautiful white neck and talking about liver and babysitters. Furthermore, he had placed Noah's occupational credentials in question.

'Anyway,' Daniel said belligerently, 'my dad knows much more than you do about dinosaurs and everything, nearly. *And* he knows about Kansas.'

'Is your dad in Kansas?' Mervyn said, attempting a little pleasant small talk with the infant. He was in the act of looking for an ashtray in which to stub out his cigarette. There were no ashtrays in Ali's house. Noah had banished them. Hattie had made a large notice which hung over the fireplace saying 'NO SMOCKING'. It proceeded, in smaller print, and with shamingly patrilineal assumption, 'If you want to smoke you must ask Noah. If Noah is out you can ask Ali.'

'He's in New York, stupid,' Daniel said. 'Kansas is a disease you get if you smoke.'

Mervyn laughed. He threw his cigarette butt on to the floor and ground it underfoot. Then he delivered his trump card. It was then that Ali knew exactly why he had come.

'Your friend Thomas Adderley will be in town tomorrow,' he said, 'but perhaps you already know. He's had some success with a play. A play about the lives of black women. The university theatre here is going to take it up. Possibly also the West End. Eva is lunching with him in college tomorrow. She's very much into the subject right now. We're all going to Johannesburg shortly, as a matter of fact. She has a research grant coming up and she means to make a study of black women's self-help groups.' Ali was not so much fixed upon bitter remembrance of a time when Mervyn had banned her, on high liberal principle, from taking Camilla to South Africa to visit her dying mother; she was not so much absorbed with the awareness that Mervyn was at that moment glowing with the pleasure of having claimed for Eva, not only a precedence of expertise in matters of the female sex, but the dual precedence of access both to her own homeland and to the company of Thomas Adderley. She was too much absorbed by a private longing for brown grass and flat-topped, flowering trees, and by a clear vision of Mot Adderley, lean and sockless, reciting Keats to her in the library.

'I do realise that you're likely to see our going there as a "sell-out",' Mervyn said, 'but this time it's not a case of "Awaydays" with Grannie – is it? People like Eva are needed there. People of Eva's calibre can help to raise the consciousness of the people.' One of the many decent things about Noah, Ali thought gratefully, was that he didn't collect free airfares and call it consciousness-raising. It crossed her mind that to get hold of Thomas would necessitate asking Mervyn for his telephone number. She would do it of course but later, over the telephone, when she felt more composed. There was no chance that she would forgo the chance to see Thomas. None at all.

'A word of advice about that handbag,' she said with malice, using all the weapons she had, as she saw Mervyn prepare to take his leave. 'I wouldn't take that handbag to South Africa if I were you. There's no consenting males act there. Carry that in the street and some upstanding white male Calvinist will consider it his duty to black your eye.' Mervyn laughed in disbelief. As he settled into the driver's seat and reached for the ignition, he snatched almost feverishly at the last area available to him in which to compete with her.

'Has Hattie mastered the one-handed cartwheel yet?' he said. 'Lucy has.' The Men Against Sexism badge, which had fallen off his clutch bag on the way to the car, was lying unnoticed in the drive. Ali picked it up and took it into the house.

ELEVEN

F OR ALI TO LIFT the receiver and dial Thomas in London was
an act accompanied by the excitement of unretractable
daring. Yet over the two decades his voice was all affable
familiarity, all agreeable surprise.

'Mot,' she said. 'It's Alison.'

'Christalmighty!' Thomas said. His laughter tumbled through
the telephone and into her lap like a bright shower of gold. Then
by some curious, gratifying miracle, Thomas came up right on
cue.

'And when am I going to see you, Alison? I am going to see
you, aren't I?'

They arranged to meet on Friday morning at Paddington,
under the clock. Friday seemed perfectly suitable to Ali who had
never kept a diary and for whom the happy expectation of seeing
Thomas again had put her prior appointment with the gallery
clean out of her mind. She knew well enough that Thursday was
out of the question, since Thomas was tied up with Eva Bobrow
and there was also the question of a childminder for Daniel. On
Thursday Mrs Gaitskell always came late: she queued for an
hour at the Co-op grocer because the shop issued its dividend
stamps in double measure on that day. For Noah this lining up
for trading stamps had always been beyond comprehension,
but for Ali it was altogether understandable that, after a week
of evenings indoors with the television and the budgie, Mrs

Gaitskell should go along for the female camaraderie of the queue. It was comparable to that other of her modest indulgences, the Bingo Hall. Since Mrs Gaitskell combined a happy knack at numbers with having little use for her winnings, Ali had become the Bingo Hall's major beneficiary. Within a fortnight she had received a small plastic doll in Highland costume; a crimping device for serrating the edges of chopped carrots, and a fiery litre of 'Macon rouge' bottled for the local engineering workers' Sports and Leisure Club.

Ali, perhaps oddly, had no doubt that in arranging the meeting with Thomas she was setting up her first venture into infidelity – and from the innuendo in Thomas's voice over the telephone she was quietly certain that his mind ran along the same lines as her own. Yet she awed herself by the precipitous boldness of her own unfamiliar gesture as she slipped her diaphragm into her handbag that Thursday evening, like an expectant bride. She added bubbles to her bathwater. In a burst of girlish elation she applied Camilla's eyelash dye to her lashes. Then to Daniel's perturbation she crimped her pale, striated hair, wondering with a kind of powerless horror as she did so what Noah might do were he ever to find her out. To be sure, he would not take it lightly, since his attitude to extra-marital entanglements had always been quite explicitly inflexible.

Ali wore pale grey for her rendezvous: a fact which in another circumstance might have amused her husband, because Ali in her silk crêpe two-piece and matching, button-over flapper shoes had once caused him to ask why she chose to get herself up in passing imitation of the Duchess of Windsor, but Ali had replied that one could surely not live in an English landscape without becoming sensitive to the delicate and varying charms of grey. There were all those silvery ladies in Gainsborough, she said, but there was not one among these with whom Noah would have cared to share his bed. They were upper-class hags all of them with washboard chests and powdered hair. Over the desk in his study, Noah had hung a dark, almond-eyed Modigliani who sprawled there naked and sensual upon a wine-red bed over his stacks of medical textbooks and journals. One arm was thrown over her head to reveal a becoming, triangular clump of dark underarm hair, while her recumbent breasts – so like Shirley's – listed gently outwards presenting dilated apricot nipples. Hattie considered the picture to be nothing short of disgusting.

'It wouldn't be *quite* so bad if she'd worn a bra and shaved under her arms,' she said, but there was no accounting for adults' tastes. None at all, Hattie thought.

Thomas came late. For almost an hour Ali stood at Paddington Station, staring into the Underground entrance where it gave into the forecourt of the mainline station and wrestled against despair. A persistent breeze had goose-pimpled her arms under the thin grey silk of her jacket and she felt it carve more deeply into those lines of middle age which had recently begun to appear around her mouth. The unaccustomed smartness of her clothes had left her feeling uncomfortably like a jilted schoolmarm and she longed to be back in her jeans. But Thomas came at last, taking the stairs three at a time on his prodigious legs and bearing an abject and wholly genuine tale of signal failure at Cannon Street. Ali breathed relief as he kissed her and took her arm. Being with him in those first few moments lifted her heart like a fairground balloon, high above the guards and stragglers at the platform gates. He was so unbelievably the same, but for the enhancing wrinkles around his clear blue eyes and for his immaculate flannel suit.

'Thomas,' she said, with a mock severity, because the suit went so against her memory of his dress. 'You are wearing a suit!'

'So are you,' he said and he kissed her and laughed and kissed her again.

'Not flannel,' she said. 'Mine is not flannel and I don't have a tie.' Thomas promptly loosened his tie. He hung it, drunkenly rejoicing, around her neck. He had been of old the only loony dresser, she recalled, on a campus full of iron-in creases and

Sta-Prest shirts. He had been the only man to bestride the aisles of the lecture halls in canvas shoes without socks; the only man who had not carried a briefcase with lecture notes. Thomas had kept no lecture notes at all, and neither, by example, had she. It had been a point of mutual pride with them to carry all knowledge in the head. He had sat beside her in lectures with his arms folded and with his immoderate legs stretched out sideways into the aisles.

'I'm lunching with a theatre manager at one,' Thomas said, sounding for all the world like a regular grown-up. 'Hence the suit. But come. We have all morning together. First I need coffee and so do you.'

'Not me,' Ali said. 'I drank two quarts of coffee on the train. I was nervous.' Thomas laughed. When he laughed his features appeared momentarily to break up into sparkling fragments and then to come together again, like water disturbed by a pebble. He was all fire and water, Ali thought extravagantly. He was all air and earth.

In the buffet, Thomas withdrew his arm and put a table between them. He lit cigarettes and tanked himself up with refills of railway coffee while Ali stared into the deepened nicotine stains between his bony central fingers and found that she had lived too long with Noah not to suffer vicariously for the violation of his lungs. It was undoubtedly good to be alone with him after all that time and yet – now that he had put the distance of the table between them – she discovered within herself a stirring of that inconvenient awe which of old had always accompanied his presence. In the past, Thomas, always set apart from the rest by his height, his dark skin, his heroic and mildly vagrant habits, had not only given shape to her girlish romanticism. He had, by those very same attributes, inspired a kind of awe which had inhibited physical approach. But now? She wished so much to banish the table and to have his arm around her; to have him embrace her before too much misgiving set in.

Thomas had seated himself opposite her with his back to the

buffet clock and she saw that he wore no wrist watch. For a man to be without a watch seemed to her faintly inappropriate these days after Noah's long example. The clock was making its way towards eleven-fifteen and Thomas's expansiveness with the time began to play upon her nerves. He had come a whole hour late and was due to lunch with a theatre manager. For her own part, Mrs Gaitskell had been contracted to watch over Daniel until school came out, but not beyond that time. Mrs Gaitskell had, as always, made things perfectly clear. She needed to be home by four-thirty to prepare her husband his tea. This was a rule of iron with her. She had been known to pass up charabanc trips to the seaside or to West End comedy shows in the cause of his tea. There was no pointing out that as a consenting adult he might find it possible – even broadening – to hazard the occasional frying of his own egg. To have voiced such a proposition would have been an impertinent trespass within another person's life and Ali would not do it. She had undertaken without fail to return by the two o'clock train.

Thoughts of the diaphragm in her handbag now intruded to undermine her poise. Had Thomas intended merely that they should pass the morning in the National Gallery? Or take a half-hour stroll together along the Embankment pooling their more recent thoughts on the work of Bertolt Brecht? A nervy under-graduate impulse came over her to close the distance between them by a resolute brightness in discourse which would make him admire her and would draw him as close to her as the kiss and the arm with which he had greeted her but had now withdrawn.

'What's the matter?' Thomas said after a while. Ali found that her hands were shaking slightly in her lap.

'Nothing really,' she said. 'I suppose I was just thinking how much you always scared me in the past.'

'*Me?*' Thomas said. '*Me* scare *you*? You've got to be joking.'

'Mainly by those unreal, rather larger-than-life looks you have,' Ali said. 'I recently saw your double on a cigarette ad. You were behaving masterfully with a white stallion.'

'And what about you, Alison?' he said. 'Talking of looks. Not only did you always look like the Ice Queen in person, but you frequently beat me at class essays.'

'*Essays*,' Ali said in disbelief. 'You were bothered about essay marks? I always assumed your concerns were global.'

'Furthermore, you got yourself entangled pretty smartish with that yobbo from the Freshers' Reception Committee,' Thomas said. 'What chance was there for me?'

'Oh God!' Ali said. 'What a mix-up.'

'Not only did you hob-nob with the senior men from the word go,' Thomas said, rubbing it in with gusto, 'but you were better at the work than I was.'

'Rubbish,' Ali said. 'I was more of a swot, that's all.'

'Then you got married,' Thomas said. 'I got drunk on your wedding day. Does that flatter you? He's made a lot of money, your ex. There's a pile to be made out of understanding concrete in Johannesburg.' Ali detected, in this last remark, elements of snobbery and bitterness which saddened her for a moment, but she shook it off.

'Thomas,' Ali said morbidly, 'our signals failed us long before Cannon Street. I'm sorry.'

'That's okay,' Thomas said, with every sign of fortitude. 'Cheers!' he said and he drained his Max-Pax, but Ali still brooded on the past.

'There was a notion strongly prevalent at the time that girls got married,' she said apologetically. 'As to the man, he was the one that happened to choose me. On the whole one didn't choose. That would have been unthinkably strident. One waited to be chosen – just as one waited to be chosen as a waltzing partner at the Saturday school of ballroom dancing.'

'I never took ballroom dancing lessons,' Thomas said. 'How was I to know all this?'

'I do admit that there were certain young women who chose for themselves,' Ali said, 'but they were the ones who had the art of making initiative look like submission. In short they had feminine wiles. I never had any of those. All I had was a head full of nineteenth-century verse.'

'Me too,' Thomas said. 'Stuffed with Keats.'

'And there *was* the business of your being such a hobo,' Ali said guardedly. 'I suppose my timorous instincts led me to a liaison with a yobbo in preference to a hobo. I imagined that you were too unconventional ever to get married. But just look at you now in your three-piece suit! You probably got married in church. You probably have a nice little monthly savings account with the Standard Bank of South Africa. You probably have two titled aunts living quietly in Bournemouth.'

'Hove,' Thomas said promptly. 'I have one titled aunt in Hove, living in reduced circumstances.'

'Well there you are!' Ali said. 'And to think I thought you were disreputable, just because you lived in a garage and went without socks. You may pity me now for my parochial assumptions. But dearest Thomas are you married? Please tell me about your wife.' Thomas drew himself up a little primly.

'My wife is an excellent woman who has no part in this morning's engagement,' he said with daunting propriety. 'Alison, I do not propose to discuss my domestic affairs with you.'

'How about your children then?' Ali said hopefully. 'Do you have any?'

'Three,' Thomas said. 'A boy and two girls. My boy is nineteen.'

'Snap!' Ali said. 'I have two girls and a boy. My older daughter is twenty. Photographs please.'

'I don't have any with me,' Thomas said. 'I don't carry my children about with me in my pockets, so to speak.' Ali smiled to think how predictably history was here repeating itself; that Thomas was raising his children in a style which would leave them free to doss in garages while she was confining and smothering hers with a great excess of care and love. She drew from her handbag a threesome of her own photographs which she handed to him with pride. Daniel prowling among cow parsley in his baseball cap; Hattie swinging on a gate with her face to the wind; Camilla recumbent, in a hammock, eating black olives from a conical paper bag. Delicious, sensual pictures. Ali could not look at them without drawing breath in wonder at her children's beauty.

'And are you happily married?' Thomas said, as he leafed through the photographs.

'Oh yes,' Ali said. She suspected that he had asked the question more to be absolved from feelings of responsibility for her than to concern himself for her sake, but she saw this as unobjectionable and took no offence. 'Third time lucky,' she said brightly. 'He's my third husband.'

Thomas smiled at her sceptically. 'I thought that only film stars got married three times,' he said.

'And crazies,' Ali said. 'You'd like him, Mot. He's a nice, reliable Jewish medic who pays the mortgage and digs the garden at weekends. He's exactly the sort of person Mrs Horowitz always wanted for Julie, but there you are. I married him instead. I wonder sometimes about Julie. Whether she ever did get married. We lost each other somewhere in the mists of time. I believe she went to Paris.'

'She's back,' Thomas said. 'For good. She never got married. I see her from time to time. She came back on her parents' account. Her father has Parkinson's disease and her mother is senile. That's life too, I suppose. Here, have your pictures back. This older girl of yours – she's a real beauty, isn't she? I ought to introduce her to my son.'

'No thanks!' Ali said overhastily, since even in jest the idea alarmed her as a tempting form of vicarious gratification.

'I have thought that it would be nice to protect her from too much charisma in men,' she said, embarking with a false brightness upon what sounded like a conversational set-piece. 'Right now she's safe as houses. Her young men are all characterised by a remarkable lack of personal magnetism. I believe that she goes to bed with them merely to gather experience.'

Thomas smiled at her indulgently, being amused by the idea. Having stubbed out his fourth cigarette, he was ready to go, but Ali kept on talking.

'Life is very different for these children,' she said. 'They don't grow up in Cambridge with that enveloping awareness of injustice. Not the way we did. Not the way your children will. One of my dear Camilla's men plays Scott Joplin on a piano which he keeps in the front garden. The instrument stands knee-deep in buttercups. When it rains he goes out and gives it an oilcloth. There's another one – a vicar's son – who wears green hair and carries A. E. Housman in his breast pocket. They all of them talk as if the purpose of life were to play Puck in trilby and spats in the latest college production of *A Midsummer Night's Dream*. We were not like that.'

'No,' Thomas said absently. 'I suppose not.'

'There were too many things which poisoned the time and the place for us,' Ali said thoughtfully. 'Had one been young in Cambridge one would possibly have demanded so much more for oneself. But being young in a place which manifestly denied the most basic personal freedoms to most of its people – how could one have hung up one's tender youthful conscience and pressed one's own personal causes? I believed, I think, in some half-formulated way, that I had no right to care about whom I married. That was wicked rubbish, of course, but I believed it.'

Thomas reached out then and put the palm of his hand on her cheek.

'It's all ancient history, Alison,' he said. 'You oughtn't to let it intrude like this. It was all a long time ago.'

'Yes,' she said. 'I know.'

'You talk too much,' he said. 'Do you know that? You always did. You always consumed your time with me delivering lucid monologues when you ought to have been in my bed.'

'Yes,' Ali said again. 'I know.'

'I don't know what you have in mind for this morning,'

Thomas said, at last, 'but I propose that we find a room somewhere.'

First, Thomas announced festively, as they left the buffet, the occasion called for wine. They would procure a decent bottle of chilled wine, he said, and would use it the more to prolong and savour the act which they had been more than twenty years in coming to. It began to dawn on Ali that Thomas had no sense of time. In this he was not unlike herself. She wondered as they walked arm in arm to the victualler why the wine should seem so necessary, given the run on time. It crossed her mind that Thomas, being, as he clearly was, such a nice man, such a loyal husband, so much less unconventional than she had always thought, could not commit adultery without first getting slightly drunk. The idea was a comfort to her; that he, as she, was perhaps wholly green in the procedures of this urgently beckoning sin.

'I have never done anything like this before,' Ali said, as they emerged from the wine shop. 'I have had three husbands, but until this very day I have never philandered. I have always married every man with whom I slept.' Thomas laughed. He stopped at a street crossing, bottle in hand, and kissed her on the mouth. There was something wildly exciting about this present contact with his teeth, Ali thought. His teeth were crowded and irregular, some of them sharply pointed, as though he had misused them to open Coke bottles in his youth. When she looked up, Thomas had fixed upon her his dazzling azure eyes which were as markedly lacking in symmetry as were his teeth.

'I like your teeth,' she said. 'You are the only man I have ever made mouths with who has eccentric teeth.'

At the hotel reception desk she watched him take a double room with bath and pay for it with his credit card. Then they giggled together in the lift over their conspicuous lack of luggage.

'Say,' Ali said, 'it wasn't half expensive! We ought to go halves on it. Go on, Mot. I'll give you a cheque.' She began to unbuckle her handbag but Thomas in his adamant refusal was all colonial chivalry.

'Anyway,' he said. 'It's Barclaycard money. It isn't real. It's plastic. Come on Alison.'

Ali laughed. 'Who would have thought we would ever be screwing each other on a credit card in London?' she said. 'Think of it, my friend.'

The hotel room was small and sparse. It was equipped with a Christian Science Bible and smelt heavily of flower-scented air freshener.

'Sanilav!' Thomas said, sniffing the air. 'It smells of lilac-scented Sanilav in here.'

'It's hyacinth,' Ali said knowingly. 'My husband grows hyacinths in pots around Christmas time. They always smell like lav cleaner.' Thomas picked up the Bible and threw it into her hands.

'Catch!' he said. 'And stop talking to me about your husband.'

'Thanks,' Ali said. 'Have you ever actually read the Bible, Mot?' she said. 'I have tried from time to time but I have to say that I find it boring.'

'Boring?' Thomas said in disbelief. He had taken off his jacket and had made a start on his shirt. 'My dear woman, I love it. I have read it twice through and I must tell you that it's gripping. It's nothing but rape, incest and vengeance from start to finish. But perhaps these things are as mother's milk to you.'

'Twice?' Ali said. 'You've read the Bible twice?'

'I read it in jail.' Thomas said. 'It was all that they would give me.' But, seeing her look so much cast down at this reference to his brief incarceration, he made light of it to revive her mood.

'I was arrested at a cricket match,' he said. 'Isn't that just like a white South African – to be arrested at a cricket match?'

'Call yourself white?' Ali said. Thomas laughed.

'Watch yourself,' he said.

'But are you all right, Mot?' she said, suddenly overcome with fear for him. 'I mean, are you safe living there?'

'Of course,' Thomas said. 'I'm a harmless, peace-loving non-comformist. The authorities know I'm no threat. I get my car tyres let down sometimes. That's the worst I can expect. You get some crackpot zealots back home, but it ain't like the IRA. Not yet. Nobody shoots you through the head when you open the door.' In the wine shop Thomas had lavishly bought champagne. He began now to twist the wire casing from the wine cork, holding the bottle cold between his naked thighs. 'As to William Lister, I never did it, by the way,' he said. 'I never drove the silly bugger over the border. Maybe I would have, had he asked me, but he asked somebody else. They borrowed my car and thoughtfully left the boot full of incriminating leaflets.'

'Fancy you having a car,' Ali said inadequately. 'You never had a car in my day.'

'Get your clothes off, Alison,' he said. 'Or are you waiting for me to rip them off you?' Ali took off Thomas's tie and pulled off her own shirt.

'I have to tell you, Mot,' she said, touched with schoolgirl shyness, 'not only do I have a most inelegant rubber diaphragm à la Marie Stopes, but I have a huge scar running the length of my abdomen.' Thomas eased the cork from the bottle with a gentle pop and took a longish swig before he answered her.

'You also have a large purple bruise on your neck where your nice Jewish medic has left his mark,' he said. He laughed to see Ali blush and spin round towards the glass and shoot a hand self-consciously to her throat. 'It's all right, he's your husband,' he said. The bruise was bedded in the well of her right shoulder: a good-sized bramble stain, standing as testimony to Noah's parting kisses at the kitchen table.

Thomas handed her the bottle. 'Lovely boobs,' he said, kissing each of her nipples in turn. Then, with a nice aplomb, he ran his tongue down the length of her abdominal scar.

Their love making was brief, abortive and less than satisfactory. As somewhere beyond them on the windless air a clock called the half-hour. Thomas shrank in agitation from her thighs.

'Half-past what?' he said sharply. 'Half-past what for Christsake, Alison? Tell me the time.' He began to grope on the floor for the old pocket watch in his waistcoat which, unbeknown to him, had rendered up its last tick at Cannon Street.

'It's half-past twelve,' she said. 'I assumed all along that you knew.'

'Oh my God!' Thomas said. 'My bloody lunch appointment is at one. I had no idea.' He swung his legs over the side of the bed. 'Listen love,' he said, taking her hand in a gesture of appeasement. 'I'll be as quick as I can. Just you wait for me, okay?'

'You'll be two hours,' Ali said.

'Hang about here with the wine and the Bible, and I'll get back as soon as I can,' he said. 'I'm really sorry, Alison.' He went to take a shower.

Afterwards Ali lay naked on the bed and watched him pull on the clothes over his stunning pale brown body. He paused to bend over her once in shirt-tails and socks, planting brief kisses on her cheek, her hair and her scar.

'Your tie is under my shirt,' she said. 'I won't be here when you get back. You ought to know that. I can't be. My babyminder has to go at half-past three. Mot, we'll say goodbye. I have loved every minute of being with you again. It has been the nicest reunion of my life.'

'Don't be so bloody ridiculous!' Thomas said in disbelief. 'Use the bloody telephone and say you've been delayed. You can't leave me now. You don't dare. In any case it's utterly absurd. My aeroplane leaves tonight. This is our only possible time together.'

'Excuse me,' Ali said, 'but it is *you* who is leaving *me*. I don't say that you ought not to, but I want it clear who is leaving whom. You ought to go now, or you'll be late. You had better jump into a taxi.'

'Alison, for God's sake use the telephone,' he said. 'It's simple enough, isn't it? I haven't seen you in bloody donkey's years.' Ali saw that Thomas, for all his advanced views on social change, could not in the gut take her babyminding problem seriously, when his own wife had always kept a full-time black servant on the premises whose labour could be summoned at any time.

Admittedly the servant, Ali guessed, would be one whose men friends and children Thomas broke the law to harbour during weekends and holidays. Admittedly she would be one whose children Thomas's own wife would have taught to read by translating Beatrix Potter into Zulu. But there was no escaping that his assumptions belonged to a privileged and servant-owning class.

'Mot,' Ali said, determinedly, quieting as best she could the insistent lamentation in her groin. 'Mot, I can't. Whether you believe me or not, I can't. Let's call it a day. Let's call it a failure of signals.' Seeing that he was feeling torn and wretched, she felt for him most strongly. She sat up and reached for her shirt, thinking that for him to have her lying there, recumbent and vulnerable, was unfair. It was to inflict too much reproach.

'I'll tell you something about me,' she said. 'Then you will think better of me. I paint. I even paint rather well. I'm going to have an exhibition in a West End gallery. Isn't that chic? Isn't that success? I want praise, Mot, especially from you. I want to hear you calling that glamorous. Don't just go off and pity me for a hang-dog fool who couldn't let you consummate one monstrously expensive screw. Admire me, Mot, please.' Thomas smiled. He brushed a trace of wetness from her eyes and kissed her on the mouth with a pleasant, assuaging conviction.

'Alison,' he said. 'You lay me out; you always did. You are one great whizz-bang marvellous woman. Even your scar is a great turn-on for me.'

'Goody bye,' she said. 'And good luck with the play.'

'Thanks,' he said.

As Thomas's footfall died down the corridor it came to her that, in meeting Thomas, she had stood up the gallery. The enormity of this omission left her stunned, but only for a moment and mainly for Noah's sake. 'Idiot fool!' she said to herself, recalling a little sadly the portfolio forgotten in her studio at home which had been ready waiting for ten days now, tied neatly at the sides with milliner's tape. Then the meeting with Thomas

146

had on balance been such a good thing, for all its failure, that it had been worth all the paintings in the portfolio. In order to paint well – really well – one had doubtless to be single-minded and ambitious. One had to walk out on a lover and keep strategically important lunch dates. In short, it helped to be a man.

Ali looked into the mirror, where her crimped hair and dyed eyelashes; her purple bruise and naked breasts, gave back to her a surprisingly seductive self-image.

There was one thing to be done and one only, she thought. She dialled the hotel reception desk and put through a telephone call to Arnie Weinberg on his extension number in the research unit. Arnie had always been the best antidote she knew against gloom. Besides, his curriculum vitae was still sitting under that Modigliani nude on Noah's desk; that lovely, yielding woman, with all the time in the world to give. Ali was ready to bet her life on it that no Modigliani nude had ever beaten a man at essays.

TWELVE

ARNIE WEINBERG HAD returned that morning on a flight from Washington in a mood so sanguine that not even the daunting state of his flat could sully it. During the week he had taken a plane to California where developments on the job front had accelerated considerably. He had flown to California to read a paper which had been warmly received and had stayed to be interviewed two days later by a line-up of committee men, most of whom had previously been present to hear him speak. This had afforded him an opportunity to parade his advantages twice. The committee had clearly thought well of him and had not waited for Noah's recommendation to come by post but had telephoned Noah for reference in New York the next day. Noah had been more than emphatic and loyal in his commendations. Now Arnie was waiting to hear from California in a spirit of fair optimism.

Yet even to a man with expectations the flat that morning had looked and smelled awful. A prevailing odour of tar and damp-rot solution had assaulted his nostrils as he opened his front door and the furniture stood in huddles under large dust-sheets in the centre of the living room. Plaster dust filled the air, along with cigarette smoke and DJ prattle from workmen's trannies. His admirable, aged landlady had appeared apologetically from the garden in her laced walking shoes to offer him sanctuary upon her ottoman for a few days. She had, in his absence, at last taken issue with the varied range of mould spores which had been growing up through the floor of his basement living room for quite some time, but the builders had come three days late. One half of Arnie was pleasantly surprised. She had always struck him as being so much endowed with upper-class calm when it came to property and decay that he had not expected any move towards reform.

'Where you have a house you have *dry-rawt*, my dear Arnold,' she would observe serenely. She spoke to him with the same cheerful detachment about her angina and her arthritis. Arnie was a great favourite with her, as she was with him. She had furnished the flat for him handsomely with a walnut-veneered grandfather clock, a set of lyre-back dining chairs and several Afghan rugs from the deceased estates of her three brothers. She had bestowed upon him a valuable roll-top desk and several canvases by Dame Laura Knight painted in the heyday of the International Artists Association. But Arnie had nonetheless begun to tire of watching rust-coloured mushrooms blooming up through the mellow chevron woodblocks of his living-room floor. The floor had been laid in the nineteen-thirties on a bed of concrete without the advantages of plastic damp-proofing membrane, and the leaking roof of the adjoining conservatory – now elegantly awash with ferns and Gothic Revival garden chairs, with their legs all in splints – had contributed a degree of seepage and surface water upon which the mushrooms thrived.

Arnie had graduated over the years from draughty bed-sitting rooms in the Abingdon Road to the more salubrious groves of Park Town where the noble proportions of the Garden Flat, the high, lichen-covered garden walls, the beauty of the rhododendrons and the benign offices of his nice old Fabian landlady more than compensated him for the aura of patrician decay. But right then he had no wish to shake off jet lag on an ottoman which he would have been obliged to share with the landlady's Persian cat, even in a room graced with two occasional tables painted by Roger Fry. Politely he had declined and headed south instead along the ornamental iron railings of the square towards the research unit from which he had attempted to telephone Ali Glazer. At the Glazers' house he was always sure of a welcome or, if necessary, a decent bed. But Ali, it appeared, was in London. That would be her date with the gallery, he thought.

'Hi, Al,' he said when her voice was shortly thereafter relayed to him from London. He was not surprised, since benign co-incidence had always played as large a part in his experience as hazard. 'How's London?' he said. Ali found her own partial nudity suddenly compromising, even over the telephone, and reached with her left hand for the bedcover which she held in a knot against her breasts.

'What makes you so sure I'm in London?' she said.

'Aren't you?' he said.

'Well, yes,' she said. 'I am. But how should it signify?' Arnie laughed.

'What's up, Al?' he said. 'Those bastards didn't like your pictures?'

'Oh *them*,' Ali said. 'I don't know. Say, Arnie, I am not enjoying this conversation. I 'phoned to talk about you, not about me.'

'Okay,' Arnie said. 'So just tell me first what happened.'

'I never got there,' she said, opting at once for candour. 'I messed the whole thing up.' There was a moment's deadly silence. 'Signal failure on the Underground,' she said. 'Cannon Street.'

'*Cannon* Street?' he said.

'Promise you won't tell Noah,' she said.

'Call them for Chrissake, Al,' he said. 'It's not that difficult.' Ali clutched decisively at the knot of bedcover between her breasts and spoke with resolution. 'I have put the arid plain behind me,' she said.

'Pardon me?' he said.

'Promise you won't tell Noah,' she said again. Arnie laughed. He enjoyed playing cloak and dagger with her against her husband. As a thoroughly legitimate form of flirtation it often heightened her spirits. Her liveliness had always pleasantly engaged him.

'My lips are sealed,' he said. 'You may rest assured, Mrs Glazer, that no word of this will ever reach the ears of the Master.'

'Thanks,' she said. 'I have a message for you by the way. It's a day late.'

'The CV,' he said. 'Forget it. I talked with Noah. It's dealt with. The whole thing is dealt with. I just flew in this morning in any case. You couldn't have got me any earlier.'

'I see,' she said. 'Well that's a mercy, anyhow.'

'My landlady is tampering with my fungi,' Arnie said. 'She has filled the air with noxious fumes. How would you like for to put me up tonight, Al?'

'Love to,' Ali said eagerly, reaching out for the balm of his company. 'Have some supper with me. There's only me and the children.'

'It's Friday,' Arnie said. 'I'm planning on working here till late. I'll take a nap in the unit and work through till ten.'

'Don't count on it,' Ali said caustically, through disappointment. 'Your victim may well die.'

'We all die, kid,' he said. 'So long.'

Ali interrupted her progress towards the railway station in Praed Street, where she had her ears pierced with a staple-gun and shot through with gold studs. The pain was momentarily intense, the blood loss slight, the satisfaction immeasurable. Through the act she felt a moment's communion with Camilla who had pierced her ears at home using a block of ice and a safety pin passed through a candle flame. She knew immediately that Noah as usual had been right. Ear piercing was mutilation and as such it exactly met the case. The mental pain which had stirred with this second casting-off of Thomas wanted a counterbalancing agony in the flesh. It wanted incision and blood. With throbbing lobes aglow like neon lights, Ali bravely put the past behind her and boarded the two o'clock train.

It had been raining heavily all over Oxfordshire in Ali's absence and was still raining now as the day turned towards teatime. Birds beaked themselves forlornly on city chimneypots and beyond the centre the air was greenly limp. Small mud lakes, like hippopotamus ponds in a model village, had appeared in the farm track which led to her house. On the sofa, Daniel Glazer was nesting under a quilt. The sound of the rain wrapped him soothingly after a painful fall. He was fast asleep but presented a parched blood-stained mouth. Where his upper-left incisor had been was now a jelly-textured gap. He had knocked his tooth out on a fence post at one thirty-five. By coincidence, at the same moment in Praed Street, a staple gun had pierced his mother's right ear lobe. Mrs Gaitskell had wrapped the small rootless milk tooth in Kleenex and had placed it on the sitting-room mantelpiece for Daniel to put under his pillow that night. The fairy would come for sure, she said. She had no doubts at all. A tooth jolted from the infant gum through violent precipitation was as valid a collector's item for any tooth-hoarding fairy as one which had loosened gradually in the course of maturation.

Ali was startled and upset. She had entered carrying a letter and a small parcel from the hall which had been delivered in her absence and she now tucked in at Daniel's feet with these to hear Mrs Gaitskell's reassurances. Both the letter and the parcel were from America. The first, from Noah's mother, contained two very small, snowy-white hand towels monographed in satin with a cursive 'G'. Towels for the doctor's hands. A scented floral 'notelet', somewhat deficient in punctuation, fell from their virginal folds, and read as follows:

Dear Alison,
Over here we call these little towels 'finger-tip towels' you can never have too many believe me! Tell Noah that his grandson (my *great* grandson!!) has been accepted for the *Gifted Program*! What a clever boy I hope your Daniel goes the same way there was never a shortage of brains in the family especially with the

men of course!! Shane's wife is due with the second one any day now God willing another brainbox but Lydia *insists* she's hoping for a girl! No more news for now

Sincerely,
Mother

Ali wrestled with an immediate and perverse desire to consign the fingertip towels as floor-cloths for the kitchen. It had never ceased to jar with her that this remote and indiscriminate employer of exclamatory punctuation marks, this obsequious and doting propagandist for the male sex, should presume to address herself to Ali as 'Mother'. A title earned by nurture, surely, not by contract? It belonged, in Ali's view, to that most dear and quite other person who had quietly died fifteen years before in her daughter's absence. A cloying usurper, Ali thought, a peddlar of undermining, homespun absurdities, and yet without her there would be no Noah. As to 'the Brainbox', whom Ali had never met, her feelings towards this young person were strongly antipathetic.

She supposed, looking back, that Camilla had been a 'brainbox' too, where Hattie and Daniel were characterised by a remarkable lack of academic precociousness on all fronts. She did not like to think that Camilla's brains could have come from Mervyn Bobrow. Nor did she care for the attendant possibility that Mervyn was actually brighter than Noah, since Noah was so much nicer. Noah had once remarked to her that since, genetically speaking, the species was constantly driven towards the norm, exceptionally bright people tended to produce slightly less bright children. Ali had gained comfort from this snippet of miscellaneous knowledge, and had inverted it, for her own convenience in the case of the Brainbox, to imply that he derived his prodigious wits from maternal grandmother's manifest deficiency in this area.

The letter was from Noah's son Shane. It had overtaken the elder Mrs Glazer's parcel en route and announced the birth of a baby daughter weighing seven pounds and five ounces. Under the announcement, in a smug corollary, Mrs Shane Glazer had written 'Born naturally and effortlessly'. Ali handed the card to Mrs Gaitskell.

'Well I'm blowed,' she said. 'Effortlessly was it?'

'If it was "natural" then it wouldn't have been "effortless",' Ali said. 'Effortless is only if somebody anaesthetises you and hacks you open.' Mrs Gaitskell cackled knowingly.

'All I know is I used to have 'em so bloody quick the midwife never could get to me on time,' she said. 'It's always been the same in our family. Our Mum were just the same. The last one come so bloody quick she were all tore up before the doctor come, poor soul. She weren't never the same after. One passage she had for the lot, ever after.' Ali gorged on the horror of it. There was nobody like Mrs Gaitskell for putting into sobering perspective the woes of one's own loins. Right now this macabre intelligence served to comfort Ali for the hollow yearning within her female parts.

'Still I've always loved the kiddies,' Mrs Gaitskell said warmly. She drew a glacier mint from her handbag and left it on the table for Daniel. Then she encased her perm in a rainproof rectangle of concertinaed plastic which she tied firmly under the chin and stepped hallwards to take her leave.

'Oh my Gawd!' she said suddenly. 'It's *him* out there. The one that burns the saucepans!' Through glazed panels alongside Ali's front door she had seen the head and shoulders of William Lister, wearing his house upon his back like a snail. 'Him that has all them blessed postcards.'

'Oh my God!' Ali said. 'Mrs Gaitskell, what shall I do?' Mrs Gaitskell had no doubts. 'Start with him as you mean to go on,' she said firmly. 'Get rid of him, Ali.'

THIRTEEN

Wᴵᴸᴸᴵᴬᴹ's ᴬᴿᴿᴵⱽᴬᴸ had coincided with Hattie's. Ali's younger daughter burst rudely past him into the hall, clawing at her mother and calling out urgently, 'Mummy can I have disco roller-skates? Rebecca's got disco roller-skates. Please, Mummy. They're so great! Becca's only cost twenty-five pounds. Say yes, Mummy. Go on – please. Say yes!' It was an invariable rule that one's children showed up as grasping materialists in William Lister's company. Ali had ceased to find it even mildly embarrassing. She stepped out into the porch, wearing Hattie like a ball and chain around her knees.

'Hello, William,' she said. Rebecca's mother, Marion, having dropped Hattie, had meanwhile executed a confident three-point turn in the drive in her gleaming Peugeot and now paused to exchange brief, parting pleasantries with Ali through the rain. At the back window were visible a sea of small siblings and friends jostling to write their names in the steam of the window panes.

'Many thanks!' Ali called out. She was fond of Marion and in general enjoyed her brief, ironic exchanges with this rather highbrow mother sunk good-humouredly in the business of child-rearing.

'Watch her head!' Marion called back over the sound of the engine and the falling rain. 'Mine have all got head-lice.' Louse-talk was a currently fashionable form of taboo-breaking among certain subsections of the professional middle class, Ali had decided. One-upmanship over head-lice was not a form of competitive behaviour indulged in by the humbler parents of her acquaintance. It was peculiar to the graduate group.

'Hattie's had them twice already,' she said, wishing to hold her own, 'don't worry.'

'Mine have them *all the time*,' Marion yelled extravagantly. 'They reek constantly of disinfectant. We've just done the steel comb and cattle-dip routine for the umpteenth time. Louse corpses dropping in their hundreds all over the breakfast table.' Ali laughed. She conceded Marion the victory.

'What next?' she said, feigning despair.

'Anal worms,' Marion called back triumphantly as she shifted into gear. 'My lot have had those too.'

William was encased from head to foot in orange waterproof overalls. He was dripping rain in copious runnels into the door mat, and on to his sodden, ill-fitting shoes.

'Is he staying here?' Hattie said, with a marked and audible lack of enthusiam. 'Why can't he stay somewhere else?'

Ali squirmed but uttered no reproof. She could never find it in her to discourage in Hattie that admirable unblinking straight-ness in handling people which Noah – with greater tact admit-tedly – exhibited also. Hattie was not gorged on guilt. Where Ali had sacrificed all her childhood pocket money to the blind box, Hattie had always been of the opinion that the poor should 'go to the bank' for money. She spent her pocket money on trinkets and sweets. She was firmly of the opinion that two Remembrance Day poppies got cut-price at a half-pence each made better sense than one got for a round ten pence. She always giggled through prayers and had spread the belief throughout the junior school that the vicar kept a half-jack of whisky in the folds of his cassock. For these and other bold attributes Hattie's company was sought unceasingly by great numbers of admiring little girls.

'I'm not stopping,' William said, pointedly rubbing his hip joint and limping into the hall. 'I am perfectly willing to sleep under the stars tonight.' Sharply he drew in breath and rubbed again at his hip joint. 'Sciatica,' he said in a whisper. 'Just a touch of sciatica – it's nothing.'

'Come in,' Ali said. 'Take your wet things off. Let's have some tea.' And she led the way to the kitchen.

William was ascetic. He was what Ali's husband called an 'ascetic pragmatist'. He was committed to poverty, Noah said, because he had no money and to chastity because he had no women. Since life had given him lots of practice, he had long been in the business of elevating these potential disadvantages to the status of a creed. On his lapel he wore a badge stamped 'Pedal Power' because he had no motor car and on his thrifty, recycled envelopes he pasted stickers which exhorted recipients to 'Conserve Trees'. Noah, as the careful nurturer of nine espaliered plum trees, chose to consider this particular exhortation a gross · impertinence, but Ali and Noah Glazer were neither of them people whose opinions William took into account. He would not in good conscience approve of either. Ali had had three marriages and wore expensive silk shirts. Decadence was her hallmark. Besides, once long ago in another country she had been the cause of his humiliation. She had lain on the grass under him at a galling initiation rite with every sign of self-possession, wholly indifferent to his agony and had connived thereafter with the enemy. William was endowed with an excellent memory and was a careful harbourer of grievance.

He had had a difficult adolescence. Having accompanied his parents from Sheffield to South Africa at the age of twelve he had · shown, at nineteen, no sign of shedding his incongruous, home-boy style. In the context he wore his shorts always too long. He committed the local outrage of wearing his sandals with socks. On holidays, he wore canvas exercise shoes into the sea. In a land of plenty his mother skimped on butter. The violent sun still burned his neck bright turkey-red and provoked swelling half-moons of sweat which drenched the underarm seams of his shirts. His gentle post-war world of watery Bovril and rationed sugar-lumps, of chlorinated indoor swimming pools and weekly baths, was always too much with him. He was no match for the indolent, brawny male philistines who roared their convertible sports cars into the student car park, or hurled their grass-stained rugger shorts at domestic servants for washing. After the ordeal of his high school days, which he had spent dodging bugle practice in the cadet corps, he had been drawn to Ali and to Thomas Adderley by a sound instinct for nosing out in them that touch of gentle aberration which made them less terrible than the rest. A similar sense of his own otherness had already drawn him into a dangerous flirtation with revolutionary politics. Now, twenty years later, as he watched Ali pour tea for him at the kitchen workboard, he regarded her with all the patronising contempt which he reserved for those of her kind who had never achieved the distinction of having had their passports impounded by the state police. There was precious little point in attempting to discuss his political work with her, he thought, since the woman was too busy fretting about her daughter's guitar practice and her son's lost tooth. William winced on his tea.

'Have you burned your mouth?' Ali asked solicitously, but William shook his head.

'Sciatica,' he said hoarsely and for the third time. 'I'll be off in just a minute.'

'Stay!' Ali cried out, rising in her chair 'William, stay. It's raining.' On the noticeboard behind him she was half aware of the postcard which Noah had placed there to warn against compassion. 'Noah is out of town for six days,' she said, making him a gift of her only defence against his presence. 'Why not stay till then?' She had offered the fact as a kindness, knowing that Noah made him uneasy. He had got off on the wrong foot with Noah from the start, poor man, Ali thought. First of all there had been that embarrassing introductory clanger when William had taken a high-minded stand against 'national stereotyping'; when Noah had come home to find a lean and hungry stranger at his kitchen table sitting before a pile of pamphlet literature. First Noah had kissed his wife.

'I'm late,' he said, 'I have had my time wasted for me by a boring, long-winded Canadian.' The stranger had bounced into action.

'Does it signify that this boring, long-winded person was Canadian?' he said sharply. 'Or merely that he was boring? What I mean is, why indulge in national stereotyping?'

Noah had stared at William for long enough to notice that the effort of making his point had turned him a deep brick-red.

'It signifies only in that I reserve the right to display what bigotry I choose in my own house, young man,' Noah said. William had chalked up Ali's husband, right then, as an enemy of 'The Struggle', and had had no cause since then to change his assessment.

Arnie came early while the family was at supper. He was bearing a gift of duty-free brandy for Ali and communed with her in his usual code.

'Croak,' he said. 'Croak, croak.'

'What did I tell you?' she said smugly. 'Sit down, Arnie. I'll get you a plate.' He bent to kiss her cheek and sat down.

'I just got a call,' he said. To Ali's ears, the phrase still conjured implications of the priesthood, or of the voice of God booming in the temple, but it no longer caused her actual misunderstanding.

'A call?' she said. 'From whom?'

'California,' he said. 'I got the job.'

'Good God, that's very quick. Well done, Arnie! Oh very well done. How deservedly rich and great you will be.' She got up to fetch him a plate and cutlery. 'I'll miss you,' she said. Arnie placed the brandy on the table where William Lister's presence had resulted in the eating being neither convivial nor brisk.

'This is for the kids,' he said, hoping to stir a little controversy in the gloom. William had, he noticed to his amusement, on this occasion consented to eat the Glazers' food, but appeared to be much against both fibre and roughage. He had made a neat pile of tomato skins and mushroom stalks on the edge of his plate and had banked up these rejects with spoonfuls of brown rice which had also been pushed to one side. Hattie in her turn was forking about in her portion to remove small, unidentifiable orangey particles which she was dumping on her mother's plate. Arnie sat down to receive his food.

'Thanks, Al,' he said.

'You won't like it,' Hattie said. She moved over with alacrity to occupy his knee. In her eagerness to claim this territory before her brother she succeeded now, as always, in leaving her thumb prints all over his lenses, but Arnie bore it with laudable good humour. The fog having uncomfortably impeded his vision, he took off his glasses and laid them on the table. They were new and rather stylish glasses, recently made up for him in Knightsbridge.

'You look funny without your glasses,' Hattie said.

'What's that stuff you're picking out of your stew, huh?' Arnie retorted. 'Chewing gum?'

'Stoo,' Hattie said, taking a well-worn giggly liberty with his accent. 'You shouldn't say "*stoo*". You should say "stew". It's oranges. From a tin. *He* put them in. They're disgusting. Yuck.'

'Oranges?' Arnie said.

'From a tin,' Hattie said triumphantly.

'Eat,' Ali said. A painful crimson flush had begun to steal up William's neck toward his ears and temples. William, having wished to buy himself the right to eat by contributing a touch of culinary originality to Mrs Gaitskell's hotpot, had without consultation tipped in a tin of mandarin oranges drawn from his own supplies. Then he had waited eagerly for praise, but his talents had once again been cast before swine.

'Oranges!' Arnie repeated mirthfully. 'Oh that's neat, William. That's real neat.' He put a hand on William's shoulder who shook him off in scorn. Only Ali among the rest ate without reserve. Having reached that stage, after induction by motherhood, where she could eat almost anything, she could now eat the children's soft-boiled eggs gone cold in the shell; she could eat the crusts of yesterday's toast, she could eat abandoned infant fish fingers impregnated with tomato ketchup. In the house of old Margaret she could gulp down tepid tea and condensed milk in a tin mug lined with fine green mould and topped with a sprinkling of dog hairs.

'It's really rather good, William,' she said but altogether without heart. It was of course godawful. An unhappy marriage of Mrs Gaitskell's enthusiasm for cornflour and William's cloying fruit syrup – but as horrors went it was small beer in a day which had begun in airy splendour with Mot Adderley and had ended now with William Lister. It was only food. She badly needed Noah, but Noah was not there. Her ear lobes cried out for aspirin and warm salt water.

'I'm going to bed,' she said. 'We'll forget the washing-up.' She poured herself a measure of Arnie's brandy and called the children.

'Come on,' she said. 'We're all going to bed.'

FOURTEEN

ALI WOKE, flanked by the sleeping children. Her head was wedged in a crevice between two pillows which Hattie and Daniel had determinedly expropriated in sleep. Daniel's bear was under her elbow. Her first conscious emotion was a quiet pain of loss. Thomas's aeroplane would by now be refuelling in Nairobi. An odour of scorched chillies and burned dripping made its way up the stairwell from the kitchen where William Lister was contriving his breakfast eggs. For the next six days, the kitchen would no longer be her own. Ali winced. The man's food habits alternated between unbridgeable modes of Transport Caff and Instant Exotic, and yet each morning these two opposing traditions clashed violently in the curried scrambled eggs.

There had been no post delivered that morning, but on the doormat alongside the bulky *Times* of Saturday lay a crumpled note from Arnie. It had been scribbled in the small hours on the back of a Pan Am ticket holder and had been pushed through the letter box from without.

'I locked myself out,' it read. 'I mean to sleep in your garage. Arnie.'

The note having warmed her spirit, Ali repaired at once to the attic study where her husband kept a small plug-in coffee machine and the last of his two French railway cups on a small tin tray. It was Noah's habit to punctuate his working sessions with strong black coffee and occasionally to lure his wife up into joining him there away from the demands of the children. Ali now made two cups of coffee and, gliding past William at the hob with the briefest of greetings, she quickly unlocked the interior door to the garage. To lurk in the garage, drinking coffee and ganging up with Arnie, offered compensation for Friday's deprivation and promised all the illicit gratification of a boarding-school midnight feast.

Arnie was stretched shirtless along the back seat of the car. His linen jacket was parcelled into a bunch under his head. On the near arm Ali noticed tenderly that the hair which sprouted from the mole on his bicep had at some time turned to grey. He stirred gently with the opening of the door and began to raise himself on to his elbows. Focusing myopically in slight disbelief, he stared at Ali with the tray. Then he reached for his glasses and put them on.

'What's this?' he said. 'Room service?'

'Coffee,' Ali said. 'That's all. I've woken you. I'm sorry. Somehow I had to.' Arnie laughed and yawned. He had always possessed that feline ability to move easily in and out of sleep.

'You haven't brought me a grapefruit with a cherry on the top,' he said. 'You call this breakfast, Al?'

'*He's* in the kitchen,' Ali said. 'He's making curried scrambled eggs. Arnie, you've no idea how it menaces me.'

'You want me to chuck him out for you?' Arnie said.

'Oh no,' Ali said hastily pursuing an instinct for neutralising conflict. 'He'll go before Noah gets back. It's all right. But why are you in the garage?'

'I went out,' Arnie said, 'I went to call on a woman I know but she was out. I forgot to take your key.'

'Go on! I thought you could pick locks,' Ali said. Arnie had long ago dazzled her by demonstrating how successfully he could pick all the family's collection of four-digit cycle locks.

'Not the house locks,' Arnie said. 'Your place is bolted like a fortress.'

'That's Noah,' Ali said. 'He likes locks. He likes to guard his goods.' Arnie smiled. He took a gulp of coffee from the cup which Ali had handed to him.

'Why not?' he said. 'He's a man of good sense. You just woke me from a dream, Al. You maybe don't realise that my hands were actually on the breasts of a naked woman.'

'I'm sorry,' Ali said again.

'That's okay,' Arnie said. 'The experience was nothing to write home about. Things were taking a distinctly downward turn. This woman she says to me do I think her boobs are beautiful so I tell her "Sure. They're great. Just great."'

'You lying bastard!' Ali said. 'You only said it to make her more amenable.'

'Right!' Arnie said. 'That's what she just said to me. "*You lying bastard*," she said "*You're only saying it so I'll let you screw me.*"'

'Then I woke you up,' Ali said. She had seated herself cross-legged in the back opposite him, wrapped as she was in Noah's bath robe. In her two interlocking hands she cradled her coffee cup which she rested on bare raised knees. She smiled now to contemplate the nature of Arnie's hectic and baroque sex life which, for all its evident percentage of success, he only ever mentioned to her in order to amuse with its failures. She had always found this impulse towards self-deprecation an endearing trait in him.

'Your life is a very different thing from mine,' she said.

'Pardon me?' he said.

'Arnie,' Ali said, 'when I telephoned you yesterday it was in point of fact from a hotel bedroom. I had stood up the gallery and had gone there to meet an old boyfriend. Naturally it all went wrong. Sexually, it materialised as one hundred per cent botch-up, so to speak. I have no experience in clandestine affairs. None at all.'

'Are you actually being serious, Al?' Arnie said. 'Is this the truth you're telling me?'

'He was my first love,' Ali said. 'People can fall in love very decisively first time. It isn't at all the laughable teenage business it's often cut out to be. It becomes a kind of Platonic ideal. A blueprint. Being human, one has this difficulty with the way things linger so in the memory. It's all right. Don't worry. He got on an aeroplane yesterday to Johannesburg. I won't ever see him again. Jesus, doesn't it all sound like *Brief Encounter*? Did you ever see that film? Rachmaninov in the background.'

'Sweetheart, you just had a lucky escape,' Arnie said.

Ali had meanwhile discovered in each eye a mild case of tears which she brushed aside with the back of her hand.

'I'm sorry, Arnie,' she said. 'I oughtn't to be unloading my personal life over you like this. You aren't my analyst after all.' Arnie smiled at her.

'Like all the best analysts I say nothing,' he said. 'I just listen, ma'am, and I collect on the fees.'

Ali paused to rotate, one by one, the gold studs in her ears which were in danger of cleaving to the unhealed flesh of her lobes. She was still sitting there with her knees drawn up, revealing a stretch of white gusset from her cotton pants, like a comely schoolgirl, he thought, on a dormitory bed. He thought protectively of her as he took in the rumpled crimp still evident in her hair and the newly violated ears. It amused him, in view of what she had just told him, that she had seen fit at this juncture to pierce her ears. The action struck him as dangerously apparent with sexual implication as far as Noah was concerned.

'Al, baby,' he said, 'do yourself a favour, will you? Don't go telling Noah what you've just told me, for Chrissake. Just you keep the whole thing under your hat.'

'I will,' she said. 'Don't worry?'

'That's my girl,' he said. 'In matters of the heart it is generally most expedient to lie and cheat.'

Ali laughed. 'There,' she said. 'So you do give advice after all. Gosh, doesn't it stink of petrol in here?' Arnie clambered past her into the driver's seat. It seemed to him suddenly gauche for them to remain there in the garage when beyond the door lay half of rural England.

'Let's go,' he said. 'Stick to me baby and we'll go places – like the letter said to the stamp. We'll take an early morning mystery tour. I'll get you back before your kids get up, don't worry.'

'You haven't even got the key,' she said. 'Not that I would doubt your ability to start the engine without it.'

Arnie drew from his pocket a small keyring and held it up.

'You left it in the garage door last night,' he said. 'How else did you think I got in?'

'I didn't think,' she said. 'Or if I did I took you for granted as a Magic Man.'

Arnie laughed. 'You got nice pins, Mrs Glazer,' he said. 'Candidly, you got two of the nicest pins I ever saw.' Ali beamed with pleasure.

'I haven't forgotten that poor lady in your dream,' she said. 'You've undermined the validity of your compliments, Arnie Weinberg.'

Arnie laughed. 'The difference is, I'm not trying to screw you.'

'True,' Ali said.

Arnie placed a hand over his naked pap with every sign of solemnity. 'I tell you no lies,' he said. 'Al baby, between friends, you got damn nice wheels.'

FIFTEEN

DANIEL GLAZER WOKE to the sound of the opening garage door. He registered, with his first blink, the slice of bright daylight which blazed through the gap between his parent's bedroom curtains and with his second the small adjacent hillock of his sleeping sister's haunches under his parents' quilt. His first thought was of his tooth which he had placed under the pillow. The thing was still there, wrapped in yesterday's Kleenex. The fairy's gold was nowhere. Disappointment weighed on his spirit. He searched carefully down at the back of the bed and in the fold of the pillowslip. He groped in the narrow gap between the bed and the cabinet but the money was not there. Ali, having been too much preoccupied with her own yearnings the previous night, had neglected to implement that benign deception. Daniel knew that Mrs Gaitskell had not meant to cheat him, but she had made a mistake. Even grown-ups could make terrible mistakes. Either the fairy had not wanted his tooth, or it had not been able to carry the money. Money was too heavy for fairies to carry. He had suspected as much all along but had been cajoled out of scepticism by Mrs Gaitskell. He didn't know now which was the more daunting – to think that his tooth had not been special enough to warrant the fairy's journey or that the poor tiny creature, having struggled from fairyland, had got bogged down in the mud pools of the farm track somewhere along the way.

In the kitchen where he went to seek comfort from his mother, he found only William, who was whistling as he packed away his fiery condiments into his Karrimor rucksack. Seeing Daniel stare, William took a shot at hearty child-centred banter and misfired.

'I collect little boys in my sack,' he said. 'Put your head in, Daniel, and see.' Daniel froze. He made no move from the spot until the telephone rang, at which point he seized his chance and fled. He could feel his heart beating in his mouth. The call was from Mervyn Bobrow, who had given thought to the idea before he telephoned that nine o'clock on a Saturday morning was perhaps rather early to be making calls, but he had weighed the propriety of the matter with his wife. Eva had had no doubts. One had to finalise numbers of one's party that evening, and if one's more nebulous aquaintances could not 'get it together', as she said, to RSVP on time then one had simply to catch them before they left for the supermarket or the squash courts. It was not difficult to reply to an invitation after all. As she pointed out, it was nothing to the trouble and expense of the host's efforts in putting the party together. Finally, as Mervyn reached for the receiver, she bestowed her attention upon the matter of suitable dress.

'Do make it clear to Alison, if she means to come for once, that this is not a jeans and T-shirt party,' she said. 'When one goes to all this trouble, one does *rather* hope that one's friends will do one proud, I think.'

The advice went undelivered since Ali was not at home and William Lister who took the call sounded more than a little aggrieved. Not only had Ali passed him by with barely a greeting that morning, but she had gone on to linger thirty minutes in the garage scantily clad with a male person to whom she had carried cups of coffee on a tray. William could not recall that anyone had ever carried cups of coffee for him on trays. To heap insult upon this implied affront, the two of them had then breezed off together half-naked in the motor car, leaving him, as he supposed, to fend for two spoilt children who would at any moment be down demanding cornflakes and orange juice. One could naturally not condone such behaviour. One's credibility as a person in the vanguard of 'The Struggle' was dependent upon upholding a scrupulous distinction between that which was 'progressive' and that which was 'decadent'.

'Has she gone out shopping?' Mervyn asked him. 'Do you know when she'll be back?'

'To be frank,' he said, 'she has just taken off in a dressing gown with a man who is not her husband. I don't think that shopping was quite what they had in mind.'

'Oh I say!' Mervyn said. He found, rising within him, a deep suspicion that Thomas Adderley — who had cried off for the Impromptu Drink as being at variance with his travel plans — had now returned to Oxford in order to consummate an Impromptu Flutter with Ali Glazer. It left him feeling up-staged. In mentioning Thomas Adderley's presence the previous Wednesday, Mervyn had hoped to make Ali suffer a little, no more. He had not expected her to press him for Thomas's telephone number or to go off with him half-naked in motor cars.

'This Lochinvar,' he said to William, 'he wouldn't on this occasion happen to be one Thomas Adderley, would he?' William gulped with surprise as the plot thickened. Thomas Adderley!

'Oh no,' he said. 'On this occasion he happens to be one Arnold Weinberg.'

'Versatile, isn't she?' Mervyn said in jest. 'Come to think of it, what are you doing in her house at nine o'clock in the morning?'

William stayed only to gather up his used matches and the last of his own supplies. He felt a little stunned by the scope of female cunning and thanked his own secular God for his gift of moral strength. Since the sun was shining, he saw no reason at all why he should linger there in the web of the female spider. He could shake the dust from his feet immediately and at the same time avoid the prospect of the children's cornflakes. He took a postcard from the pocket of his windcheater and wrote in parting haste at the kitchen table.

I have left your egg pan to steep in Fairy Liquid. The eggs I used were all my own.

Yours, William

SIXTEEN

W HEN NOAH TELEPHONED from the research unit, Ali was
working on the oranges. She had experienced the greatest
difficulty in representing these simple elliptical shapes and had
found repeatedly that they would not present themselves in an
obedient stack upon the canvas, but alternated, with each
attempt, between tumbling giddily outwards and rising, overlarge and ominously surreal, in the context of columbine and
pasture. The composition was not restful. The background itself
was proving peculiarly insistent and, while it was true that with
the kitchen window thrown open like that tendrils of columbine
curled in over the casement and two snapdragons had of late by
her neglect grown up through a crack in the stone with startling
rapidity, Ali did not wish to imply any disquiet in the work by
depicting these things as encroaching so near. There was no
reason why, in portraying that abundant tangle, one should
necessarily open the floodgates. Nor why one should tolerate
those orange orbs which hummed in the foreground like suspended detonators. She detected in these the picture's beginnings, an insidious implication of excellence which had never
been present in her painting before and she wished to resist it,
being alarmed by it. It was the best picture she had ever
embarked upon.

To hear Noah's wonderfully grave and level tones over the
telephone was a considerable relief, for in his speech the notes

barely rose and fell. He would stay only to check his mail, he said, and would then call a taxi and head for home.

'Come quickly,' Ali said, 'because I've missed you.'

Noah stepped from the office ante-room loaded with Jiffybags and envelopes, two of which he held between his teeth. He heard the incongruous retreating clomp of ill-fitting hiker's boots upon the hospital floor and, glancing leftwards, was surprised to see the back of William Lister passing through the distant plastic doors at the end of the corridor. Next he acknowledged the entry of Arnie Weinberg into the ante-room with an amiable lack of ceremony denoting long-standing friendship.

'What the hell's William Lister doing around here?' he said, speaking through the envelopes in his teeth.

'Search me,' Arnie said, who had not seen him.

To Arnie's knowledge William had only once before graced the research unit with his presence. He had unexpectedly accompanied Ali who had arranged to meet her husband in the canteen for lunch. Arnie smiled to remember how on that occasion, William – firmly refusing all food – had sat out the half-hour with a glass of water in front of him watching the weaker brethren busy themselves at the trough.

'He came to eat lunch, maybe,' Arnie offered wittily. 'I guess he just came by to starve in public.' He promptly emitted a short, somewhat brutal laugh. 'How was your flight?' he said. Noah became aware at that moment that clenched between his teeth was a recycled envelope exhorting him to conserve trees.

'Oh shit!' Noah said. The letter was brief and oddly childish. It contained no salutation and ran as follows:

This is to let you know that your wife has not been idle in your absence but Arnold Weinberg could probably tell you exactly what I mean. Does the name Thomas Adderley mean anything to you?

Yours sincerely, William Lister

Shaking slightly, Noah folded the letter and put it into his pocket. Cases were rare indeed where Noah would readily have given credence to William Lister's sanctimonious avowals, but Thomas Adderley was, unfortunately, just such a case. Mot Adderley: the Nigger in the Woodpile! The rough-shod golden hero of his wife's arrested youth.

'Oh shit!' he said again.

'What's up?' Arnie asked.

'Nothing,' Noah said. 'Nothing at all. Call me a taxi, will you?'

'Sure,' Arnie said. William's aspirant snipe at Arnie had, ironically, passed Noah by. He had merely read the wretched thing as casting Arnie in the role of informed bystander, which indeed he was, and had no intention at all of discussing the affair with anyone but Ali. He then proceeded systematically to sift his post, most of which he committed, after brief examination, to the wastepaper basket. The salvage he placed neatly upon his desk, fastened with two bulldog clips. Then he stepped out to wait for his taxi.

Ali had moved with a sketch book into the kitchen garden, by the time he came, in order to work with unwonted zeal upon the whorls of a columbine. The time was two o'clock and the sun being high, she wore her hair pushed under the crown of an old straw hat. The bundled hair laid bare the familiar groove of her neck and the sight of it caused Noah an emotion close to physical pain as he approached. He became simultaneously aware both of his own advancing age and of that range of poignant amorous failures which had afflicted his bygone youth. The combination left him bruised and raw. In a moment his own memory had cruelly run him by an undermining pageant of his past.

He saw himself suddenly at fifteen, hovering where the much-loved Jean made cakes in her mother's kitchen. He saw himself kiss her until the muffled giggles of her friends in the broom closet caused her to burst out with uncontrolled laughter. What Noah had read as love requited, he then in that sniggering denouement saw as a heartless conspiracy by a monstrous regiment of women. He saw himself again, at thirty, open a door upon Shirley supine on a bed; one of her nipples was in the mouth of a naked stranger whose bucking haunches she enclosed within her own raised knees. Now, as Ali turned her head towards him in welcome, Noah saw, as it were behind his eyes, the vivid fall of a safety curtain on which was clearly stencilled 'The rest you must not see'. It surprised him even as he stood that the mind could summon to the case so strong, so apt, so theatrical an image.

'Hello, my love,' Ali said. She rose and kissed him warmly. Then she proposed coffee which he promptly refused. 'Have you eaten?' she asked solicitously. Then she followed him indoors and watched him plant his bag on the kitchen table.

'I've eaten,' he said. 'Excuse me. I have a headache.' He proceeded up the stairs towards the attic where Ali discovered him minutes later, stretched on the convertible bed which Camilla had once stained with urine. His eyes were fixed upon the ceiling; his hands were under his head.

'I'm very glad to see you,' she said. 'I'm sorry that your head hurts.' She stepped forward and, sliding a cool hand between the buttons of his shirt, brought it to rest on the furrow of his sternum. She could feel there the heavy rise and fall of his breathing. 'Do you need anything?' she said. 'Aspirin, perhaps? Are you all right, Noah?'

'D'you see anyone last week?' he said. Ali considered the matter.

'A clutch of largely unwelcome callers,' she said lightly. 'William came. He spent a night here. So much for my predictions. Noah, it was raining cats and dogs when he came. Really, I couldn't turn him away.'

'Who else?' Noah said.

'Mervyn,' she said. 'The word must have gone out that you were in transit, I reckon. He came to harangue me about his *drinkfest*. Anyway you missed it. So did I. I passed the thing up. Noah, do you not find it increasingly difficult to believe that I ever shared a roof with that person, let alone a bed?' Noah's heart bounced under her hand, but the warning passed her by.

'Who else?' he said with a perplexing tenacity.

'Arnie was here for a day or two,' Ali said. 'His house was being fumigated. He appeared just in time to lift the gloom over the supper table which William's presence had induced. The children will be glad to see you, Noah. Daniel bashed out a tooth but he's fine. Hattie is anticipating that you will collect her from school today. That's if you can make it.'

'Thomas Adderley?' Noah said. 'Did you see Thomas Adderley?' Ali removed her hand smartly from his shirt.

'Yes,' she said. 'I had coffee with him. Last Friday. Noah, you must understand that it was wholly innocuous.'

'Funny that it slipped your mind,' he said.

'I had coffee with him,' she said. 'As I told you, it was innocuous.'

'Did you go to bed with him?' Noah said. The question was not one to invite flannel. One could but answer to it 'yes' or 'no'.

'Strictly speaking, yes,' she said. 'I did. But Noah, please, it was innocuous. It wasn't at all what you think.' Even as she said it the defence struck her as utterly ludicrous. To be 'naked in bed' as it were and to 'mean no harm'. 'What I mean is not so much that it was innocuous, I suppose, as that it was absurdly brief and sexually wholly unsuccessful. It taught me that sex is infinitely better at home. I think that it also taught me to put away my past. I'm truly sorry, Noah, but it's over. I can only hope that you will believe me.'

'Get out of my room,' Noah said.

'Please,' Ali said. 'I want to try and explain the thing to you. It was something I had to do. It had to do with making the past lie down.'

'I don't want to hear it,' Noah said.

'I love you,' Ali said. 'I think that I know that more certainly than before.'

'I have asked you to get out of my room,' Noah said. Ali made a move but she turned towards him hopefully in the doorway.

'I wish that you would at least tell me to "shift my ass",' she said. 'Then it wouldn't feel so terrible.'

'Alison,' Noah said ominously, 'will you get the hell out of my room?'

SEVENTEEN

AT THREE O'CLOCK Noah got up and shaved. Shaving was not a thing he cared to undertake in aeroplane toilets and he had therefore delayed the exercise until he had reached his own bathroom. Before he drove to collect his daughter from school he delivered to Ali, with a pointed glance and murderous implication, one small tray complete with used dark green coffee cups which he had lifted unwashed from the floor of the garage. It seemed manifestly obvious to him that, twenty years on, Mot Adderley still got his rocks off inhabiting garages.

Being by nature a punctual person, he arrived comfortably in time to hear the school's dismissal bell, and was consequently surprised to find that Hattie was not disgorged among the chattering swell into the entrance hall. In Hattie's almost empty classroom he encountered a cleaning woman, scraping crushed wax crayons from the floor with a palette knife, who grumbled quietly, to nobody in particular, that it made you wonder what sort of homes the children came from. Hattie's teacher emerged, oblivious, from a cupboard with a box of tangled embroidery threads and a pile of Binca cloth upon which the children had begun, but never completed, some ham-fisted cross-stitch. She put down the box when she saw Noah and tripped jauntily towards him through the wax crayons in flat, gold dancing pumps. She flashed him a wide, painted smile calculated to charm the male of the species.

'Hello there, Dr Glazer!' she sang out.

'Good afternoon,' Noah said stiffly. He had very little time for this particular young woman whose educational methods had always seemed to him both complacent and diffuse and whose dress offended his expectations of sobriety in the profession. To have an aspirant siren in striped clown's overalls bear down upon him with all the daunting force of her youthful charm made him wish his daughter was educated by nuns. Though the classroom was too advanced to be equipped with an old-fashioned blackboard, he could see that on the pinboard alongside his elbow, where there was displayed a necklace made by the children of unwashed foil milk bottle-tops interspersed with cotton reels, she had twice written the caption 'Our Jewellery' with the third 'e' omitted.

'Pardon me,' Noah said compulsively, and he tapped with his fingernails at the pinboard. 'But aren't we in England? It's my belief that on this side of the Atlantic jewellery has three e's.' In response the pedagogue bestowed upon him a patronizing glance and chuckled prettily.

'You will find Harriet in the library,' she said. 'I expect she hasn't heard the bell. I sent a group of them to the library to practise their "take-away". Quite a few of them are wobbly on "take-away".'

'Oh really?' Noah said, but she appeared armourplated against his sarcasm.

'I sent them off to play shop,' she said. 'Giving the right change can be a great help with "take-away".'

'How about if they give the wrong change?' Noah said. 'If all of them are wobbly, who's to know the difference?' To Noah the knowledge that his daughter had spent the afternoon playing shop with empty custard cartons, coming, as it did, hard upon the knowledge of his wife's infidelity, induced in him a mildly punitive instinct against the female sex which was not altogether surprising in a person nurtured in the lap of Mrs Glazer the Elder. He believed that his only daughter wanted taking in hand

– a requirement which neither her mother nor this present devotee of current educational fad was capable of meeting. Right now, she clearly also wanted lines of subtraction sums in straight rows.

'Ma'am,' he said stiffly, 'as I understand it you regard any form of systematic or rigorous instruction as an archaic form of oppression.' Hattie's teacher opened her mouth very wide for a moment which gave her the look of a glossy tropical fish.

'If you mean that we leave the children free to discover their own levels and interests,' she said, 'then I'm proud to say it's true.'

'Forget it,' Noah said. He moved off in haste lest she foist upon him what always fell upon his ears as inexplicable, contemporary jabberwocky. As he made his way acrosss the courtyard, Hattie's teacher gazed pityingly after him, not only for his unfashionable views, but also for his lack of clandestine decency in venturing to air them so readily in public. Taking up her basket, she made for the staffroom, in order to portray his dated heresies for the amusement of her colleagues.

Hattie's teacher had been right about one thing and one only, Noah decided, as he approached the library. The remedial subtractors had not heard the bell. The volume of noise emanating from that traditional quarter of silence was enough to drown out the impact of all extraneous clamour. The 'take-away' scheme, begun in good faith but without adult supervision, had early on disintegrated into chaos as each of the more strident among the youthful traders had refused in turn to relinquish the coveted post of shopkeeper to the concept of rotation without armed struggle. Cartons and cardboard money rained through the air amid acrimonious accusation. Since some children had begun to raid the library shelves for missiles, a significant variety of child literature was now displayed upon the floor. It gave Noah no surprise to detect the voice of his own little daughter as the loudest among the party nor that, upon entering, he found her covetously guarding what remained of the funds. But Hattie was not only dominant and strong-willed. Drunk as she was with her own power, she was also warm-hearted and affectionate. At the sight of him she immediately abandoned the proceeds of commerce and ran forward to embrace him warmly.

'Daddy!' she said. 'My Daddy!'

'Sweetheart,' Noah said. He did not drive her directly home, but drove her westwards into the city. Shrewdly playing Ali's game of stolen treats in cafés with a vengeance, he ensconced her in a tall café chair and gave her the menu. As he sipped at a small, sugarless espresso, he watched his pretty, ebullient daughter plough with relish through a monstrous wedge of chocolate gateau embellished with whipped cream. He watched her wash it down with banana milkshake from a tall conical glass.

'Is that nice?' he said. Hattie nodded and swallowed.

'Can I have some more?' she said.

'Sure,' Noah said. He raised his hand for the waitress. 'Hat,' he said. 'How about if I were to send you to a real good school? Would you like that, sweetiepie?'

'Do you mean a school that calls homework "prep"?' Hattie said with an eagerness which took him by surprise. 'Do you mean a posh school?' Hattie was at that moment in a frame of mind to capitulate on all things 'posh'. During her father's most recent absence, she and her friend Rebecca had been teased and mimicked outside the sweet shop by a group of older boys who had called them 'posh'. It had occurred to Hattie for the first time that there were those in this life for whom she and Rebecca would always be perceived and envied as being a cut above. Besides, in the midst of defending themselves, they had discovered an unexpected pleasure in pulling rank. This recent conversion had been given strength by a change in reading matter. Hattie had moved on from pony books to boarding-school stories in which gabardine raincoats and lacrosse sticks were offered as items of glamour to be striven for by all little girls of sound mind.

'Do you mean I can go to a school with a real uniform?' she said. Her dark eyes shone with excitement. 'Oh *please*, Daddy,' she said. 'Oh *please!*' Reaching out to him in gratitude, she besmirched his jacket lapel with whipped banana and chocolate flake, but Noah was content to let it pass. Where he had expected considerable resistance, there had been none at all. The thing had been a pushover. And the knowledge that his wife would have strong moral objections to the scheme came to him right then as an added source of satisfaction.

'I bought you a beautiful book, Hat,' he said. 'An illustrated version of the *Iliad*. You've heard of Homer, have you?'

'You mean Oklahoma?' Hattie said irrepressibly. 'Yes, of course I've heard of it.' Noah laughed.

'And Daddy,' Hattie said. 'When I go to my new school, can I have a new pencil case?'

'Sure,' Noah said.

'And a kitten?' Hattie said, pushing her luck.

'No,' Noah said. 'Not a kitten.'

In making the proposal a reality, Noah wasted no time. By noon of the following day he had made tours of inspection round three imposing assembly halls and had interviewed the headmistresses of three private girls' schools in the county environs. His favourite among the heads wore an oatmeal tweed suit with lapel pin and sturdy 'Style-Eeze'. Her hair she wore like the Queen's. The girls sat twice-yearly examinations in June and November, she said, and were required among other things to take Latin, Needlework and Theology. Regulation felt hats were compulsory in the winter months, and cotton hats in the summer – both complete with grosgrain hat bands in the 'house' colours. Earrings were not permitted in any form, and no exceptions were made even for what she called the 'foreign gels'. By teatime Noah had gratefully submitted the registration fee and Hattie was over the moon. She could hardly contain her impatience to go out and buy her hockey boots. The thing was a *fait accompli*.

It was not possible for Ali to argue the issue effectively with Noah since communication had been reduced on his part to an offensively polite minimum, where on hers it had moved from initial attempts at ingratiating supplications towards such curt, barbed sniping as his markedly scarce presence in the house would allow. Even at bedtime there had been precious little scope, since Noah had transferred his hypoallergenic pillow and his current bedside matter to his study, where he had slept alone since his return. He had aborted all attempts she had made to raise the subject of her lapse in constancy by repeating firmly that he did not want to hear it, and by leaving the room on the pretext of being 'busy'.

Ali began irritably to resent Noah's incessant industry as a male ploy designed to confer status. There was no way in which a man could have position these days without his being in command of a desk top and two telephones, she thought. The trick was to board aeroplanes often enough and to march about in corridors with wallet files. Then one was undeniably 'busy'. Men were always busy. Thomas Adderley had even been too busy to make love to her properly. Ali could not envisage ever being busy in a way which would prevent her from putting the wants and needs of others before her own. She now saw this as a trait traditionally much praised in women, but one which stripped her both of position and of bargaining power. At the same time it was with some distress but with no real surprise that she watched Noah move rapidly from that benign but regressive assumption which endows a 'good' woman with more gentleness, more nobility, more steadfastness than any man, to its equally regressive but less benign counterpart, that in transgressing, such a woman becomes automatically more fickle, more scheming, more morally frail and more villainous.

This stance, injurious as it was towards half the human race, bore the inevitable stamp of cultural inheritance. Noah was not to blame for it. But his behaviour over Hattie's schooling was altogether different. Here she refused to see what he had done as in any way a sensible thing in the circumstances, but as a means of punishing her through her child. He was visiting his wife's sins upon his daughter and was bringing on to the battlefield an unlovely artillery of law and order. Ali's instincts were outraged. She regarded her regular afternoon walk to the village school where she encountered the casual cluster of female friends with their indigo jeans and striped pushchairs as part of the amiable ritual of her life. It lifted her heart to see her dear, bold Hattie barge out of school at the end of each day in jaunty dungarees and bright stripy jumpers. She loved Hattie's unchecked flying hair and her feet shod in pastel training shoes and glitter socks. To trade this comfortable scenario for its alternative at the private girl's day school was a prospect abhorrent to her apprehensive nature. She envisaged a gauntlet of pushy, donnish parents in threadbare overcoats and laced brogues, skimping on personal outlay in order to pay the school fees; competing together over which of their precocious offspring had earliest passed the viola examination to Grade Seven. She fancied she was already familiar with the type of parent whom she had encountered regularly in bookshops and supermarkets, refusing to buy Richard Scarry books because they contained 'American slang', or barking in loud class-bound voices over their thrift in having chosen the 'fourpence-off' breakfast cereals in preference to the ones that everybody liked to eat. She had always felt for their pitiably grey-clad, priggish offspring in plaits and knee-length hose. Was she now to join the clan and gloat in her turn over pennies saved on freezer bags?

'I'm surprised that you imagined the head will have her, since she's been so badly taught,' Ali said coolly, attempting to conceal from him the anger and the terror which the ruddy mottling around her throat was all too readily revealing. 'As I understand it, the entrance requirements are rather stiff,' she said.

'Bullshit,' Noah said. 'They need the fees. What they're after in there is girls' asses on seats.'

'There are quite enough precocious "asses" in this county to fill the seats twice over,' Ali said. 'Anyway, I thought it was a church school. I'd be interested to find out what brand of Christianity you intend to profess.'

'Quaker if necessary,' Noah said grimly. Ali gulped.

'May you rot in hell,' she said.

'Thank you,' he said. 'As it happens, it won't be necessary. Religion is not an issue. Institutions merely ask these questions so that, in the event of serious accident, they know which holy man to call in. That's all. I have, incidentally, taken out an insurance policy to cover any possible accident.' The man, Ali thought, had become wholly impossible.

'Hattie will refuse to go,' she said, clutching at straws.

But upstairs, Hattie, in her neatest script, was writing her name over and over on the back of an envelope in a state of delirious excitement: 'Harriet Rachel Glazer, Form One B, St Katharine's School for Girls'. She was hammering out, by repeated endeavour, the most suitable forward slope for a person about to be blessed with daily 'prep' and a grey felt school hat.

Things went rapidly from bad to worse. First, since Noah was unhappily present to witness the fall of a head-louse from Hattie's hair into her breakfast cereal, he required the entire household, including Mrs Gaitskell, to douse their heads in sheep-dip and to stay home working on the corpses with fine steel combs. This measure, which kept Hattie from a birthday party that afternoon and brought destruction to Mrs Gaitskell's new 'set', served also to show up Noah at his most offensively managerial. Second, Ali woke alone in the small hours, still reeking of DDT, to find herself wracked with what felt like third-degree labour pains. The spasms were both unaccountable and intense, but she saw through the night alone chewing on her pillow to muffle groans, and groping in jack-knife position for Disprin on the bathroom shelf. At dawn she telephoned the doctor who responded by paying her a prompt home visit. He examined her on the sofa while the household slept, pressing down on the uterine area with the palms of his hands. Ali gasped with pain.

'Tender?' said the doctor. Ali wondered whether it was a condition of entry into medical school that the candidate first assimilate the terminology for undermining pain. 'Tenderness' and 'discomfort' were the words which Noah favoured for describing the ache accompanying bee-stings, or an abscess in the gum.

'It actually hurts like hell,' Ali said, fearing all the while that Noah would rise at any moment from his monastic pallet in the attic. The GP took a plastic glove from his medical case and drew it over his right hand before making a brief internal examination.

'How long has the diaphragm been in position?' he said.

'Oh my God!' Ali said. 'Well over two weeks.' The thing had been in since the Friday when she had met Thomas in London. The doctor winced and laughed at once. He gave her a small, friendly pat on the buttocks. Then he placed a sheet of paper towel under her haunches.

'Allow me,' he said. The thing came out like dead squid, reeking offensively of perishing rubber and stale secretion. It contained, in addition, a small pool of recent menstrual blood. The GP blotted her crotch with the paper towel before with-drawing it to wrap the pungent diaphragm and the used glove. He handed her the parcel.

'Let the dustbin have it,' he said. 'If my memory serves me well, you've had some trouble with contraception in the past, Alison.'

'Yes,' Ali said. The doctor smiled.

'Get Noah to have a vasectomy,' he said, probably half in jest. The word fell as guiltily on Ali's ears as if he had boomed 'neuter the cuckold!' through the house. It wracked her with a small involuntary shudder.

'Oh no,' she said. 'We might want to have another baby.' The GP chuckled knowingly. His practice was riddled with women of Ali's age who were indulging in conception as a last pre-menopausal fling. He knew the breed. He wrote out a prescription for a new diaphragm and handed to her from his sample collection a four-day course of antibiotic capsules with effect specific to the uterine area.

'That infection will clear up within two days,' he said. 'Don't worry about it. Take the full course and give my regards to your husband.' He shut his case with a brisk snap and walked out into a dawn chorus of strident bird twitter.

It was Daniel who had left the box of Tampax opened on the kitchen table. He had drawn it from a plastic carrier bag he found in the kitchen and had helped himself to 'just one'. That was the rule he had negotiated with Ali, that out of each box he could have 'just one'. They were intriguingly like white mice to him with their cottonwool bodies and nice string tails. And the cardboard casings, too, were so invitingly phallic; so silky smooth in the way they shuttled in and out of each other. Ali wondered sometimes whether Daniel was the only child in the world who had specially asked for a whole box of Tampax to himself in his Christmas stocking.

Noah, as he ate his granola, eyed the product with none of his son's enchantment before taking off for his research unit.

'Does one deduce from the presence of tampons on the breakfast table that you are, at least, not pregnant?' he said. 'Or do you buy them merely for your children to demolish?'

'Get lost!' Ali said, pricked at last into heated response. 'You bloody pompous bore.'

'Watch your language,' Noah said. To 'get lost', in a manner of speaking, was Noah's exact intention, since his schedule would not allow him to remain much longer at home in any case. He was booked within ten days to fly to Toronto for a week, prefaced by a four-day conference in Bologna. Within three weeks of completing his obligations in Toronto he was due at Princeton. Since he also had work to accomplish with Barbara in New York City he planned to forgo the early summer retreat with Ali in Cornwall and pass the interim in New York. Cornwall had always bored him and had been an annual concession to Ali. This year he was in no frame of mind to make concessions to her. He meant instead to work productively in New York and, in so doing, exorcise his anger and hurt. He had no doubt that he would return to her in the autumn, but right then he wanted what, to himself, he called 'space'. He snatched up his jacket, and took care as he left the house to trace a judicious perimeter wide of the windows, fearing the sudden crash of falling flowerpots.

EIGHTEEN

Noah had already departed for Bologna when Camilla returned for a weekend early in June. Being accustomed to her stepfather's movements, his absence did not surprise her. It merely deprived her of the pleasure which she always took in his company. Since she had brought a new boyfriend with her, it deprived her especially of the pleasure he gave her with his caustic appraisals of her male companions. That these pleased her as constant evidence that Noah really cared about her was perhaps surprising, but Camilla had always relished Noah's scrupulous pastoral care as much as her small half-sister defiantly resented it. Hattie was not placed as Camilla was to perceive anything uncommonly benign in a man who brought one hot chocolate in French railway cups and told one to watch one's language. Since she had not served a prior sentence of infancy under the guardianship of Mervyn Bobrow, there was nothing in it to surprise her. There was now nothing to surprise Camilla in Noah's current absence; only in that he meant to be away so continuously through the summer and that – when she had idly commented upon the Italian Linguaphone tape in the cassette recorder – Ali had replied, not with her usual affectionate irony upon Noah's self-improvement projects, but with an unguarded whiff of animosity.

'He might have got on faster had he tried learning Norwegian,' she said. 'He might have found it more in conformity with his own moral rectitude.' Camilla chose to object.

'What do you mean?' she said.

'All that northern puritanism,' Ali said airily. 'All that carping about nicotine and white sugar. I reckon the Italians wouldn't find it *simpatico*.'

'Rubbish!' Camilla said. 'The Italians will love him.'

'If I talk rubbish,' Ali said irritably, 'why do you come here and waste your time in talking to me?'

'I came because I need your help,' Camilla said candidly. 'I need you to help me make a ball-gown.'

Camilla's attendant boyfriend was called Matthew Carpenter. Ali had at first mistaken him for a casual fairground attendant, but he was, like her daughter, an undergraduate. He wore his hair close-cropped and had bleached his weekending Levi's in violent, random blotches to a leprous mottling which was echoed in the mottling of his recent acne scars. Under a pair of striped braces he wore a T-shirt which said, 'Go on, admit it – you're after my body'; an assertion which, with its high-handed imputation of motive, had from the first left Ali speechless with annoyance. Moreover, he had spent the first mealtime playing film buff over the propagation of a Spanish film director whom he had relentlessly called 'Bun-well', while poor Daniel had tried in vain to introduce his trick banana.

'Not "Bun-well"; "Boon-you-ell", you idiot!' Camilla had said heartlessly, while Ali marvelled at her daughter's newly acquired snobbery, but Matthew Carpenter had remained untouched by it.

'That's right, Camilla,' he had replied, as if commending her from the heights of his dais. 'Bun-well. Franco Bun-well.'

'Luis,' Camilla said. But Ali could not feel sorry for the boy. There was something in his irrepressible striving after effect that reminded Ali of Eva Bobrow, whom she had met that morning in the coffee shop. She had gone there in a last-ditch attempt to reach Noah's heart through his palate, but all in vain. He would not listen to her. He had gone off in a huff to Bologna, announcing that he would not return until August. Ali had once given money to a beggar man on the Embankment who had said to her, 'Don't just give me money, Missus. Listen to my story.' Ali felt similarly cheapened now that Noah's bank account was readily available to her while his ear was not available to listen to her story.

'I met Eva Bobrow in the coffee shop, Camilla,' Ali said. 'She was pressing two posters on the proprietor for his pinboard. One was for the Monteverdi Vespers in the college chapel and the other was for a "Working-class Lesbian get-together for Inner Peace" in Leamington Spa. I kid you not.' Camilla refused to smile.

'Is some predictably backward political point being made here?' she said – she who allowed her stepfather to get away with using words like 'dyke'. 'Are you saying that a person who likes Monteverdi can't also support gay lib or Inner Peace?' It was one of those moments for Ali when she missed Noah almost beyond bearing. Noah would have understood exactly why it was funny. He would have known without explanations that it was not the causes in themselves, but the rolling of cause and allegiance into so composite a ball; the whole package. Besides, who else was there in life with whom one could pool one's lurking bigotries, if not with one's dear husband who was now regrettably absent?

'I'm sorry, Camilla,' she said humbly. 'Let's get on with our sewing.'

Ali was glad to take over Camilla's dress-making because it diverted her from the oranges, which continued powerfully to glow and hum like goblin fruits. She contemplated defusing the picture by scrawling 'Outspan' over the orange globes or by painting out the background and replacing it with a static interior arrangement of drapes and vases, but as it was she left the painting to shine out uncompleted in its excellence while she turned gratefully to Camilla's dress. There was something so much tamer in the satin moire and the tailor's tacks; and such a rich material gratification to be got from adorning an object so worthy, even for the arm of Matthew Carpenter. Ali wondered sadly whether it was still appropriate to hope that one's daughters would find happiness in men and marry suitably. To hear the nightly turn of the key in the door of Camilla's bedroom which she shared with Matthew Carpenter made Ali itch to bite her nails.

Camilla took leave of her mother with the ball-gown over her arm in a dry-cleaner's bag.

'Thanks, Mummy,' she said. 'You're a genius.'

'Just a competent needlewoman,' Ali said. 'Enjoy yourself, my darling.'

'Say,' Camilla said, as a parting afterthought, 'is there a Byron in the house? I need one, to write an essay.' Finding it hard to deny her daughter anything, Ali sought out the vellum-covered book with an unexpressed reluctance. Having it once more in the hand, she envisaged Julie Horowitz at forty, now stridently lecturing her pupils from the prescribed OUP edition. Did she remember either the book or its recipient? It was more than two decades since that high-minded theft, but Ali was resolved within a moment. For Julie Horowitz she would stand up the Cornish coast that summer and fly to Johannesburg! For Julie Horowitz she would board all the aeroplanes it took. This year she and the children would have a really adventurous summer holiday. She would venture far, far afield and be back to impress Noah with her newfound boldness upon his return. If the loathsome Bobrows could take wing for Johannesburg when they had no business there but consciousness-raising, why could not she? And if Noah himself could constantly bestride the world from Bologna to Mexico, why not? An impatience seized her for Camilla to be gone. When Camilla had gone she would dial International Directory Enquiries and telephone Julie.

Camilla blew dust from the nap of the cover and examined the fly-leaf with interest.

'My God!' she said. 'Barmitzvah? What's this? Is this Noah's by any chance, or is it a relic from Mr Bobrow's ethnic past?' 'Mr

Bobrow' was a piece of distancing terminology which Camilla had adopted in her teens and, having found it served effectively, she had ever since retained it.

'There's no necessary crime in ethnic allegiance, Camilla. Nor in ritual,' Ali said. 'Some of us like religion and some of us like Inner Peace. There you have it. It belonged to a nice old man who now has Parkinson's disease. Look after it for me.'

'Is it catching?' Camilla said smartly. Ali, knowing how much she and Camilla meant to each other, wished that love would not so often get in the way.

'His daughter was my friend Julie Horowitz,' she said. 'She stole it for me once. I value it.'

'*Stole* it?' Camilla said with mock horror. 'God, I thought Mr Bobrow was the one who lifted books.' She turned to Matthew Carpenter who had that morning replaced the black T-shirt with a sunny yellow string vest. 'My family are all bibliophile klep-toes,' she said with inverted pride.

'Mine are all librarians,' Matthew said, wishing to air the skeleton in his own family cupboard.

Over the telephone Julie barked out her extension number, sounding abrupt and commanding. Every inch a Horror Witch.

'Hello, Julie,' Ali said. 'It's Alison.'

'Now listen here,' Julie said aggressively, 'I don't know any Alison. Would you state your business please, I'm busy.' Ali controlled an impulse to laugh out loud. It was intriguing to her to hear Julie's childhood forcefulness transformed into prickly middle age.

'Julie,' she said firmly, 'It's Alison. Alison who ate all those marshmallow fish by the swimming pool once. Remember?' There was a moment's pause before Julie's manner cracked.

'*Alison?*' she said. 'But my dearest angel Ali-pie, where have you been all my life? You never bloody wrote to me. You got bloody married and you bloody vanished into the night.'

'Sorry,' Ali said. 'It was dreadful of me. But I have thought of you so often.'

'Christmas card?' Julie said. 'Couldn't you have sent me a Christmas card, stating name and address once in twenty years? How do you plead?'

'Guilty,' Ali said. 'How are you?'

'Terrible,' Julie said, with gusto. 'Just beginning to realise what "long in the tooth" means. I've got receding gums.'

'I've got my teeth all wired together,' Ali said eagerly. 'Capped, crowned, bridged and cantilevered. Do let's compare tooth rot.'

'I'm forty,' Julie said.

'I'm forty next month,' Ali said.

'I'll bet you've got fewer fucking wrinkles than I have,' Julie said with feeling. 'But we'll let that pass. Are you visiting the Homeland at long last? When are you going to see me?'

'I'm telephoning from Oxford,' Ali said.

'Oxford *England?*' Julie said.

'What do you think?' Ali said. 'Oxford Blauwildebeestfontein?'

'You must be a bloody millionaire if you can afford to make early morning calls abroad,' Julie said. 'Are you acquainted with the charge rates?' Ali laughed. Tight-fistedness had always seemed to her a characteristic of the rich. Julie's forthright lack of ceremony had helped to close the gap.

'What are you doing?' she said.

'Marking shitty student essays,' Julie said. 'How about you?'

'Nothing,' Ali said. 'Julie, can I come and see you?'

'What's the catch?' Julie said suspiciously. 'You dump me for twenty years and then you want lodging rights. You're not having a nervous breakdown, are you? Nurturing isn't in my nature. I do enough of it with my parents. They have entered into a state of geriatric decline.'

'I'm sorry,' Ali said. 'I'm not having a nervous breakdown; not to the best of my knowledge.'

'Terminal illness?' Julie said. 'Tell me the catch.'

'I have two young children. That's all,' Ali said. 'My husband is working abroad right now.'

'How old?' Julie said.

'He's nearly sixty,' Ali said.

'Jesus, I mean the kids, honey-child,' Julie said with some impatience.

'Oh,' Ali said. 'They're nearly nine and nearly five.'

'So they're eight and four,' Julie said. 'Okay. If they don't put a ball through my French windows. Or break the china. They can come too. I really don't see why not.'

NINETEEN

JULIE HOROWITZ MET ALI and her two younger children at Jan Smuts Airport, where she materialised as an elegantly under-dressed and rather glossy middle-aged woman with an impressive sun-tan and discreetly hennaed, well-bobbed hair. She offered her cheek to Ali for a kiss, smelling of French perfume and breathing mouthwash.

'I told you you'd have fewer wrinkles,' she said. 'And these are your gorgeous babies. Hello kids. Get your bags off the conveyor belt and look sharp, Ali-pie. Now is not the time to act like the Lady of Shalott. Are you as dreamy as ever?' Ali laughed.

'It's good to see you,' she said.

'The car's just outside,' Julie said. 'Come on.'

On route, from the wheel of the car Julie turned to the children.

'How far can you lot swim?' she said. Hattie blinked back at her, screwing up her eyes in the unfamiliar, un-English brightness.

'Ten metres,' she said. 'Twenty-five with a float.'

'Me too,' Daniel said.

'Liar!' Hattie said. 'He can only swim five.'

'I meant five,' Daniel said. 'I forgot.'

'*In armbands*,' Hattie said ferociously. 'He has to have arm-bands or he sinks.'

'I forgot,' Daniel said.

'In my garden is something you won't forget in a hurry,' Julie said fiercely. 'In my garden is an unfenced swimming pool.'

'Oh goody!' Hattie said.

'Oh goody, my foot,' Julie said. 'It's the winter. You will both be kept tied to the jacaranda tree if you venture near it without a grown-up. Just once. Understood?'

'Yes,' Hattie said.

'How about you, Daniel?' Julie said. 'Don't you talk?'

'Yes,' Daniel said in a whisper from under Ali's large straw hat.

'In this town the major cause of infant death is drowning in suburban swimming pools,' Julie said. 'I speak of white infants of course. Lucky little pinkoes like you. Black infants die most often of malnutrition. Harriet, why does your brother wear that hat? Is he hiding from me?' Hattie giggled.

'He pretends to be Huckleberry Finn,' she volunteered eagerly. 'He's always talking to himself.'

'He looks more like Mary Pickford,' Julie said. As the youngest and dreamiest of three children herself, Ali identified strongly with Daniel. Yet her heart went out to Hattie who suffered so terribly at times from jealousy. Sibling displacement was an experience which neither she nor Daniel had ever had to live through. She thought now of a clapping rhyme which Hattie and Rebecca chanted in the kitchen some days, and hoped that it had no prophetic implication for the case in hand.

> Susie had a brother
> His name was Tiny Tim
> She put him in the bath tub
> To see if he could swim
>
> He drank up all the water
> He ate up all the soap
> He tried to eat the bath plug
> But it wouldn't go down his throat.

It shocked her that Julie had not fenced her pool, or drained it for the winter.

'Ali-pie,' Julie said, interrupting her thoughts. 'What do you mean by bringing your son here in bermuda shorts and a poove's hat? It's unpatriotic. Why don't you get his hair cut?' She drove with a masterful know-how through the complex erosion of highways where Johannesburg's mining magnates had once held sway in graceful pilastered houses. 'You must see many changes,' she said sarcastically. 'I mean with regard to concrete and steel. All our significant changes here have to do with concrete and steel. For the rest we jog along as always. One step backwards; one step forwards; two steps sideways. Funny place.'

'Funny peculiar or funny ha-ha?' Ali asked gloomily. Julie, though Ali loved her, was proving a little abrasive.

'Both,' Julie said.

'I'm told that my ex-husband has made money in concrete.'

'Oh yes,' Julie said. 'He's a pillar of society. And rather good-looking. Shapely, bald cranium, peppered with freckles. He gets interviewed on the television sometimes, sandwiched between the interminable nature programmes. Cranes heaving in the back-ground and teams of blacks striding about in boiler suits. Would you like to meet him?'

'Not particularly,' said Ali. 'He was never really my type. I think I'd rather watch the nature programmes.'

Julie laughed. 'That's what you say,' she said. 'After you've seen the umpteenth antelope leaping gracefully across the screen you'll eat your words. The television here is afflicted by a glut of witless nature. That edifice presently impeding your sightlines, by the way, is the Rand Afrikaans University – speaking of changes as we were. The "Volk" are changing their class accoutrements, Ali, but not their voting habits.'

Time and distance had allowed Ali to forget until now that Julie, like many English-speaking South Africans, was capable, when referring to Afrikaaners, of sounding a bit like Goebbels on the Jews. 'Time was when they were just a bunch of Dutch white trash,' Julie was saying. 'Just a bunch of proles. They slept in their underclothes; they tapped wheels on the railways all week and revved their Harley-Davidsons at weekends. Nine barefoot, snot-nosed kids at every doorway scratching at flea-bites and veld-sores. Do you remember how we used to say an Afrikaaner was someone who was always tinkering with his brake-linings?'

'Not really,' Ali said.

'Well these bloody jumped-up Boers in there have mechanics to fix their motor cars,' Julie said. 'They wear cuff-links; they play cricket. They also play the stock market.' She nodded backwards with a lively venom towards the retreating edifice of the Rand Afrikaans University. 'Afrikaners in Park Town,' she said. 'Jesus doesn't it rankle! The "Volk" are into capitalism, Ali. They cleaned up cheap after Sharpeville and look at them sitting pretty now. Do you remember when "capitalism" along with all the other "isms" was a Jewish conspiracy cooked up to undermine the moral fibre of the race? Even Cubism was suspect.'

'You sound a wee bit like an inverted Nazi,' Ali said. 'Do you realise that?'

Julie laughed. 'Nazi? I'm a Jew. But as to these buggers, one used to believe that the Final Solution lay in importing three million Harley-Davidsons. In that respect, times have got more complex. I have to collect my post on campus,' she said. 'We'll have lunch in the student caff, if that's okay with your children. It's early days, however. What are we doing? Do you fancy a little urban anthropology before we nosh? Let's make a pre-prandial foray into the Rosebank Shopping Centre. It will amuse your children.'

At the shopping centre where she parked the car Julie purposefully brushed aside a collection of maimed beggars and blind basket-sellers to guide her visitors into the air-conditioned opulence within. The place was a hymn to conspicuous consumption where Persian carpets spilled from shop doorways and gold jewellery twinkled abundantly from behind electronically guarded plate glass. At the Bendy Babes clothing boutique

Hattie pressed her nose to a window display of gold lamé bikinis and diminutive disco-clobber for pre-pubertal females, and found that covetousness overcame her.

'*Please*, Mummy,' she said. '*Please*, let's go in. It's all so fantastic! Only to try on. Not to buy anything.'

'Your father would have a fit,' Ali said, feebly, whose own idea of pre-teen party dress was still the Liberty lawn smock worn with sash and ankle socks. Julie pushed open the door.

'Let's stir things up a bit,' she said wickedly. 'It sounds to me as though your father is in receipt of too much deference, what with him sixty and all. Come on, Harriet, I'll treat you.'

'Please,' Ali said. 'You oughtn't to.'

'I'm rich, remember,' Julie said. 'Don't get your knickers twisted, sweet Ali-pie. You keep out of this.'

Ali and Daniel idled awkwardly in the air-conditioned arcade, until Hattie emerged ten minutes later, the radiant owner of a fake leopard-skin two-piece comprising footless tights and matching sloppy Joe.

'Isn't it hideous?' Julie said amiably. 'You could suppose that the entire stock had been made for child prostitutes.'

'If you're so rich,' Ali said, 'Why do you pass up maimed beggars in the streets?'

'Oh *them*,' Julie said. 'To give alms is merely to prop the system. Furthermore, you don't in your innocence suppose that they're *freelance* beggars, do you? They're just front-men, Ali. Behind every one of them lies a big-time crook who's lining his coffers with the bulk of the proceeds.'

'Rubbish,' Ali said. 'You're just too jolly tight-fisted to make a few hand-outs to blind cripples. Confine your paranoia to rich Afrikaaners. Why worry about rich blacks?'

Julie laughed. She barged unrepentant through the same half-dozen limbless paralytics on her way out to the motor car and set off hell-bent upon a winding whistle-stop tour of the city which caused Daniel to throw up into the crown of the straw hat. In Yeoville Julie pointed with puzzling gratification to tyre marks scorched into the tarmac, as evidence of proletarian Afrikaner youth – as yet untouched by cuff-links and the Rand Afrikaans University – who had executed wheelies in the meaner streets on motor bikes. Outside the Fontana Bakery in Hillbrow, the paving slabs moderately thick with off-beat amorous couples, Ali saw the first and only Rastafarian of her stay.

'You see before you the five square yards in South Africa where amorous clutchings are proportionately gay and proportionately multi-racial,' Julie said. 'It is also probably the only five square yards in the country where whites are likely to mug blacks.'

'How was Paris?' Ali said. 'Tell me something nice.'

'Far away,' Julie said. 'Let's not talk about it. I'm like whatshisname in *Great Expectations*. Jagger's clerk. I won't talk Weymouth in the courts of Chancery. If you want to stay sane in this place you cling to the clichés. "Europe's okay, but it's nice to be back in SA." Ali-pie, the sun shines here, even in the winter. Not like in Paris. Nothing but drizzle and bloody dog-shit all over the streets. God, Ali, but it's nice to see you again!'

In Fordsburg Julie drove with a perverse but holy anger past the empty, eyeless houses standing as testimony to the State's recent removal of Asian shopkeepers.

'Lunch, people,' she said suddenly. 'My stomach tells me it's grub time. Let's go and see what's cooking.'

In the campus caff where they lined up for pastries and fruit juice the student population, predominantly white and glossy beyond Ali's local rememberings, was scattered about among transglobal melamine-topped tables and Duralex glassware. A graceful young man, lounging like a young Athenian in a kitchen-boy suit, made startling elegant haute-camp of that badge of black subjection. The female rump before Ali in the queue was clad in pressed white baggies, sexily brand-labelled 'Bang-Bang'. Ali found it pleasing, but not so Julie.

'Prudery and titillation have always made fond bed-fellows,' she said. 'If some local factory were to brand-name their jeans

"Fuck-Fuck", it would bring the place to a standstill. The double-entendre is precisely what makes it so acceptable.'

A significant minority of students clustered around the cash desk were wearing sweatshirts emblazened with computer print-out portraits of Steve Biko.

'But doesn't it make you nervous?' Ali said. 'All this wearing of hearts on sleeves in what is generally considered to be a police state. All this standing up to be counted. What happens to them all when the tanks roll?'

'When the tanks roll, I predict that most of this crew will be sitting behind desks in Houghton and getting on the 'phone to their stockbrokers,' Julie said viciously. 'It's a familiar process called mellowing. It happens to us all.'

'Not all,' Ali said. 'It doesn't happen to all. You may be right about some.'

'Okay,' Julie said, conceding the point as if it made no difference. 'It happens to some.'

They sat at a table already partially occupied by two coiffed undergrad starlets in backless glass slippers who, having eaten their fill of yoghurt and apples, were now retouching their mouths in turn, with a shared lip-brush.

'If my Mom's bloody maid hasn't ironed my bloody jeans for tomorrow's demo, I'll bloody kill her, no kidding!' announced one of the starlets, shutting her compact with a commanding snap. She rose promptly to her feet, having offered the grist to Julie's mill. But it did not signify, Ali thought, that a handful of the affluent young sowed their oats in the furrows of protest politics and moved on. There would always be those, like Thomas, who were steady and true. 'I'll sight you, Sandra,' said the starlet. 'I've got Psycho II at two. Then I've got Socio. and Soc. Anth.'

'This is a mad place,' Ali said. 'Julie, why do you live here?'

'Why not?' Julie said. 'The blacks live here, don't they? Most of them have no choice. To up and leave as we did – that was hardly a heroic gesture. It was merely to demonstrate that us white folks owned not only this country but the whole world.'

'Yes,' Ali said. But she wanted to say simply that being back there had seemed to burn Julie up inside.

'Speaking of our respective domicile,' Julie said, 'there is somebody else here right now from Blauwildebeestfontein like you. Did you know that? A literary genius in residence. He hangs out here in the caff with a clutch of indigenous admirers.' In the far corner, following the direction of Julie's indicating arm, Ali observed with little surprise that Mervyn Bobrow was holding court.

'He says that he's writing a novel,' Julie said. 'South African writing is very chic right now, of course. He'll stick around here in the Wits caff for two months and then he'll go off and write some highbrow *skiet-endonder*, choc-full of dust and barbed wire, for which he'll get a publisher's advance and, following upon that, a sheaf of admiring British weeklies saying that he's captured "the valid smell of the veld". As if those poor *uitlanders* could tell the smell of the veld from the smell of frying chapatis.' Mervyn Bobrow, accompanied by his delighted youthful coterie, had begun to make his way to the exit.

'He's asked us to dinner tonight,' Julie said. 'I told him I had a friend.' So that was it, Ali thought. She had come six thousand miles to dine with the Bobrows!

'And does he happen to know that the friend in question is me?' Ali said.

'Not a bit of it,' Julie said. 'But you're coming with me. Have you met him then?'

'I was married to him once,' Ali said.

'To *him*?' Julie said. 'First a prospective prince of concrete, then a Jewish genius and then a Jewish doctor? Well done, Ali-pie! If my mother weren't senile she'd be inflamed with envy on my behalf. I confess to a small twinge of it myself.'

'Nonsense,' Ali said. 'Julie, you always had more men than I'd had hot breakfasts. They were like bees around hollyhocks with you.'

'Maybe so,' Julie said. 'I never had the art of keeping them. I was always too much capable of looking after myself. It's called "bossiness" in women. You're lucky. Being vulnerable comes naturally to you. You may get knocked around, but you'll never be alone. With me – only sissies ever wanted to stay with me. Who wants sissies?'

'Daniel's a sissy,' Hattie said, trading loyalty in the hope of achieving a slice of the discourse, but all in vain.

'I aren't,' Daniel said. 'I'm a boy.'

'Sissies are *always* boys, dumb-dumb,' Hattie said.

'How's Thomas?' Ali said. 'Thomas Adderley.' Julie laughed.

'Lovely – and married,' she said. 'Thomas thrives. He grows straight and true in this place. God knows how. He used to teach school, do you know? The silly bugger took his Grade A mind and went teaching in a government school. Of course, most male schoolteachers go in straight lines to headships but not so Thomas. He got thrown out. He had some distinctly Cubist ideas where it came to the teaching of History, I believe. Anybody with sense knows that school History is a case of facing Mecca and chanting Blood River and The Great Trek five times a week. What do you suppose is the matter with our darling Mot?'

'I heard tell that he wrote plays,' Ali said. 'You can't eat plays, can you? How does he eat?'

'I give him my salary,' Julie said.

'Jesus!' Ali said, and it crossed her mind that she probably owed Julie the price of a hotel room in Paddington. 'I'm sorry, Julie. And I said you were tight-fisted.'

'So I am on the whole,' Julie said. 'But I believe in his talent and I have considerable shares in gold. I have strong vested interests here in a system which Thomas would like to see in sackcloth. Do you enjoy these contradictions, Ali-pie?'

'Only when I'm with you,' Ali said.

'These two small persons, here,' Julie said abruptly, changing the subject. 'Were they got upon you by the genius or the medic?'

'The medic,' Ali said. 'I have a grown-up daughter by the genius who is at Cambridge right now.'

'I see,' Julie said.

'And you?' Ali said. 'You never had any?'

'Not me,' Julie said. 'Not even a pussy cat. I don't like nurturing, remember.' Ali wondered whether it was altogether idiotic to hope that some wonderful, aberrant Afrikaner from the Rand Afrikaans University would fall in love with Julie at a cricket match and dazzle her with the brightness of his cuff-links. She decided that it was.

Mrs Bobrow glanced anxiously around the dining room that evening. The anonymity of the place, with its standard campus-issue furniture, was disturbing to her confidence. Teak veneer and plastic foam did not justly reflect one's personality. Since the evening's menu was, she flattered herself, 'exotic', she had given time and effort to getting the extending table as much as possible into line. Two miniature 'table forests' and a box of moss and pebbles stood equidistant from two glass carafes containing reeds and green bamboo stalks, and yet the suspicion remained with her that the thing looked set for a Rotary Club lunch. At home one's dining table had Jacobean legs, even if there was some doubt about the authenticity of the top. In short one had an infrastructure supportive to one's projection of self. Yet it was ludicrous to be anxious. Being a 'woman-in-one's-own-right' as one was – and God only knew there were few enough of the species in these hallowed groves of bridge-club and coffee-morning wives – this ought surely to expunge one's unease about the unacceptability of paper table napkins, for example. For the paper table napkins Mervyn was wholly to blame. She had sent him out expressly to buy cloth napkins that morning, but he had returned without them. He had passed the time instead dazzling undergraduates in the student café. And even now he was not yet home. Mervyn had not been himself lately, she thought. He had been snappish and unpredictable. He had begun to cut corners in the scrupulous division of domestic labour which they had always upheld and had had the effrontery to use as his excuse that the flat 'came' with a servant. A hopelessly decadent black woman who coated the bathroom fixtures each morning with a half-inch layer of scouring powder before going on to monopolise the Bobrows' telephone for the best part of the day. Eva had been obliged to play the 'White Madam' and buy a padlock for the telephone dial. The woman used Fairy Liquid as though it grew on trees and pinched the Bobrows' gin. It piqued Eva that so much of her creative energy was consumed these days in watching the housemaid in a place where Mervyn appeared to be thriving. It compromised her progressive credentials. Mervyn was becoming chronically manic. He had shirked on his commitment to supervise Lucy's holiday project-work. She had begun to suspect him of being a little sweet on the Horowitz woman and for this reason she had played matchmaker for the evening and had invited along a charming Norwegian expert in police repression whom she had met during the course of her researches into black women's self-help groups. Now Mervyn had once again upset her plans by inviting Ms Horowitz with a female friend. A person from Europe, to be sure, but one for all that who would effectively upset the symmetry of the seating arrangements.

The self-help groups, to say true, had begun to get Eva down. She had found them a great disappointment. False-consciousness was everywhere and Methodism, along with a variety of more extreme manifestations of patriarchal Victorian evangelism, appeared to be rife among black woman machinists and garment workers. She had made the observation recently to Thomas Adderley, who had been unsuitably sanguine in reply. He had quoted to her what he called an old local adage, that whereas once in South Africa the whites had got the Bible and the blacks had got the land, the thing was now reversed: the blacks had the Bible and the whites had the land. But Eva, as she had put him down for his levity, had reminded him that the thing was no laughing matter. As far as the women's movement was concerned, a preoccupation with the after-life was a severe impediment to the way forward. Thomas could not see why. Christianity, like all religions, he said, contained the inspiration for advance as well as retreat. In the context, salvationism lifted people up. It gave them dignity, unity and hope.

Eva returned to the kitchen thinking of Thomas Adderley, who was to be one of her guests. To be sure, his thinking needed sorting out, but he was at least 'somebody' in this no-man's-land. A person whose name held some cop among readers of the *Observer*. Earlier in the day she had toiled assiduously over her Chinese pork parcels which now lay bound and gagged in an unsuitable Pyrex roasting dish pocked with scorched meatglaze marks left by careless previous tenants. The chilled lentil soup stood in the fridge in a monstrous aluminium saucepan in which it would have been more fit to boil a week's handkerchiefs. There were no decent pots in the flat. At home, Eva thought wistfully, as the doorbell rang, one had Le Creuset oven-to-tableware, which was the birthright of every superior cook.

Ali had met Thomas on the afternoon preceding the Bobrows' dinner party when he came to call on Julie. The meeting was easier, more agreeable, more lacking in emotional intensity than either of them might have feared. Both had seemed to have lived through and beyond the episode in Paddington and no reference was made to it, even when Julie left them together at a garden table under the lemon trees and went to answer her telephone. Thomas took a nice but not overwhelming interest in Ali's children, whose game of hop-scotch on the paving-stones caused him to remark upon continuity and innovation in children's games. His wife was a nursery schoolteacher, he said, and he had thus become vicariously acquainted with a vast range of clapping rhymes over the years. Ali was glad to have him mention his wife to her in that easy way and wanted rather to meet her, but it was soon apparent to her that, while Thomas was a frequent visitor, frequent enough to be familiar with the placing of every household object which Julie had called upon him to fetch – like the deck-chairs and the daily papers, for example – Lorna Adderley was not. Then Julie returned across the lawn. 'Thinking of our engagement tonight,' she said, in her loud, exuberant voice, 'are you aware, Thomas, that our mutual friend here was once married to Mervyn Bobrow? *Married* to him, my dear! Ali has a remarkable capacity for espousing men, admittedly, but marriage to him. Is that a state one could remotely envisage?' Thomas merely smiled.

'Not me,' he said.

'To be sure, you are the wrong sex,' Julie said. 'Though one has to admit that poor Mr B's handbag lends an air of sexual ambiguity to the case. Tell us about being married to him, Ali, we are all ears.'

Ali groped for one of those masterfully noncommittal phrases which Noah had always used in reply to her early quizzings about his first marriage.

'It was kind of long ago,' she said. 'It doesn't signify.'

'God knows,' Julie said. 'Among marriages you get all sorts. I propose, regarding tonight, that the four of us meet at the staff club and drink ourselves into a fit state for the occasion. Lorna will come, won't she?'

'Yes,' Thomas said. 'She'll come.'

Mrs Adderley turned out to be a quiet, sweet-faced and plumpish woman; a fine-skinned blonde whose looks had early lost their bloom under the harshness of the southern sun. Her hair, which was drawn severely from her forehead, was fixed with a regiment of steel hair slides alongside the ears and her only concession to personal adornment consisted in a pencilling of thin, outdated arcs over her eyelids in place of absent eyebrows. She seemed to Ali the kind of woman whose competence and authority would come into their own among children rather than adults. Ali, who warmed to her, was made awkward, not by the fact of her being Thomas's wife, but by the knowledge that Julie was undermining the woman. Not only was she supplying Thomas with sums of money vastly beyond the means of a nursery schoolteacher, but she was, right then, pushing her own combination of intellect and Parisian chic beyond discretion. It seemed to Ali a gross rudeness in her friend that she consumed the half-hour in the staff club bantering wittily with Lorna Adderley's husband on the subject of an esoteric letter controversy currently raging in the *Times Literary Supplement*, and a lesser rudeness in Thomas himself that he allowed it to continue. It puzzled her. Noah, she felt sure, would never have let such a situation come about. But then, Noah was Noah. She knew him by now to be a better thing than Thomas. Thinking of Noah right then induced a sudden melancholy which transferred itself by association to Daniel. Poor Daniel, who had been so tearful at parting from her that evening; so loath to have her go out.

'How old is your little boy?' Lorna said, with the impressive clairvoyance of a quiet, observant woman, but Julie was right then calling to them both from the hat stand where, with the help of Thomas, she was reaching for coats.

'Quaff your gin, you two, and hurry up!' she was saying. 'The sooner we get there the sooner we can all go home again.' On her way out, Julie, while illustrating a point with a flourish of the arm, caught her gold bracelet in Thomas's coat button.

'Oh my God!' she said. 'We have become inseparable.' After a brief struggle she unfixed the bracelet from her wrist and strode with Ali towards her car, leaving the object dangling carelessly from Thomas's coat front. 'We'll see you there,' she said.

At the Bobrows' apartment, things did not promise well. Eva did not like surprises and Ali's appearance as Julie's friend was naturally galling to her. While her past efforts to enlist the Glazers' presence at her social functions had repeatedly met with failure, Ali had now appeared unexpectedly when she was least welcome. In the circumstances, Eva remained determinedly affronted. But Ali's transgression was soon overshadowed by a greater transgression on the part of Eva's husband, for Mervyn had not returned.

The meal began without him. It had to since the pork parcels could not wait for ever. Several of Eva's brave conversational gambits rose and fell like failed soufflés as his absence became both conspicuous and unnerving. Julie had lapsed into a disobliging silence as she sniffed out tomato ketchup in the soup with a cold, uncharitable talent for chemical analysis. The Norwegian, who had been invited to pair with her, appeared to be wholly occupied in admiring Ali's pale, Quakerish physiognomy. Manfully Mrs Bobrow tried lifting the spirit with a condescending jibe against local cuisine.

'I have dined out, since coming here, on more unimaginative roast-and-two-veg than ever before in my life,' she said. 'But where cooking is left to the servants, while the women play tennis and bridge, the culinary traditions are lost.' While Lorna rose politely on cue to praise the food, Julie rose all too predictably to play devil's advocate.

'I have always had the greatest difficulty myself in telling Stork from Omo,' she said with a wholehearted insincerity. 'But then we grew up, us colonial hicks, on two standard puddings: bananas set in red jelly and baked custard. They were all the maid could make. Do you remember it, Ali? Dora's curds and whey?' It was at the conclusion of this provoking utterance that Mervyn entered at the wide French windows. One eye was torn at the corner and dramatically encircled with bluish smudges. The clutchbag dangled from his wrist. Eva emitted a cry but Mervyn fended her off, almost as though he did not know her. He stalked tiger-wise towards the table with a gleam of triumph in his amber, feline eyes. Lorna Adderley dabbed a little nervously at her mouth and laid her knife and fork neatly on her plate at twenty-past four. Mervyn came to a stop and struck an attitude. He began to speak, like a ventriloquist, in a voice not unlike Noël Coward's.

'Sorry I missed the party,' he said. 'I was propositioned in a bar. A rough sort of hang-out where a brace of muscle-bound white hearties mistook my sexual leanings. Naturally, I turned them down. "Be assured," I said' – and here his voice rose high and precious and his 'r's rolled like a Scotsman's – ' "the tattoos on your forearms repel me. I would rather offer my body to a team of Zulu shift-workers than to the likes of you. I plump for 'brown' not 'brawn'. I have no taste for the Master Race." '

He sat down then to await the company's praise for this the latest of his daring forays into the nation's lowlife, smelling the while of blood and sweat. Then he blinked twice and fixed his eyes on Ali.

'Alison,' he said suspiciously. 'What brings you to my table?' A compromising memory of Ali's accurate prediction regarding the clutchbag now rose to snuff his elation. 'What the hell are you doing here?' he demanded unpleasantly. 'Eva! What the hell is this woman doing in my house?' But Eva had gone for an ice-pack.

Ali saw the wheel turn painfully before her. 'Sit worthy friends: – my lord is often thus. Feed and regard him not.' Mervyn had reverted to playing Supertramp, only this time, mercifully, it was someone else's problem. Eva's problem. She was not obliged to stay and watch as the show evolved. In her mind she was Noah all those years ago on the night he had proposed marriage to her, standing sanely and squarely in her living room with Angie's gin bottle in his hand.

'Weep all you like,' he had said. 'Weep and let it fester. It's all you can do.' It had shocked her a little at the time but Noah – precisely because he had not presumed to save the world – had so successfully managed to save her. She could let the thing fester and walk away from it. It was, as Noah would have said, 'No problem.'

'We ought to go,' she said. 'Julie – the babysitter. And I have some telephone calls to make. I would like to telephone my husband.' Julie got readily to her feet.

'It's true,' she said. 'We really have to go.' The Norwegian expert in police repression pressed them earnestly to stay, but

Eva, clutching the ice-bag, looked tired, grateful and relieved. Behind them they heard her begin to gather up the plates. Julie's bracelet was left forgotten in the hallway, where it hung from the buttons of Thomas's coat. As she swung her car in the drive, making a wide arc of light from her headlamps which for a moment blazed gloriously in the azalea hedge, Julie heaved a sigh.

'Say, wasn't the grub something else?' she said. 'I believe that I have left one of my molars behind in the sweetmeats.'

Daniel Glazer did not trust the babysitter. He had never before had a brown babysitter with a funny accent and a funny beret, whose status in the house seemed somehow perplexingly marginal. She was not comfortable there. Mrs Gaitskell had always been a believer in ebullient bedtime romping as a prelude to sleep, but this person had not presumed upon any physical closeness. She had not even presumed upon the upholstered living-room furniture, but had taken a small hard kitchen chair from the back veranda and had brought it through into the white man's region for the evening where she sat uneasily with her head bent over a scarlet rectangle of knitting. Daniel could not be sure whether the faint clicks he heard emanated from her throat or from her needles. There was no way of being absolutely sure that she wasn't the wolf-lady like the babysitter in the story they had had at nursery school.

Daniel tried hard to stay awake until his mother got back but he did not succeed. Yet he slept fitfully. He woke shivering to find he had thrown off his covers and that the winter night was unexpectedly chilly, given the previous warmth of the day. He was startled to remember that he had left his precious soldiers on the back lawn that afternoon where he had been playing at shooting the pink ballerinas.

Ali, having thought once to dilute Daniel's relentlessly stereotypical male war-play, had tried valiantly to buy him some plastic womenfolk along with his plastic soldier men, but the toy industry had been against her and the pink ballerinas were all she had been able to find. Naturally, the ballerinas, in their un-armed, saccharine pinkness, had not quite met the case, but had nonetheless proved useful to Daniel in his fantasy-play during which they were often to be found prostrated in various attitudes of devastation at the base of the kitchen table or under the climbing frame, while the soldiers stood in triumphant rows upon the summits, with their guns poised. To Ali's mild chagrin, Noah had always found this pattern of play not only highly amusing but also reassuring, since he felt that it proved Daniel to be making a wonderfully normal job of adjusting to a slightly crackpot mother who had been eccentric enough to have bought him the ballerinas in the first place.

Daniel wrapped himself in his bed quilt, pushed his feet into his training shoes and tip-toed into the living room. The babysitter had dropped off in the chair. The knitting dangled near the floor, and her beret had pushed itself askew on her head in sleep. Daniel struggled with the key to the back door. It turned with a startling, tell-tale squeak which caused a moment's irregularity in the sleeping black woman's breathing. Then all was well. A cricket shrilling in the hedge fell silent as he touched the grass. Above him Daniel saw that the stars were marvellously, giddily bright. The soldiers lay illumined in a square of light which fell from the kitchen window on to the grass. Beside them lay the box, throwing its shadow before it in a dark, elongated parallelogram. Daniel ran to them over the grass with a beating heart and knelt to gather them up. It was then he saw and heard the cat.

The cat was a stray. Unusually for a female, it was ginger. It was very small and thin, but for its great swollen belly which swung like panniers on either side of its ribcage. It ran to Daniel eagerly for comfort, emitting occasional jerky little cries. Under its tail the animal's small distended vulva was edged with blood. Though Daniel had no idea of it, the cat was experiencing a modest feline version of that discomfort accompanying the birth of a footling breach. Daniel stroked its head between the ears. He let the bed quilt drop and he followed its lead to a narrow chink at the back of a small brick shed alongside the swimming pool which the animal had chosen for its nest. Daniel crouched at the chink between wall and hedge for a good twenty minutes, his childish, predatory stalking having taught him unusual patience. It was too dark for him to see anything. He could hear that the cat, after one squeak louder than all the rest, had begun to purr. There was a wetness about it and a funny smell.

Daniel remembered that in his hand-luggage his mother had allowed him to pack, from his jungle survival kit, a much-favoured item which, under the influence of his father's trans-atlantic idiom, he still knew as 'a flash light'. He ran back across the grass, passing the abandoned soldiers on his way. Inside the house the black woman slept on. The only danger, with his brief scuffle in the sports bag, lay in the possibility that Hattie would wake, who shared the room with him, but that danger seemed happily to pass. He returned to the shed by the swimming pool where to his amazement he saw that the cat was already suckling two dampish, rat-like babies with flattened ears and hairless paws. She appeared at the same time to be chewing up a dark, gory little parcel attached to an equally gory rope between her hind legs. Daniel squatted beside the chink, keeping a respectful distance. He felt a sense of wonder and privilege – as one of the Magi – to witness such a birth under the vivid southern stars. He had no urge to interfere; only to watch. He was glad that Hattie was not there, who would have been making a lot of noise and itching to dress the kittens in Sacha doll clothes like the cats in Beatrix Potter. He knew that the mother cat was hungry because she was so thin and he knew that she would be thirsty. She needed milk.

He returned to the house where he found that, while all the crockery had been put away in high-up cupboards which he could not reach, there was an open shelf of funny things within his grasp. The explanation for this shelf was that Mummy's friend Julie Horowitz was so rich that she could afford to waste her money on china that she didn't like. Daniel liked all of it. There was a teapot shaped like a camel designed to spew tea out of its mouth, and several rather lecherous-looking toby jugs. A couple of mugs said things in pointy gold writing that Daniel could not read, but the nicest thing of all was the jampot house which Mummy had fallen upon earlier in the day with recognition and delight. It was just like one the Zulu maid had had when she was a child, she said, and she'd always wanted one the same. It looked like a thatched English cottage with its lid made into the roof. Daniel took off the roof to use as a saucer. Then he took from the fridge a litre bottle of milk and went back with his equipment to the cat. There were now three suckling kittens and the gory parcel had vanished. Daniel filled the roof of the jampot house with milk and held it out to the mother cat. She lapped greedily, stippling his hand with cold, white droplets of milk from her tongue.

Then suddenly Hattie was there, coming up behind him.

'What are you doing?' she said. 'I've been watching you for ages from the window.' Daniel gasped. In haste he switched off the torch.

'Nothing,' he said, realising suddenly how cold he was. 'It's nothing.' He stood up and faced her, holding his arms guiltily across the narrow corridor to bar her vision.

'Show me!' Hattie said. 'Show me or I'll tell about you being near the swimming pool.' Daniel began to cry.

'Show me!' Hattie said. She shouldered him from the access and took the torch from his hand. In the scuffle, Daniel knocked over the milk which ran eagerly into the dry, red earth below the hedge.

'It's kittens!' Hattie said with real delight. 'Oh, Dan, aren't they lovely!' The kittens by now had dried out into a presentable, striated fluffiness, one orange and two grey.

'It's a secret,' Daniel said. 'Please don't tell the grown-ups.'

'No,' Hattie said. 'Of course not. The ginger one can be mine. Yours can be the two grey ones.'

'But they don't belong to us,' Daniel said. 'They just sort of belong to themselves, Hattie.'

'The ginger one is a girl one,' Hattie said, reaching out to lift it from the nipple. 'Yours can both be boys. I don't mind if you have two.'

'But they don't belong to us, Hattie,' Daniel said again. 'You shouldn't pick them up. They're too new.'

'Mine is called Susan,' Hattie said. 'She *wants* me to pick her up.'

TWENTY

BACK IN ENGLAND the coming of the summer vacation saw Camilla move, with an undergrad girl friend, into a Brighton seafront flat, borrowed on a student grapevine for the month of July. For both girls, accustomed to the more sober and landlocked atmosphere of Cambridge, the seaside town presented a novel delight. Construction workers whistled at them from airy scaffolding each morning as they set out to hobble over shingle on rope-soled shoes and take the water before the crowds. Then there were the irresistible shops. Such bargains were to be got from the period clothing boutiques. Such a wealth of crenellated satins and old silk nightwear. Such quantities of nineteen-forties Bally shoes – Bobbie Shafto shoes, buckled and tongued. Camilla bought a pair of grandad long-johns with buttoned calico flies and button-on singlet top, which she afterwards dyed in a saucepan to the colour of blackberry fool. The effect was astonishing. Shrinkage reduced the legging to mid-calf and caused the top to meet the pants with difficulty, in gaping scallops around the buttoned midriff. Through one of these enticing apertures was visible the perfect, concave swirl of Camilla's newly tanned navel.

The flat lay towards Kemp Town; the rambling ground floor of a house faced with cracking stucco. Gull splat and sea-spray coated the tall window panes. Within all was sticky from the sea. A pile of sticky unmatched crockery stood on a sticky kitchen shelf. There were several sticky, slim-waisted Ovaltine mugs. Sticky ashtrays, of which there were many, had all been pinched from south coast hotels. The furnishings were sparse and random. A small mangey bridge table – the only table – stood with a wobbling leg in the grand bay window, covered with oilcloth. The sofa, a sea-green 'Put-U-Up', had been smothered in a variety of hairy plaid travelling rugs and stood facing an antique harmonium called 'The Chicago Cottage Organ'. This last, when opened, revealed above the keyboard a row of perfect ivory stops labelled in gilded Gothic script. Dulcet, Dulcimer and Aeolian Harp.

Camilla's girlhood piano lessons had not passed in vain. Struggling at first with the dormant bellows, she filled the air each evening with a cosy medley of Victorian hymn tunes. The place was Home Sweet Home. The girls had never been happier. Towards evening they drew their knees up on the Put-U-Up, drank instant coffee from the Ovaltine mugs and developed a wholly unserious fantasy, about living there for ever, which was, of course, sadly impossible. They would acquire a small tabby kitten, they fantasised, and would feed it on fish-heads bought from the old men near the Palace Pier. They would grow old there together, stepping out on winter mornings to throw toast crumbs over the balustrade at the pigeons.

'We'd have run out of money by Michaelmas,' Camilla said resignedly, but money, Emily said, was not a problem. They would acquire a rich Arab student as a lodger, who drove an Audi. He could sleep on the Put-U-Up. She and Camilla would live on the rent and borrow the Audi. They could even share the Arab if he were a thinkable proposition.

'My stepfather drives an Audi,' Camilla said, idly contemplating the limited uses of stereotypes. '*And* he's allergic to cats.' It occurred to her that Noah would not be able to step over the threshold of the Brighton flat without placing his oxygen supply at risk. The plaid rugs alone would constrict his bronchial tubes.

She was loyally resolved never to preside over a household where her stepfather could not dine with her in comfort.

'I've never had a stepfather,' Emily said. 'Only four stepmothers. There used to be a new one practically every time I came home from my boarding school. What is your real father like?'

'Nut case,' Camilla said blandly, aware as she said it how easily one could misrepresent, with a facile colloquialism, a formative reign of terror. Only the previous day she had recalled on waking the time when Mervyn had taken her by the hand at the age of six, or was it seven, and had led her without knocking into the bathroom where a guest was rising from the tub. Mervyn had at that time embarked upon a phase of loudly propagating greater sexual emancipation.

'My daughter is a shrinking violet,' he said by way of explaining his intrusion. 'She needs a more robust exposure to the nude male form.' But Camilla remembered that the guest had made decent haste to wrap his loins in a bath towel.

'Bugger off, Mervyn,' he had replied hotly. 'Show your daughter your bloody prick!' Camilla couldn't remember who he was, nor whether he ever came again. In recollection she could never envisage his face. Only the fine black hairs on his legs, and that there was something disturbingly wrong with his penis. She knew now what had been wrong with it. He hadn't been circumcised.

She dreamed the next night about Arnie Weinberg. It surprised her that in the dream he kept a collection of antique boxes crowded together on a glass shelf in the living room of his Park Town flat. Most were made of wood and some of silver. One of the boxes was made of a delicate greenish alabaster. There was also a miniature wooden captain's chest with recessed brass handles. In the dream Camilla saw herself offer him the small papier-maché box in which she kept her earrings, but Arnie laughed and told her nicely to keep it. Then he kissed her. Not on the cheek as he had done when she had won the hundred metres at school, but on her open mouth. Yet he had turned down the gift of her box. He had not wanted it.

Camilla opened her eyes right then to the vision of Lord Kitchener on a poster. He was displayed opposite her bed, moustaches bristling, and pointing an accusing finger at her. The poster's caption had been altered from 'Your Country Needs You' to 'Have you taken the Pill?' It had been pinned there by one of the flat's regular female occupants and its presence consistently irritated Camilla who prided herself on remembering to take the Pill without prompting. She made a point in this respect of differing from her mother. She was determined not to be scatty. It was out of fashion for women to be scatty. Camilla was surprised and elated by her dream.

'Who would have thought it?' she mouthed into the air. Alike as she and Alison were, Camilla – now at the edge of adulthood – was always readier than her mother had been at nineteen and twenty to confront her own sexuality. Camilla at nineteen would not have shirked on Thomas Adderley. She would have taken him on rejoicing and worked the whole thing through. That was perhaps her blessed advantage.

The telephone was ringing in the next room. It was summoning home Emily, whose grandmother, having witnessed, with quiet resignation, the recent demotion of her son's fourth wife, had died that night in her sleep. Beside her on the table her son had found her heart pills, her arthritis tablets, a large bottle of liquid paraffin and a photograph of her granddaughter Emily in the college garden with her beautiful, amber-eyed girl friend, Camilla Bobrow.

Emily's tearful departure at once turned Camilla's mood. The construction workers' morning catcalls ceased to amuse her and the gulls in the evening cried to her forlornly, like the lost souls of the dead. The cottage organ echoed back at her in the tall, sparsely furnished living room with funereal implication and she quickly abandoned it for the Byron which she read on the Put-U-Up, making desultory notes towards an essay. There was nobody left to telephone. Ali and the small children were out of the country – a fact which on reflection she found unprecedented and worrying. Noah was as usual suspended somewhere between continents which she found not so much worrying as distinctly inconvenient at this juncture. Dear Noah would soon have paid her train fare home to Oxfordshire. They would have breakfasted together as of old in the family kitchen and dined out in restaurants or gone to the pictures. Matthew Carpenter was, to the best of her knowledge, doing Morocco on his thumb. It was with some shyness, but no real doubts, that she finally rang Arnie Weinberg one evening in the lab. To propose that he come down for the weekend seemed a great liberty but, to her joy, he agreed to come at once. He was by temperament flexible and inclined to make spontaneous decisions. The seaside suited him and he had always had a large soft spot for Camilla. It was clear to him, moreover, that the girl was lonely and forlorn. It shone through all her determinedly seductive accounts of the pizza bars and the cottage organ. Next morning early he threw his swimming trunks and a frisbee into the back of a small hired Fiat along with his minimal clothing supplies. He had already sold his own car, in preparation for the move to California. Along the way he acquired a two-litre bottle of Valpolicella with a plastic stopper and a box of marrons glacés.

Camilla was overjoyed to see him. She had spent the morning preparing his lunch. Step by step from her paperback Elizabeth David she had jointed a free-range chicken and simmered it in cream and Gruyère cheese. An aroma of garlic and fresh tarragon hung about her as she approached him down the steps in the puce interlock combinations. He laughed out loud with pleasure at the sight of her.

'Those knee-highs are something else, Cam!' he said. 'Kid, you look great. You got style.' He had the wine and the frisbee and the chestnut sweets in the crook of his left arm, but he held out to her his right hand which she took.

'They'd probably look better on you,' she said, since their hip size was not actually dissimilar.

'Don't you believe it,' he said.

'What I mean is, they're really made for men,' Camilla said bravely. 'I can't quite muster the right bulge under the fly-buttons. You've got new glasses Arnie. They look most terribly expensive. Are they tax deductible?' Arnie laughed.

'There's not too much gets deducted from my tax,' he said. 'Only from my salary.'

'I've made lunch,' she said. 'A real four-star heart-attack special. It's all cream and chicken fat.' Arnie ate undaunted, wedging the toe of his Adidas shoe under the wobbling leg of the bridge table to stop the wine from slopping. He had not break-fasted and the sea air whetted his appetite.

'Now I want the organ,' he said. He balanced himself gingerly between two jutting springs on the Put-U-Up and contemplated the gentle spread of Camilla's rump on the music stool. Camilla played him a stanza of 'Jerusalem', but somehow in Arnie's presence the fair dream of the Holy City was no longer an automatic joke. She stopped and turned on the stool to face him.

'Arnie,' she said, 'you don't happen to collect old boxes, do you?'

'Boxes?' Arnie said. 'How do you mean, "old boxes"? You mean cartons from the grocery store? Right now I got plenty. For mailing my books to the States.'

'Forget it,' she said, 'I was only asking. Hey, Arnie, don't you ever hate your name? What I mean is, don't you ever wish you had a more glamorous name? You're quite a glamorous man, really.' She flushed a little, because he looked at her with such blank incomprehension through his dishy new spectacle frames. But she carried on regardless. 'If you were to call yourself "Arne", for instance,' she said, 'then you would sound like a Danish architect.'

'Are you kidding?' Arnie said. 'A Danish architect – what for?'

'Or "Arno",' she said. 'Then people would think you were Italian.'

'What for?' Arnie said again, thinking amusedly that it had been a long time since he had last heard a woman talk such wholehearted nonsense to him, especially one with such a nice East European name, but that Camilla was both delectably pretty and hopelessly young.

'You figure that to be Italian is more glamorous than to be a Jewish medicine man from Country Club Road, Middletown, Connecticut?' he said. Camilla flushed more deeply.

'Oh no!' she said. 'I didn't mean that *you* weren't glamorous. I only meant your name.' Arnie tried crossing his legs on the Put-u-Up, but gave up in further physical discomfort. He picked up the Byron which lay on the sofa beside him and opened it at random. Twenty-five years on, it still fell open at the page where Julie Horowitz had pinned it one summer evening to con the lines by heart which were printed there. She had done so in defiance of the English teacher's instructions, which had been to memorise the first two pages of *Lycidas*.

'She walks in beauty, like the night
Of cloudless climes and starry skies;
And all that's best of dark and bright
Meet in her aspect and her eyes:
Thus mellowed to that tender light
Which heaven to gaudy day denies.'

Arnie read the poem through to the end. Then he shut the book.

'Let's take a walk,' he said. 'Let's get some coffee.'

In the coffee bar a young Italian waiter, flicking at the table top with a kitchen cloth, stopped to kiss his fingers to Camilla and promptly became voluble on the subject of her exposed navel. Venus had once come to earth, he said, and had taken up residence in an inn in Bologna where the innkeeper, having spied through a keyhole on the goddess undressing, had been bewitched by the beauty of her perfect umbilicus. He had gone at once to his kitchen and created *tortellini* to celebrate its form in pasta. The waiter made the small circular shape with his finger and thumb before breaking off to kiss his fingers once again.

'What's *tortellini*?' Camilla said.

'You come tomorrow,' said the waiter urgently. 'You ask for Mario. Tomorrow I make for you *tortellini*.' Arnie gave the order for coffee and waited for the man to go.

'Mario, huh?' he said. 'What happened to Arno?' It was then that he became aware that the poetry book was still in his hand and he put it down on the table.

'Your book,' he said. 'Sorry, I took your book.' After the coffee Camilla led him to the shore, where, expressing a sudden urge to bathe, she pulled the singlet over her head and walked topless into the sea in long-johns. Arnie who lay clothed on the pebbles, sweat-shirt bunched under his head for a pillow, watched her walk gingerly towards the water on tender feet and contemplated the Byron. She returned hugging her breasts with goose-pimpled arms, because she had no towel, and came to a calculated stop, standing astride his pelvis. Water dripped from her long-johns on to his trousers.

'You're dripping water all over my pants,' he said but Camilla stayed where she was. She shook her short hair briefly like a small wet dog, scattering droplets on to his shirt and on to the red vellum of the Bryon cover.

'I know,' she said. 'Do you often read poetry, Arnie?' She crouched down over him on her haunches.

'Only when I watch you walk, Camilla,' he said a little dryly. 'Get up, kid. You're sitting on my balls.'

'I know,' she said again. 'I'll get up just as soon as you tell me you don't like it.' It came to him then that Camilla wore no underpants beneath the long-johns and that stray dark curls of damp pubic hair were protruding through the fly-buttons. 'Pass me my top, would you?' she said. 'I'm cold.' She pulled the buttoned singlet over her small high breasts, shifting her weight subtly but provokingly on his pelvis.

'Get up, Cam. You're a baby,' he said.

'I'm twenty,' she said.

'I'm thirty-nine,' he said. 'Do you behave like this with all the men you know?'

'Don't insult me,' she said. 'If you don't like me to touch you, just tell me so and I'll stop.'

'Cam,' Arnie said. 'Let's not pretend that I don't know you're one gorgeous piece of ass. You are also a baby and Noah's daughter. Now will you kindly get your half-naked crack off my crutch?' He lifted one knee to throw her but its effect was only to bring her face nearer his own.

'I'm Noah's stepdaughter,' Camilla said. 'Anyway, Noah believes I'm so promiscuous as it is that he'd probably be quite relieved to think that I fancied you. He thinks I always go for effeminates.'

'And quite how promiscuous are you?' Arnie said.

'Probably no more so than you,' she said. 'Anyway who's going to tell him? Not me.'

When Arnie kissed her, it was so much like the dream that Camilla was tempted to ask him yet again about the boxes. She knew that she had been there before. She knew 'the sweet, keen smell' and 'the glass beyond the door'. She knew the sounds of sighing. She knew the startling, corporeal dream of Jerusalem and that at all other times in her past when she had opened her mouth to other men's mouths, it had been as a mere taking of childhood lollipops. She knew that she had entered into the House of Love.

'Easy, baby,' Arnie said struggling against her manifest intensity, but he knew as he had always known that she was away and out the most perfectly beautiful girl he had ever seen and that to make love to her would be like climbing into the blossom end of a pear.

'Excuse me,' Arnie said, moments later, pausing in front of the chemist shop on the way back to the flat. 'But I don't have any rubbers.'

'I do,' said Camilla. 'I've got lots of them.'

'I see,' Arnie said. 'Do I take it then that, as far as you are concerned, this event is right on schedule?'

'Oh no!' Camilla said. 'Honestly. I always keep them with me, that's all. I don't even use them as contraceptives as a matter of fact. I use the Pill. I've been on the Pill since I was fourteen.'

'Is that right?' Arnie said sarcastically.

'Noah got me put on the Pill, because it gives women smaller periods,' she said. 'I used to bleed so heavily that I twice got put on a hospital stretcher with a drip in my arm.'

'I never knew that,' Arnie said. 'Nobody told me.'

'I keep contraceptive sheaths only because Noah's put the wind up me about VD,' she said. 'I decided to make men use them as a condition of entry.' For a moment Arnie was rendered speechless with admiration.

'Congratulations,' he said. 'You have the whole thing quite properly wrapped up. You bulk-buy in plain wrappers through the mail, I assume?' he said.

'I buy them in Boots,' she said proudly. 'Over the counter. At first I went to the Family Planning Clinic, but they gave me those sturdy, durable things – passion killing like wellington boots – so now I choose my own. I don't buy any of that fancy, gimmicky stuff with stipples and luminous tints, I have to tell you. I buy only the plainest, most expensive kind.' Arnie wiped his glasses on the hem of his sweatshirt.

'Is this a consumer survey you're offering me, Cam, or is it a decent screw?' he said.

'Sorry,' Camilla said laughing shyly. 'By the way, can I borrow your sweatshirt please? I'm slowly expiring with cold. I feel like a frog.'

'Croak,' Arnie said as he peeled the garment off. 'Baby, I feel like a frog-prince.'

Arnie woke around midnight with a cramp in his leg. He groped for his glasses and turned on the bedside lamp. Being brass and badly earthed, it gave out a small electric shock on contact. All the bedding was on the floor. From the wall, Lord Kitchener's gaze was distinctly unfriendly. Beside him, sprawling naked on her belly in sleep, Camilla had colonised nine-tenths of the bed.

He eased the palms of both hands under her at rib and haunch, and heaved her over.

'Move, Cam,' he said. She stirred faintly and, without waking, drew her thumb into her mouth and sucked.

'I don't believe it!' Arnie said. 'Hey, Cam, you're sucking your thumb – do you know that? You're a baby.' He pulled lightly at her hand below the thumb, but the sole effect of this reproof was to make her clamp on more tightly in sleep and to emit several small contented grunts like a nursing infant.

'Jesus!' Arnie said. He kissed the lobe of her pretty shell-like ear and found his mouth tasting of sea-salt. This was no surprise to him, since he had kissed it earlier that evening and knew – recollecting now the innkeeper and the matchless umbilicus – that Venus had risen from the sea. Yesterday – was it yesterday? – Camilla had risen from the sea herself and had walked towards him across the pebbles like a night of starry skies. Where, he wondered, had she put that sexy poetical Barmitzvah book? She had placed it beside her on the bedside cabinet alongside her packs of Durex. 'With love from Uncle Sam and Auntie Ida.' Oh sweet Camilla! And who the hell was Uncle Sam? Uncle Sam! Arnie raised his eyes by association to Lord Kitchener. Then he got up and wrapped himself in a bedsheet from the floor before stepping over yesterday's dropped clothing on his way to the lavatory. Raised up from the rest, Camilla's damp combinations were drying out over a chairback.

She was still sleeping soundly when he returned, but had in his absence accomplished a diagonal, expansionist manoeuvre encompassing the whole surface of the bed – a manoeuvre which had left her rear end fortuitously illuminated within a charmed circle of lamplight. Arnie laughed quietly. He seated himself upon the outer edge of the bed to fix his gaze upon the place where Camilla's inviting, youthful pubes met in a perfect neat seam below the larger cleft of her buttocks. Tenderly laying back her lobes with both his thumbs he pushed an index finger through the seam. It closed around him like a warm-blooded sea-anemone. The woman was unbelievable. It entertained him to reflect upon how deliciously sexy she was. Even in sleep she performed like the pick of *Playboy*'s preppiest masturbation fantasies. Ali's kid was dynamite. He had always known it for a fact. Suddenly he jerked his finger inside her.

'Quit sucking your thumb and hand me those rubbers,' he said. Camilla opened her eyes for a moment and heaved her rump upwards as she mumbled inaudibly through her thumb.

'Pardon?' Arnie said.

'I said don't stop because I like it,' she said. 'I said not to use the sheaths. Please, Arnie, I want you not to use them.'

'I'll use them,' Arnie said. 'Hand them over.'

'Please.'

'Cam,' Arnie said. 'I'm telling you to hand them over.'

Sunday was Arnie's last day. During that time he dazzled her, not only by winning three successive free games on an inter-galactic war machine in one of the amusement arcades, but by making a stylish U-turn over a traffic island as he changed direction in the hired Fiat while heading out with her for lunch in a country pub. He said goodbye to her after a brass band concert in the grounds of the Royal Pavilion where – when an audience of elderly ladies rose from their folding chairs for the National Anthem – Arnie rose from his knees on the grass with Camilla standing upright on his shoulders.

'Nice work, partner,' he said afterwards, as he lifted her down. 'You're balletic. Did you ever do that before?'

'It was all you,' she said. 'You held me up. Do people learn tricks like that in medical schools?'

'I learned it one time in a clown school,' he said. 'In Paris. I left it to work with Noah.'

'I'd really like to come back to Oxford with you,' she said. 'Shall I do that, Arnie?' Arnie kissed her hand.

'You stay right here,' he said. 'I'll be back on the weekend.'

'All right,' she said.

'And watch out for Mario,' he said. 'Remember, he's glamorous.' She stuck out her tongue at him as a parting gesture, but long after he had lifted her from his shoulders her feet had still not touched the ground.

TWENTY-ONE

J ULIE HAD HELD OUT for some days to Ali the promise of Thomas Adderley's new play which was to open within the week at a local arts theatre.

'I have not always cared for what he writes,' Julie said, 'but this time I have no doubts. This time I assert without reservation that Thomas has found the soul and the voice of the place.'

'Dust and barbed wire?' Ali said in jest, since she was not accustomed to hear Julie praise things.

'Ali-pie,' Julie said earnestly, 'what Thomas has written will make you rise up and shout Hallelujah.'

Thomas, as it turned out, could not go to the opening night of his play. He was intercepted that evening by the security police who had reason to suspect that he had been in receipt of subversive literature. This was perfectly true. Thomas had the previous day received, unsolicited in the post from England, a stack of inflammatory pamphlets which had come, with a covering letter, postmarked SE9.

'Yes,' Thomas told the police captain. 'I did receive such a parcel. I destroyed the contents immediately.'

'I'm glad to hear you admitting to receiving it, Mr Adderley,' said the policeman. 'Had you denied it, I have a warrant here to search your house, and another for your arrest.' He produced the items from his inside pocket and laid them on his desk. Twenty years earlier Thomas might have quipped that neither warrant was strictly speaking necessary, given that the police had powers to search and arrest without them, but he was older now and wiser. He no longer enjoyed such academic debating points. He valued his quieter life.

'We want you to cooperate with us, Mr Adderley,' the policeman said. 'Have you got any idea who is sending you these things?'

'None at all,' Thomas said. He knew that it was always unwise to lie to the police who, if they caught you at it, had from there on the moral upper hand. Neither was it wise to tell the truth. It was always best in these cases genuinely to know as little as possible. Therefore, while his eyes had yesterday involuntarily begun to scan the covering letter, Thomas, by a strong effort of will, had wrenched his brain from the brink of assimilating what the note had actually said. He felt now that, while the owner of that small neat handwriting burned unmistakeably before his mind's eye, the names of people whom the letter had listed as parties to whom the pamphlets were to be handed on had genuinely fuzzed in his mind.

'Any instructions enclosed?' said the policeman. 'Names of other recipients perhaps? Come on, Mr Adderley, you're a sensible man these days. We've been watching you for a long time now and we know you've kept your nose clean. We're very pleased with you.' Thomas found himself uncomfortably sullied by praise. He longed for a cigarette as he watched the policeman smoke.

'We have reason to believe that these subversive materials have been sent with covering letters to persons like yourself,' the policeman said. He paused to suppress a smirk of satisfaction before airing an example of the terminology he had recently learned in the police Marxism course. ' "Fellow Travellers", so to speak, Mr Adderley,' he said. 'Your political friends will be calling you a sell-out these days. You might as well talk to us. You can discuss these things with us as between old friends here.'

'If any of my friends are political,' Thomas said, 'then they are wise enough not to tell me so. I have no answer to your question, Captain. As I told you truthfully, I destroyed the parcel immediately without reading any covering letter.'

'And how, precisely, did you destroy this material, Mr Adderley?' said the policeman.

'I burned it,' Thomas said. 'In the envelope.'

'Perhaps you kept just one or two?' said the policeman. 'Just as souvenirs from London South East 9.'

'I burned them all,' Thomas said.

'Now why do such a thing, Mr Adderley?' said the policeman. 'A man like you. It is no secret to either of us that you would like to see great changes here in our country, not so?'

'I burned them because revolutionary heroics from SE9 have no value for me,' Thomas said. 'No validity.'

'You believe that a revolutionary should put his money where his mouth is so to speak?' said the policeman. 'Or is it that you don't like to take your line from Hampstead, Mr Adderley? You prefer to take it from Moscow perhaps?' Thomas reflected that SE9 would be rather a long way from Hampstead. In spirit probably further away than certain subsections of Johannesburg. Possibly Bexley; possibly Eltham Park.

'I don't take my line from anywhere,' he said.

'Mr Adderley,' said the policeman, 'to be frank with you, you have very few secrets from us here. If any more of these "parcels" arrive addressed to you, you would be very well advised to inform us of their arrival immediately.' Thomas said nothing. 'Anything you wish to report to us will always be treated as a matter between good friends,' the policeman said. He smiled unexpectedly. 'Good evening to you, Mr Adderley,' he said. 'You may go. Enjoy your "first night",' he said, and winked.

'Thank you,' Thomas said.

'My regards to your friend Miss Horowitz,' the policeman said suddenly. 'Or is it "Ms"? Now there's a woman for you, who really likes to chew nails.'

Had the theatre boasted a curtained stage, Thomas would

have arrived in time to see it fall, but it did not. The theatre was more of the warehouse and scaffolding variety, with a central, wooden dais raised on agit props. What greeted him instead was the frozen tableau of his final scene where a black woman, neither heroic nor cowardly, but tenacious, cunning and, above all, enduring, stood at the graveside of her husband and son who had been shot dead in a township riot while she had been off doing time in jail on a pass offence. Her papers had not been in order. And he arrived in time to see and hear the audience stamp their feet and roar. Ali felt that before her eyes another huge, surviving Mother Courage had dragged another hand-cart through another troubled age and clime. She did not speak; she could not, but her heart said Hallelujah. Around her the crowd both black and white had risen and begun to sing '*Nkosi Sikelele Afrika*' – that rich and moving hymn which constitutes the alternative national anthem. No person spoke upon leaving, except for Eva Bobrow whose voice rose audibly in the silence as she addressed herself to the expert on police repression.

'I found in it a disappointing lack of political *explicitness*,' she said. 'A lack of *explicit* commitment; a degree – shall I say – of *emotionalism*? Thomas!' she called out then, as she spotted him at last in the crowd. 'Ah, Thomas, there you are! We missed you during the performance, but you were backstage, of course. Jurgen and I have a good few bones to pick with you. Item one. Your excellent play at no time took on *directly* enough either the Women's Movement or the police. Another time we would both of us really like to see you *more directly take on the police*.' Ali saw Thomas's face shatter for a moment into that startling, elemental laughter which broke him up into glittering fragments, like water disturbed by a pebble.

Julie was not a person who went in for overzealous minding of children. She favoured them at all times unseen and unheard. Daniel was grateful for this whenever he was left in her care. He was glad that, after simple exhortations not to 'break anything' nor to venture close to the swimming pool, Julie would put on her glasses and direct her attention towards preparing her lectures, or else she would scan the financial columns of the newspapers, or bury her nose in what she called the 'tee-el-ess' which was also a sort of newspaper. For one thing he didn't care for her and for another he liked to go his own way in her wonderful garden, playing Mowgli behind the shrubs or secretly feeding the mother cat on bits of bread and milk. For this he always used the jampot house, not only because he could reach it, but because it gave him very good cover. If Julie happened to encounter him, she would laugh and ruffle his curls and accuse him of borrowing from her 'gallery of horrors' to make a 'cosy little billet for his soldier men'.

On these occasions, when his mother left him with Julie and took the car to the shops, Hattie would always beg to go along because she liked the shops so much and she would always beg her mother to buy her things. But Daniel had no time for shops. He was in this respect his father's son. Shops were boring places, he thought, except for ice-cream shops – and Julie kept ice-cream in the fridge anyway. He always preferred to stay behind, deftly avoiding the intrusions either of his hostess or of the black baby-sitter lady in the funny beret, who came in once a day to launder and clean. The only danger lay in the possibility of his being interrupted by Julie as he went about his secret ministrations to the mother cat. Julie was inclined to take her mid-morning coffee at the poolside, sometimes on her own and sometimes with Ali, or with a man called Thomas Adderley. That way she caught the crisp morning sun on the terrace before the pool area turned to shadow. There was something perplexing to Daniel about the way Julie and Thomas behaved together when Ali wasn't there. It was much more sort of close and married-looking. But Thomas Adderley didn't live in Julie's house. He came and went like a visitor.

On this particular Monday morning Ali was out with Hattie and Daniel had just successfully accomplished a third week in secret feeding of the cat. He saw to his surprise that Julie and

Thomas had fallen asleep with their arms around each other. Beside them were empty coffee cups and discarded novels. He stopped in his tracks with the jampot house in his hands. Surely only married people hugged like that in their sleep? Then, to his relief, he heard his mother.

When Ali and Hattie came home Daniel saw that his sister was wearing a new T-shirt and a funny cap. The T-shirt had writing on it and a picture of a big yellow sun. He ran towards them eagerly, because it was strange to be there alone at the poolside with Julie and Thomas being so close and married-looking and asleep.

'Mummy!' he said. 'Mummy!'

For Ali to find them lying there, the two great loves of her past, was like the final closing of a book; the ending of an era. The thing had a kind of dreadful symmetry. Intermittently, through-out her adult life, she had consumed so much of her soul in longing for Thomas that she was strangely glad, now, to lay the burden down. What she saw before her rose as another pile of broken glass and running sores which in her blessed privilege she could step over and leave alone to fester. She accepted that, as the unsavoury tenets of extra-marital rough justice operated, Julie had something of a claim on Thomas, but she had taken him in Paddington to be a loyal and monogamous husband; had taken him for a fellow initiate in the arts of adultery. This he now clearly was not. Ali was disappointed. She put a finger to her lips and beckoned Daniel to come away with her into the house.

As he crossed the paving-stones, Daniel fell sprawling. He almost fell into the pool. Julie's shoes had tripped him up. The jampot house fell in pieces with a high, resonant explosion and when Daniel rose up he saw that he had broken the skin on both his knees. Julie sat up sharply to attention. Daniel had run whimpering into his mother's arms.

'Never mind, my baby,' Ali was saying. 'It's just a jampot house. Just a little silly jampot house. We can try to find another one just the same.'

'Damn you, child!' Julie said harshly. 'You have broken my jampot house! I was planning to give it to your mother. Your visit here was expressly conditional upon your not breaking any of my china.' She rose, angry and compromised. Thomas meanwhile slept on. 'A letter came for you, Ali,' she said. 'I have it in the house. It came care of me at the university. Perhaps it is from your husband but I think not. Having spoken to him, as I did this morning, I cannot think he would address his letters so idiotically. He telephoned for you this morning. He'll probably try you again.' Julie softened. She put her hands on Ali's shoulders and gave her a kiss.

'Dearest Ali-pie,' she said. 'We've had some very good times.' She turned and looked back at Thomas, still recumbent on the stones. ' "The salmon falls, the mackerel-crowded seas",' she said wistfully. 'My birthday is next week. I'm forty-one. Yours is in two days. We'll eat strudel together in Hillbrow, eh, to celebrate our middle age before you take yourself home. You're booked to go home next week, aren't you? Your medic tells me he means to be back in Oxfordshire in twelve days' time, Ali-pie, and I took him for a man whose word was good. I have to tell you that I took to him very strongly in general. He's American. You never said.'

'Yes,' Ali said. 'No.'

'In fact you have said almost nothing about him,' Julie said. 'You have been very good. Your personal life has been in a state of minor crisis, I suspect. That was the catch. That was why you came, wasn't it? But you haven't bothered me with it. I have quite enough bother on right now, of course, what with the gardener having had an axe wedged fatally in his wretched skull the week before you came. Of all the aspirant applicants for the job not one of them has a pass-book in order. Did I tell you? Times have been difficult for us all.'

Ali shivered. There were times when Julie's abrasiveness occurred to her as a compelling form of self-torture.

'Jesus, Ali,' Julie said. 'What is that child of yours wearing? Who tells you to buy her such fascist T-shirts?' Hattie's new

235

T-shirt, wheedled from Ali against her better judgement, came with a matching yellow eye-shade and said, in an arc of upper-case lettering over a smiling, full frontal sun-face, 'Sunny South Africa'. 'Take that thing off at once, child!' Julie said. 'You can't wear a thing like that in my house.'

'I can,' Hattie said staunchly. 'I will. Anyway, it *is* sunny here.' Behind them Thomas cleared his throat. He was blinking and smiling and raising his cup.

'Cheers, Alison,' he said. 'All it wants is a little amendment; a small addition. I propose "More Power to the People in Sunny South Africa".' Oh Thomas!

Ali's letter, though unsigned, had clearly come from Arnie who, upon returning to the research unit after a third weekend in Brighton with Camilla, had been moved by the sight of Noah's imperfect typing which had thus far spent the summer sitting idly in the roller of the office machine. He had added a corollary of his own to it and had despatched it to Ali, with Camilla's help, care of 'The Horror Witch' at the local department of English.

'% asyouwillsee = $^3/_4$' ran the corollary, 'i have)finally £ =)taught % myself to $ touch $^5/_8$ -type/6. HAPPY BRITHDAY % AL/?!'

'Bon voyage, Ali-Pie,' Julie said at the departure gate. 'I can't say that I don't envy you. To have a nice bull-necked Yankee medical hunk waiting for me back in temperate Blauwildebeestfontein – that would be one hundred per cent better than a slap in the face with a pickled herring. Perhaps he would like two wives?'

Ali laughed. 'To speak frankly, I would say that you have Thomas. Or, at least, part shares in him. Julie, do you love him?'

Julie shrugged. 'Love,' she said. 'You can keep it. But you, Ali, with your three marriages. You must believe in love. Do *you* love him? You always used to. Don't pretend you didn't.'

Ali scanned her emotions, not for the first time since that

protracted denouement from Paddington to the poolside, and discovered that she did not. But she worried for him. Worried for his precarious safety in such an explosive and baffling place.

'No,' she said. 'He's yours, for all I care.'

'To speak true,' Julie said, 'he's not much of a proposition in reality. For all his size and loveliness, he is not altogether corporeal, if you know what I mean. Thomas is too good for this life. Too good and not good enough. Goodbye, my dear friend and don't think too badly of me. Go home and enjoy your medic.'

Ali laughed and kissed her. 'Thanks for having me, Julie,' she said. 'I never incidentally said that my husband was bull-necked.'

'He sounded like a seventeen-inch collar to me over the telephone,' Julie said. 'I call that corporeal. Goodbye, Ali.' She placed in Ali's hands as a parting surprise the jam pot house, artfully and secretly glued for her by the curator of a local musuem. Ali bit her lip to fight back tears.

' "Friendship is like china",' she said, ' "Precious, frail and rare"'.

'Are you actually quoting me this doggerel?' Julie said. 'Or are you making it up? What are your sources for this nauseating snippet of folk poetry?'

'You are,' Ali said. 'But that was long ago.'

Ali had no idea until the plane had been airborne three hours that – zipped in among Hattie's hand-luggage which she kept upon her knee to ensure for periodic intakes of air – was a sleeping three-week-old kitten.

TWENTY-TWO

Ali's reentry into England did not prove easy on the nerves; not for a person to whom the prospect of smuggling held out no charms. Guiltily she followed the green light at Heathrow Airport, with its attendant implication that she had 'nothing to declare'. The kitten behaved beautifully, and, as Ali had taken the further precaution of doing what Arnie Wienberg had once advised in the circumstances – namely of 'getting in line behind a party in turbans and saris' – the British customs officials had been too busy venting a measure of controlled, racist harassment upon her forerunners in the queue to concern themselves with Hattie's hand-luggage. Hattie had been very naughty to bring the kitten in like that, without asking, but Ali had not the stomach to scold her for it. The child had wanted a kitten for so long, and here was that rare and wonderful thing, a female ginger, like its mother. Of all cats, ginger tabbies had always been Ali's own favourites. She foresaw, with relative stoicism, the prospect of feeding the tiny creature at four-hourly intervals through the night with a medicinal eye-dropper until it was ready to lap and, with considerably less stoicism, the repercussions from its presence in the house where Noah was concerned. Noah would be furious at a time when appeasement seemed the better part of discretion.

In the airport car park she found that the Audi had been broken into and had had one of its front windows shattered, but worse was still to follow. Misgiving struck her heart as she saw that the house – at the mercy of Noah's untended climbing plants since May – had already begun to take on the look of Haunted Castle and that the front door stood wide open. An unmistakeable smell of dripping and scorched chillies hung thickly on the air in the hallway above a pile of unopened mail. Ali mounted the stairs with trepidation, like Mother Bear returning from a walk in the woods. Someone had most certainly been sleeping in her bed, since several starkly prolific semen stains now graced the dark brown nether sheet. The shower leading from the room had not yet drained of its water, which floated steamily in the run-off, sporting a surface film of warm, soapy scum and sloughed particles of skin.

'William Lister!' Ali said, but above the bath, suspended from the clothes line, hung a black nylon brassiere in size 38D.

The kitchen, under Hattie's prohibitive 'NO SMOCKING' sign, yielded up as further evidence a box of used matches lying beside a pile of wood ash in the grate. The children had already run off, oblivious, to their bedrooms, so eager to rediscover the pleasures of old toys. At the bottom of the garden William Lister was raising a mallet as he drove a wedge into a section of dead elm trunk. Beside him stood a new and impressively large woodpile. The size of the woodpile struck Ali forcefully as hideous evidence that William, together with the owner of the 38D brassiere, was planning to ride out the winter right there on her premises. Though he waved to her with a casual greeting when he saw her at the window, William did not cease from his labours until he had cleft the trunk neatly in six and had added the pieces to the woodpile. Then he laid both mallet and axe on the ground and made his way to the kitchen door. He stamped his feet heavily on the mat and wiped his forehead on one of Ali's table napkins, which she watched him draw out of his pocket.

'Phew!' he said. 'Chopping wood; it's thirsty work I can tell you, but really – with all that diseased elm lying there unused in the woods, I don't understand why you people ever resort to expensive fuels.'

Ali's immediate thought was that he had let the oil storage tank run dry or that the electricity supply had been cut off. William was meanwhile displaying his calluses for her with undisguised satisfaction.

'You are making a woodpile,' she said unnecessarily and, discovering a sudden, desperate need for hot tea, she cast her eyes over the workboard for the kettle, which she could not see.

'Full marks, my dear woman, for brilliant deduction,' William said. 'That I am, indeed.' Something had happened to William, Ali decided morbidly. It was not merely that he had lost all sense of reality, nor that he had never used words like 'indeed' to her before. The nylon brassiere and the semen stains stood as ominous pointers to the awful truth that William had come of age where women were concerned, and that he was now demonstrating for her benefit how well he could handle the weaker sex. William had become a card-carrying understander of women.

'Welcome home, beautiful,' he said. 'You've had a nice little touch of the sun. It makes you look younger. I'm afraid I can't offer you any tea until I've got this grate of yours cleared out and the fire made up. It draws terribly I may say, this fireplace. Your kettle has been on the blink since this morning.' Ali stared at him in a state of contained indignation which came as a prelude to rage.

'It could just be worth mentioning that Noah's had all the flues bricked up,' she said. 'Brick-dust and wood-smoke give him asthma. I hope you realise that whatever else you have been doing here, you have also been in danger of burning down my house.' William chuckled dismissively.

'As to your husband's asthma,' he said. 'It is a well-known fact that it's an ailment rooted in psycho-emotional problems. Noah wants to look beyond his chimneys for the cause.' Something was happening to Ali which – for all that Mervyn Bobrow might have dismissed it as a mere rising obsession with 'utensils and territory' – was in truth another coming of age. Tutored in the poignant resolution of her own sex by the power of her two unlikely spinsters, Julie Horowitz and old Margaret; sustained by the uncrushable and enduring Mrs Gaitskell, Ali had at the last discovered her strengths in the knowledge that she had somehow marvellously cast off all residual yearning for Thomas Adderley. That liberation which had begun after Paddington and had reached its recent completion beside Julie Horowitz's swimming pool had already started to celebrate itself in the painting of the oranges to which she now longed to get back. She addressed William Lister in the confident voice of one who had discovered not only that she could get on and off aeroplanes without terror, but that she could do so with an item of unscheduled livestock concealed in her children's hand-luggage.

'If you've buggered my kettle, William Lister,' she said, 'you will also – before you pack your bags – clean out the grate and telephone a plumber to fix my shower. Finally, you will get your fancy-woman's underwear out of my bathroom. You have ten minutes, starting from now.' William began to stave her off with a shot at amiable condescension.

'I refuse to let you quarrel with me,' he said. 'If I allow you to quarrel with me, you will only hate yourself for it tomorrow, believe me.'

'On the contrary, I will love myself for it,' Ali said. 'What I am saying to you, William Lister, is get out of my house! Take your stinking streaky rashers and your recycled matches and never darken my doorstep again.'

Further verbal sparring was aborted by the ringing of the telephone.

'It'll be that wrong number again,' William said. 'I've been getting it the whole week I've been here. Some demented crone keeps ringing up from a call-box and raving about a fire.' Ali nonetheless made haste to answer it, as William moved for his rucksack. By the time she had come off the telephone – though the cheque for the kettle was nowhere, and the brassiere and the grate were untouched – William had mercifully gone from her house. The caller was old Margaret whose voice quavered more thinly than ever.

'They've got me at last,' Margaret said. 'I've joined the bloody coffin queue. I've been committed.'

'Coffin queue?' Ali said. 'Where are you?'

'Knees up Mother Brown,' Margaret said. 'Bedpans. The bloody works. The poor old hags, they all stink. I hoped you might look in. Spread a little cheer for me with a half-jack of brandy and some fags. Hide them under your coat, mind, or they'll claw them off me sure as God made little rotten apples. They're all thieves in this hole. Rogues and thieves.'

'Which hole?' Ali said.

'There was never a bloody fire you know,' old Margaret said. 'Though the doctors said there was. The bloody neighbours called the fire-brigade – and the ambulance. There was nothing but a lot of smoke. A potful of singed ox-heart. One of my turns must have come on over the dog's dinner.'

'Oh Jesus!' Ali said. 'What are you saying to me?'

'I'm geriatric,' Margaret said. 'I'm no longer at home.'

Several tall firemen had led her into the waiting ambulance where they had called her 'granny' and had given her reviving puffs of oxygen. 'I'm not your granny. I'm a spinster,' Margaret had said with dignity, before they had taken her to the hospital. A week later the general practitioner, whom she had acquired on Noah's recommendation, had signed the certificate for her admission to the old people's home. The pugs had been despatched to a dogs' home, including the one small female in season who had been discovered behind chicken wire in an upstairs bookshelf alongside a copy of *Major Barbara*. A house-clearing agency, on behalf of the landlord, had made short work of the plastic bags and the carrot-top trees. A builder's skip now stood outside the front door of what had been Margaret's house, and a contractor's board had been fitted to the cracked front window.

The renovations, while they were naturally a minor nuisance to the Bobrows' tenants, promised considerably to enhance the value of Mervyn's property which had suffered over the years from its proximity to substandard housing.

'I'll come,' Ali said, hating herself for having been absent in Margaret's hour of need. 'I'll come today.'

Ali made her way first to Mrs Gaitskell's flat in the hope of being able to deposit the children there for an hour while she visited old Margaret. She discovered that lady clutching her gut at the cooker as she boiled up a brick-like pudding for her husband's tea.

'He likes to come home to a good, solid pudding,' Mrs Gaitskell said, 'though I shouldn't be on my feet. I had a scrape last week for cysts on the womb.'

'Womb?' Ali said. 'Cysts!' Mrs Gaitskell's gynaecological usage constantly brought home to Ali how squarely and straight that person faced up to the whole hazard-prone area of the female body as a substandard piece of design. It seemed to her realistic and courageous.

Mrs Gaitskell expressed herself delighted to have the children for an hour, in spite of Ali's concern for her. They would be 'no trouble' she said, and she directed them at once to the large bag of glacier mints which stood perennially upon the sideboard. Ali left them on the sofa; a contented threesome, cracking boiled sweets between their molars and coaxing the budgie to peck at his cuttlefish.

In the old people's home, Margaret sat in the day room like a hollow-eyed boarding-school girl waiting for the dawn of an exeat weekend. The curtains and the gloss-paintwork in the room were lilac. Lilac, she had decided, was a colour to be tolerated only on lilacs. The room was overcrowded and smelled of rubber pants and urine. She missed the smell of dog and boiling pig melts. A concentration of aged persons lined the walls in walking frames. Faces from Hogarth and crowded into the workhouse.

'Watch your handbag!' she said hoarsely, because Ali had at that moment approached her through one of the lilac doors. 'There's a lot of thieves in here. They nick your clothes when you're asleep. They'd stop at nothing.' It was true that the inmates were between them attired in a curious predominance of purple nylon cardigans, but then the dress of Margaret herself was not unworthy of notice. She was clad in a motley layering of unfamiliar clothing, most of it bearing tweedy labels and held together with safety pins. Seeing Ali stare Margaret held forth a fine wool scarf to reveal the Jaeger label.

'Tit for tat!' she said and cackled briefly. 'If you can't beat 'em, join 'em. I've joined them, Ali, I can hardly tell myself from all the rest.'

'I can,' Ali said, helplessly. 'I always will.'

In a nearby café where the two of them repaired for lunch, Ali cut up a section of rare-grilled sirloin for Margaret and watched her dribble beef ooze on to the familiar shirt-front.

'No wonder the upper classes are so oversexed, it's all this bloody protein,' Margaret said. 'You can forget about protein back in the hole. We're always eating "slip down". The bloody nurses are at it all day long. "Eat up dear; it's all just slip-down." Doesn't it make you spit?'

'Yes,' Ali said. She saw that Margaret had already directed a goodly chunk of her defiant spirit into the time-honoured, institutional channel of complaining about the rations. It depressed her. Margaret had lost weight. Her dentures appeared no longer to fit her gums and she had developed a compulsive tendency towards sucking on them for relief. Ali passed over the brandy which Margaret secreted greedily in her handbag. In a flash of clairvoyant foreknowledge, Ali saw that Margaret would shut herself in the loo with the brandy that night and down the bottle at one sitting; for to measure it out in modest nightly doses would simply be to invite having it expropriated either by the inmates or by the staff. Brandy would be her ultimate 'slip-down'. It seemed to Ali extraordinary that Margaret, who had survived a decade in relative plumpness on egg-white and cracker-biscuits, had now, within three weeks of joining the 'coffin queue', shrunk by a third of her girth. Her skin hung in wrinkled swathes at wrist and jowl. It came to Ali that a violent disorientation, coupled with a few harsh frosty nights and the odd half-jack of brandy, was probably all it would take to expunge the willing flesh. Margaret's skin had become curiously transparent. Before the meal was over, she had fallen asleep in her chair.

The appearance of an itinerant gardener the following afternoon struck Ali not only as comic relief, but as a gift from heaven, prior to Noah's imminent return. He wore his loam-drenched, tea-cosy hat resting on three warts which were clustered between his eyebrows and stated his terms decisively as he slurped his tea from a saucer at Ali's kitchen table.

'Missus,' he said sternly. 'Bill Parsons is the name. Mister Bill Parsons. I'm a poor man, Missus, but I'm honest. An honest man, Missus, if you get my meaning.' Ali nodded vigorously, wishing to have it understood that she did not doubt his honesty. Not for a moment.

'Ten pound and I do the lot,' he said. 'Digging over and planting out. I do an honest job, Missus, and what do you say to that? Ten pound for the benefit of an honest man's work?' Ali had begun to believe he had been scripted by Bottom the Weaver.

'I'd rather pay you by the hour, Mr Parsons,' she said. 'That's if you don't mind. I do not wish to exploit you and it might take longer than you think.' Since Mr Parsons had reached that stage of deafness where he took all verbal response as personal affront, he merely glared at her formidably as he twiddled his hearing aid.

'Now look here, Missus,' he said. 'I'm an honest man. Honest and hardworking. I've got my own tools and my own mower. Five pound now, and the balance tomorrow. I can't say fairer than that. Ten pound to me, and to you the whole muck-heap digging over and planting out with wallflowers.'

'Oh no, Mr Parsons!' Ali said most emphatically. 'No radical changes, please. My husband would not care for that at all. Definitely no wallflowers. I would like you simply to tidy the beds and trim the climbers. And mow the grass, of course. We do have a mower. There is absolutely no need to bring a mower.'

'Oh aye,' Mr Parsons said, twiddling his hearing aid impatiently in the face of so long an interjection. 'It's like I said, I've got a decent mower and all my own tools. You've no need to fret yourself, they're good tools all of them and no rubbish. Five pound down and I'll be back at sunrise quick as ever you can say "Jack Robinson".'

'Yes,' Ali said. She was intrigued by the way he had modified the gesture of forelock-touching whereby he wedged the right thumb deftly between the three warts and the ribbing of the tea cosy, and jerked upwards a half-inch and down again.

Mr Parsons did not appear in the morning but he came towards the end of the afternoon, reeking heavily of five pounds' worth of best bitter and trundling a monstrous petrol mower in a wheelbarrow. Ali, all that day, had been wholly absorbed with her painting.

'Nothing too radical, Mr Parsons,' she said in casual greeting and she retreated at once to the oranges. The painting was evolving beautifully. It had excited her all day to watch it grow and change. From the outset it had had the quality of being somehow beyond her control. She now perceived this as a strength and not a weakness. The painting was growing through her, catching, as it did so, a multitude of vivid, provoking ambiguities.

'Mummy!' Hattie said in agitation. 'Come quickly! Daniel is crying. Mr Parsons is mowing Daddy's plants. Mummy – he's *mowing* the flowerbeds!'

Mr Parsons had managed with remarkable speed to convert a section of the front garden from Haunted Castle to Scorched

Earth. He had razed one of the wide herbaceous borders, severing the clematis and several small shrubs at root. Then he had forked over the ensuing devastation and had arranged within it four rows of wallflowers spaced at twelve-inch intervals from each other. As Ali rushed, headlong and gesticulating to stop him, Mr Parsons switched on the mower. The situation was impossible. Not only did the object render her speech inaudible, but it threatened to cut her off at the ankles. Over the din, Ali believed she heard him shout that he was honest; honest and hard working. His machine came drunkenly towards her, guzzling the last of the hollyhocks. Ali made a final, heroic rush upon the object and found herself somehow fortuitously assisted in the assault by the timely interference of a tall dark-haired woman, who in that instant had taken Mr Parsons by the shoulders and had wrenched him from the handles. The mower rumbled heavily to a halt.

'Now lookee here, Missus,' said Mr Parsons aggressively into the silence. 'You'd no call to touch that mower. 'Tis mine. Nor no more had you call to interfere with an honest, hardworking man about his business.'

'*Honest!* Don't make me laugh!' said the stranger with unusual vehemence. She had the voice of Ethel Merman and the profile of Barbra Streisand. She was also very properly dressed in the style of a Bonwitt Teller ad in the *New Yorker*. 'You absurdly drunken yokel; you incompetent old sot!' she said. 'Quit screwing up her garden, okay? She'd like for you to stop it!'

The effect on Mr Parsons was remarkable. He jambed his right thumb obsequiously into position between the warts and the ribbing and began immediately to bow out backwards towards the gate, as if taking leave of royalty.

'Now beat it, you jerk!' said the stranger. The instruction was quite extraneous. The mower and the wheelbarrow, which he had left behind him in his departing haste, later materialised under scrutiny as the property of the local parks department.

'Hi!' said the woman warmly. She held out to Ali her finely

boned right hand on which the fingernails were varnished bold scarlet. 'I'm Shirley,' she said, 'Shirley Glazer. I guess you're Alison. I take it that you people missed my card. I'm here for a conference at the hospital. I came by a couple of times last week but you were out of town. Your boarder entertained me most hospitably.'

'He was no boarder,' Ali said. 'He was a usurper. I threw him out yesterday.' Shirley Glazer coloured a little and laughed.

'Oh really?' she said, recovering fast. 'And I just threw out the gardener. We'd make an excellent team. Are those two cute little kids your kids, by any chance? Noah's kids? My god, but aren't they small!'

'I'm big,' Daniel said. 'Go away.' Shirley laughed again. She clearly thrived on stirring up contention.

'You look like Noah,' she said to Daniel with a kind of amiable challenge. 'But your colouring is all different. I guess the colouring just came as a different package, huh?' Daniel said nothing. Ali, as they walked towards the house, found that she was rudely sizing up Shirley Glazer's boobs as an undisputed 38D, but the woman was pushing sixty! She was, moreover, at once intimidating, capable and well-presented. What could she possibly want with William Lister? What could any woman who had once been married to Noah want with William Lister?

'I'm kind of sorry about your boarder,' Shirley said. 'Personally, I thought that he was cute. A little slovenly in his personal habits, maybe, but kind of charming, no? So utterly stiff and British, if you'll pardon me. And so earnest in his politics. I have strong radical leanings myself, as Noah will doubtless have told you, but I have always also been a hedonist. I am a radical hedonist.'

'Noah has told me nothing,' Ali said truthfully. 'But what exactly is a radical hedonist? Are you a socialist who can't live without mixer taps?' Shirley laughed.

'Those too,' she said. 'Mixer taps and sex. I have to admit that I always found capitalists to make better lovers.'

'I see,' Ali said. 'I do not speak from a great experience in the field, but I would hazard that almost anybody, across the ideological spectrum, would make a better lover than William Lister.'

'Now that's not fair,' Shirley said. 'And it's also totally untrue. For a start, he's heterosexual. That is a rare thing in a man these days. In the States, at least. I can't speak for Great Britain. I've been here just over a week.' Ali laughed out loud. Shirley was already so markedly unlike Noah in her penchant for instant self-exposure that it made her wonder how the two of them had ever got through an evening together, let alone a decade.

'The polarisation of the sexes,' Shirley said earnestly, 'is symptomatic of the growing crisis of capitalism.'

'I see,' Ali said.

'I'm serious,' Shirley said. 'You try calling up a couple of men in New York City next time you're a little stoned on New Year's Eve and wanting masculine company. Ten to one they'll be out propositioning each other. I spent last New Year's Eve listening to Mr Schubert on the stereo.'

'There's a lot to be said for it,' Ali said. 'I do a lot of it myself.'

'That's an okay attitude for a person who's married,' Shirley said. 'Alison, for all that he's maybe insufferably pompous, your husband is a real, A-line hetero.'

'Thank you,' Ali said.

Shirley had seated herself at the kitchen table and had taken out her knitting. She had set down two completed front halves of a prodigious cream-coloured cardigan rich in cables and diamond patterning, and had drawn a hank of oiled fisherman's wool from her bag which she had looped over a chairback for winding. Ali was almost tempted to offer her outstretched thumbs for the task, but she had taken it upon herself to find a clean enough saucepan in the house in which to boil some water for their tea. There was still not one available which did not reek of turmeric and crushed cardamom pods.

'Oh hang it, we'll drink this,' Ali said, feeling faintly

debauched. She banged down on to the table a bottle of bourbon plus two glasses. 'Bourbon is a woman's drink,' she said. 'Before Noah, I was married to a lunatic, you know. I am not a woman *wholly* devoid of experience.'

'Jimmy Beam, oh my!' Shirley said. 'A lunatic, you said? I can fully appreciate that Noah might make a very satisfactory antidote to a lunatic. But do you not find him – oh excuse me – a little tediously attracted to notions of anal sex?'

'No,' Ali said firmly, wondering why she took no offence at the question. 'I do not. Noah has always readily accepted that I am insufficiently eclectic in sexual matters.'

'I guess the poor man harbours latent homosexual urges along with all the rest,' Shirley said outrageously. 'And which man would not, who had that sweet-tongued grey-haired witch for a mother?' Ali began to discover that the pleasure to be got from listening to Shirley was largely gained from having someone else to be wicked for one. It was like hiring an assassin. 'There's the card from her in the hall,' Shirley said. 'I recognised the hand-writing. Don't you ever get to opening your mail? Somewhere in that pile is a card from me giving you the dates of my conference.'

'I will,' Ali said. 'But I will not yet.'

'Forget it,' Shirley said. 'mine's obsolete and "Mother's" is the annual New Year card. A prefabricated miscellany of tabernacle kitsch plus her own barbed platitudes within. I opened mine already. Say, I'd sure like to take you guys out to eat someplace, you know that? When I say eat, I'm talking food. Is there some-place around here that will sell us food? I don't mean some no-good British hamburger dump that serves up rubber mats between cold buns.'

'There's the *Saraceno*,' Ali said hopefully. 'They don't do mats in buns.' She had not been to the *Saraceno* since the night Noah had taken her there with the baby, to escape the Bobrows' scrag end.

Throughout the meal Shirley talked about her past, and all in front of the children. She talked with a vivid and conspicuous lack of restraint which compensated Ali, in one half-hour, for a decade of Noah's reserve. She and Noah had gone to the same high school in New Jersey, Shirley said, where by the age of twelve her already burgeoning breasts had begun to thwart a long-held aspiration to become a world class athlete. By fifteen her beautiful, wide mouth, which all through grade school had got her dubbed as 'Nigger Lips', had come into its own as a double-attraction, along with her breasts, for a catholic selection of high school boys in the back rows of movie houses. Noah was not the best of the bunch, she said, but he was surely one of the best. And he was later lent advantage by having survived the war. She had met him again, by coincidence, she said, on a kibbutz where she was about to make her journey through Zionism into socialist hedonism. Noah was about to injure his back. He was charmed and won by her liveliness. Like many a sober and cautious young man, he was attracted by the prospect of a wife who danced well and loved company.

'*Kibbutz?*' Ali said in bafflement and surprise, because the person Shirley was talking about was a person she did not know. They were married shortly thereafter in the proper, traditional manner. Shirley was already pregnant, but only just. The honey-moon was spent, unbelievably, in the Cotswolds, not a million miles from where Ali and Shirley sat eating aubergine pie. Shirley remembered the trip mainly for Noah's irritating and inveterate tourism and for her own abysmal morning sickness and powerful food cravings. She had been so angry on one occasion, she recalled, that when Noah had returned without maple syrup to the B and B in Stratford-upon-Avon, she had threatened to throw up the landlady's breakfast forthwith into the washbasin and to poke it down the sink with the bristle-end of Noah's toothbrush. The event had taken place in the year in which Ali had cut her first adult teeth. She had also, in that memorable year, cut her teeth of literacy on the first of the Beacon Readers.

For a wedding present, Noah had given her a fine gold chain, Shirley said, measuring exactly twenty-four inches in length, to wear around her waist. The idea had been to ensure against an increase in girth – pregnancies excluded. She had worn it for almost twenty years and had removed it only for the duration of her pregnancies. Both times, with the assistance of diligent and systematic exercise which came easily to her, she had been able to reassume the chain within two weeks of having given birth. Ali was startled to think of her husband as a man who would, so to speak, confine his bride in chains, and offered up grateful, silent thanks for the advancement which twenty-odd years can, in certain cases, wreak in the soul of a man. The object reminded her vaguely of *La Chaîne Haute Fidélité* which had long been a feature of the toy cupboard, and had finally made its way thereafter to a Labour Party jumble sale.

'Shirley,' Ali said, 'What made you take it off? Divorce?'

'Sterilisation,' Shirley said. 'One naturally takes one's jewellery off prior to anaesthetic. I never put it back. Pardon me, Alison, but have you actually been sterilised?'

'No,' Ali said firmly. 'I have not.'

'I recommend it,' Shirley said, 'for the sexual freedom it affords.'

The next day, coming upon Ali over her painting, Shirley engaged in a generous effusion of praise.

'Finish it,' she said. 'I want to buy it.'

'I had in mind sometime,' Ali said politely, 'to show it to my husband. He only saw the beginnings of it.'

'Forget it!' Shirley said. 'I'll pay you two thousand dollars for that painting.' Ali drew in breath.

'But it isn't even finished,' she said. 'I should need a month at least to finish it. It's tricky. It needs a decent, strong north light. And then, I have the children to care for.'

'Finish it,' Shirley said. 'I want it in four days. I am leaving, as you know, after the weekend.'

'*Four days?*' Ali said. 'You must be mad.'

'I just changed my mind,' Shirley said. 'I propose to pay you three thousand dollars for it. Finish it.'

'Three thousand dollars is roughly equivalent to the cost of all our airfares to Johannesburg,' Ali said. 'It's actually one hell of a lot of money.' It occurred to her that there was potential stature to be gained from footing the bill for one's own airfares, especially now that Noah would be watching his spare cash in order to pay Hattie's detestable school fees. But one would of course be kept most *terribly busy*. Busy as Noah. There would be no time at all to sleep. No time to shop or buy food. One might even – like Thomas Adderley – be too busy to make love properly. Who could tell?

'It's actually one hell of a painting, Alison,' Shirley said.

'I've never really been busy before,' Ali said. 'Not for money. Not since I taught school.'

'I'll pay in advance,' Shirley said. 'Finish it, Alison, I want it.'

TWENTY-THREE

Noah RETURNED to England on a flight from New York after an uncongenial and largely wasted summer. He had hated his absence from Ali and – having been undermined in advance by the apparently precarious state of his marriage – he had found the travelling more tiring than usual. Then, while Ali's telephone call from Johannesburg had been all that was affectionate and conciliatory, it had done him no good at all to learn that she had gone halfway across the world, moved, she had said, by an old copy of Byron, but to the very spot which happened to harbour the person of Thomas Adderley.

It was towards the end of this period in New York, while brooding upon this morbid circumstance, that Noah had accidentally set down his left heel into a broken paving-stone in Little Italy, where he had gone to lunch with Barbara. The jolt had caused the immediate onset of his all too familiar spinal problems and for the next few days he could shuffle about only with the greatest difficulty. Being reluctant to embark on a relationship with a new therapist so shortly before his return to England, he had prescribed himself a course of powerful muscle-relaxing tablets which had caused him to sleep out the better part of four days. He had then enlisted the aid of the kindly Barbara to massage the soft tissue around his sacroiliac joints. Being addicted to productive labour, Noah had fretted and fumed during his more wakeful moments, since the affair had seriously thrown out the schedule which he had previously devised with Barbara.

Then, when he had finally left her – armed with a silver-topped walking stick which had once belonged to her father – he had been obliged to pay a time-consuming visit to his son Shane in New Haven whose wife had so recently given birth to his second grandchild. It had rankled with him terribly that Ali had not been there to undertake the buying of gifts for the Brainbox and his sister, and that he, instead, had had to hobble grimly around FAO Schwartz, leaning on a walking stick, before heading out for Grand Central Station.

Now, on the flight for home, being full of back-pills and pain-killers, he dozed off frequently, but woke each time to find himself fervently craving the company of his wife. The sound of Ali's voice over the telephone line from Johannesburg had induced an urgent ache in the testicles which no mere osteo-narcotics would ever annul. The bald fact of the matter was that he had not been to bed with her since the first week in May and, notwithstanding his current spinal incapacity, he sustained himself in and out of sleep on a strident, swash-buckling fantasy of propelling her into the bedroom and peeling off his shirt which he would use to bind together her naked, milk-white wrists.

'Get your sweet ass on the bed!' he said, waking to find that the day had dawned and that he had said it in the hearing of a Pan Am stewardess who was at that moment looming over him with a fiendishly citric morning reviver. He reached promptly with his right hand for the orange juice and with his left for the central agony in his lower back, which was shooting out a radius of burning needles into the area of his left haunch. At Heathrow Airport he made his way to the car hire desk and subsequently drove himself home with his jacket bunched artfully into the small of his back.

The first thing which confronted Noah upon his return was Mr Parsons' section of blitzed herbaceous border, planted out grid-wise with wallflowers.

'Holy shit!' Noah said, vehemently, swearing vengeance and blood for his desecrated clematis. 'Al!' he bawled from the driveway, leaning crotchily on the silver-topped walking stick. 'What the hell's been going on around here?' The second thing, which confronted him a few seconds later, was a vision of the wrong wife seated like Madame Defarge at his kitchen table, prodigiously accomplishing a cream-coloured cardigan.

'Hi!' Shirley said. 'How are you?'

'Where's Al?' Noah demanded sharply.

'Busy,' Shirley said. 'Hey, cool it, Noah. Your wife is busy.'

'What do you mean she's busy?' Noah said, indulging the unusual extremity of raising his voice. 'I just got off a goddam plane, for Chrissakes. I expected her to be here!'

'Right now she's busy painting,' Shirley said. 'Twenty-four hours a day. She's out with her easel, chasing cows. Take a seat.'

'Not just now thanks,' Noah said. 'Just now I'd like to find my wife. I'd also like to find out who's been busy with my plants.' He moved forward, wincing stiffly as his weight shifted.

All the while Shirley had not stopped her knitting, but now she put it down on to the table and stared hard at him.

'Pardon me for uttering a truth so brazenly self-evident,' she said, 'but Noah, your back is in spasm.'

'Sure,' Noah said conceding the point reluctantly. 'Right now it's not too comfortable.'

'My poor boy,' she said. 'Don't be so pompous with me. You are in considerable pain.' She got up very promptly and swept the table clear of her knitting. Then she flicked briskly at stray crumbs with a kitchen towel. 'Can I help?' she said. 'You want to strip to your shorts and lie right here on the table? It's a better height for me than any of your beds.'

'Thanks,' Noah said weakly. 'Shirl, you're a doll.'

'Watch your language!' Shirley said. 'I'm no doll. I'm a chiropractor.' She helped him to step up with the aid of a kitchen chair and arranged his limbs expertly in appropriate attitudes.

Then she blew on her hands and rubbed them together removing surface chill.

'You've gotten a little overweight, my friend,' she said. 'But I guess that darling, talented wife of yours has no objections to your girth. How is it you got so lucky?' Noah intermittently gave out small shameless grunts as he let the marvellous, violent grinding of cartilage wash over him.

'Other side now,' Shirley said. 'Right side please, with your back towards me. Relax, Noah.'

'Shirl,' Noah said. 'You're a great lady. How is it you always knew so exactly what I needed?'

'Professional know-how of the best kind,' Shirley said. 'Don't get metaphysical with me.' She ran her fingertips searchingly up the length of his spine, uncovering his subtle misalignments. 'On your back,' she said. 'Just fix your eyes on the pinboard now. Relax, Noah.' Noah eased himself over and allowed his cranium to rest heavily in the palms of her hands. As he stared out towards the North Korean Working People on William's postcard, he gave a moment's passing thought to the brotherhood of man. Then Shirley wrenched with a wonderful deftness at the vertebrae of his neck.

'Shirl,' he said. 'Tell me something. How are things with you these days? Like are you happy or unhappy?'

'I'm in shape,' Shirley said firmly. 'Don't you worry. I jog. I find that it channels compulsions. You maybe ought to jog, Noah? Maybe not. Maybe it would kill you. Too many people need you right now. This is tender, am I right?' she said. 'Just here?'

'That's right,' Noah said. 'Exactly there.'

When Noah stepped gingerly from the table he felt much better; tender but refurbished by that laying on of incomparable hands. Only the ache in his testicles still burned unabated.

'Better?' Shirley said. Noah was moved.

'Much better, thank you,' he said. 'Shirl, you want to know something? Once I loved you deeply. I was always loyal to you. Why was it you treated me so badly?'

Shirley swiftly took up his clothes and handed them to him in a bundle, without flinching. Then she reached for her handbag and her knitting.

'Get your shirt on, Noah,' she said. 'Cover all that gross, ageing flesh and don't be absurd. Bye now and take care! Tell Alison I'll come by tomorrow to collect my picture.'

'Picture, my ass,' Noah said unpleasantly as he fastened his shirt buttons. 'What picture? What the hell have you been up to, Shirley? What are you doing here in my house? It was you that got to work out there on my garden.' Shirley laughed. She lingered for a moment to help him with his cuff-links.

'I gave a lecture at the orthopaedic hospital,' she said. 'Subsequently your adorable wife happened to sell me a painting. Her most recent painting. She's busy finishing it.'

'Not that painting with the oranges?' Noah said. 'But that's her best painting. She's gonna keep that painting.'

'Wrong,' Shirley said. 'I just paid her three thousand dollars for it. You could try making her a higher offer, but I'd contest it. She already sold it. To me.'

'*Three thousand dollars?*' Noah said. '*Are you crazy?*'

'Like you value it so much, she must let you have it for nothing?' Shirley said. 'I paid her in advance. The money is already spent. She used it to buy three air tickets to Johannesburg. The picture's mine.'

'Shirley,' Noah said shrewdly, 'since when did you care so much for owning paintings? What you want is to own a part of my wife. Is that a way of getting to own a part of me, I wonder, or are you merely wishing to set the cat among the pigeons?'

Shirley laughed. 'I guess that all my life I was a cat among pigeons,' she said. 'Be reasonable, Noah. You get the artist. I get the picture. Just bear in mind that Alison is busy right now. Your wife is honouring a commission. I want you to remember that. Right now her time is worth around two-fifty dollars an hour. Have a nice day.'

TWENTY-FOUR

A LI HAD GONE OFF that morning in pursuit of the cows. The farmer had moved the herd to graze in new pastures which had constituted a minor set-back for the completion of the painting, but the problem was now all resolved. Ali had set off early and had followed the herd, scarcely stopping to dress herself. She had merely drawn from the cupboard the first comfortable garment to hand, which had turned out to be the old Adidas pants in which Noah dug the garden. Finding these considerably too large in the waist, she had resorted to a sizeable fold and had fixed it with the first available pin. This had chanced to be the Men Against Sexism badge which had fallen from Mervyn Bobrow's handbag. The painting had temporarily taken over Ali's life. Joy in the task of completing it had produced a fervent light behind the eyes and had lent a fire to her appearance from which no unbrushed hair and outsize gardening trousers could detract.

She had sent Hattie to Brighton with Arnie that morning, in the latter's hired Fiat, since Arnie – who had given up his flat and taken up residence for his last week in England in the Glazers' house – had offered himself for the job of fetching Camilla. Daniel had spent the morning catching up on sleep under the eye of Shirley who had, for the third day running, come to relieve Ali from all familial obligations, and in the execution of this service she had been uniformly splendid. With her conference over and her amorous life temporarily in cold-storage, she had thrown herself single-mindedly into the task of caring for Ali's children.

She had driven them to London the previous evening for a West End performance of *Toad of Toad Hall* and had brought them home still bright-eyed at midnight after a carnivorous buffet in the Piccadilly Hotel. Earlier in the week she had coerced both children into brisk country walks, heaping lively scorn upon Daniel's aversion to nettles and mud and effectively repressing Hattie's assertions that all properly conducted walks led in straight lines towards ice-cream shops. To Ali's greater amazement Shirley had got both children to bathe without protest and to ingest a fresh green salad tossed in oil and vinegar.

It was only when Ali returned from the fields to find Noah's hired car in the driveway and to hear the strains of Count Basie on the record player that it came to her how giddily time had raced. Noah's return threw her into a mood of immediate joy. She raced into the house, passing her husband's bags in the hall, and came to a stop in the sitting-room doorway. Noah, having been frustrated in his efforts first to find his wife and next to take a shower, had retreated there to the sofa with the previous day's *New York Times*.

'My dearest Noah,' Ali said. 'You're back! I wasn't there. I'm so sorry.' Noah drank in her appearance gratefully from head to foot before he spoke.

'I see that you have become a Man Against Sexism,' he said.

'Oh,' Ali said. 'It's Mervyn's. He left it here ages ago. I am using it to keep up my trousers. That is to say, I am using it to keep up *your* trousers. Isn't it elegant? I ought to have got dressed for you but I have been so terribly busy.'

'I heard,' Noah said. 'Shirley told me.'

'I liked her, I must tell you,' Ali said. 'She's been here for ten days at a conference.'

'I heard,' Noah said again. 'She told me before she left. She'll call back tomorrow lunchtime. She said to tell you.'

'There's just one thing about her I've been saving up to ask you,' Ali said. 'Between you and me, does she ever stop talking about her sex-life?' Noah shrugged.

'I read on a plane one time about a tribe in the Pacific,' he said. 'They have a "doing chief" and a "talking chief". I guess Shirley's just had to make the transfer from one chieftaincy to the other.'

'Oh no!' Ali said. 'Not at all. She's not been idle, I assure you. As a matter of fact, she's been initiating William Lister.'

'I don't want to hear it,' Noah said. 'Al, you're looking good. How is it your husband's absence so markedly improves your looks?'

'It's the sun,' Ali said. 'And the whole business of going home and finding it isn't home after all. Home is here with you. I have found it settling, Noah. I feel better. How are you, my dearest man? Do you think that you could see your way clear to stepping forward and holding me? You see, I have missed you so terribly.' Noah's mouth as he kissed her tasted pleasantly of stale airline coffee. Then she laid her hand on the bulk of his groin.

'If that's all for me then I'm flattered,' she said. 'I'm also greatly relieved.'

Noah smiled. 'For whom else do you imagine?' he said, but Ali shrugged.

'I don't know,' she said, 'but I have harboured an intermittent fear that one of those fun-loving DJFs in the personal columns of the *New York Review of Books* would have snapped you up – especially since Shirley told me about the great shortage of able-bodied heterosexuals in the US of A.'

'Bullshit,' Noah said. 'They're maybe no longer lining up at her door, that's all.' Noah spoke brutally, through an old hurt which Ali had never before suspected or understood. Meanwhile, Noah had removed the Men Against Sexism badge from the Adidas pants in the interests of easier access. 'Get your dia-phragm,' he said. A shock-wave jolted Ali from the beginnings of pleasant erotic abandon.

261

'Oh my God, Noah,' she said. 'I never collected the new one!' Slowly and deliberately, Noah withdrew his hand from the exercise pants and wiped female juices irritably on his trousers.

'So what happened to the old one?' he said murderously. 'Al, this better be good.'

'The bald fact,' Ali said, 'is that the last time I used the thing, I forgot to take it out. It went nasty. It began to grow a kind of disgusting mustard cress up my crotch. I had one truly horrendous, scary night with contractions and hot flushes. The doctor put me on penicillin. You were asleep in your study at the time. I ought to have woken you and told you, but I didn't like to in the circumstances.' Noah beat his fist quietly against the door jamb, raising his eyes to heaven as he felt the elevating, airborne fantasy of the previous night decay and fall around him.

'You screwed up,' he said. 'I might have known you would. Goddammit, Al. How is it that you can't so much as practise infidelity without being grossly unhygienic along the way?'

'It could be that I'm too chronically monogamous to "practise infidelity" without flagellation,' Ali said. 'As to the great "infidelity", Noah, I'd love to know how you found out. I have tried hard not to believe that Arnie told you.'

'William Lister is your man,' Noah said reluctantly. 'He wrote me a letter.'

Ali's mouth dropped open. 'The miserable swine,' she said. 'However could he have known?'

'He guessed, maybe,' Noah said. 'Forget it, Al. I did tell you not to let him in.'

'True,' Ali said. 'Too true. And now I'll tell you something else about my epic indiscretion, shall I? It might at least be of interest to you to know that it never got off the ground. There wasn't the time. What with the signal failures on the railways and the botch-up over the babysitting, the man barely had time to admire the good-size purple bruise you'd kissed on my neck before we had to jump back into our clothes and say goodbye. Neither of us was wearing a functioning watch. In short, he never *came*, Noah, for what that's worth to you. He had a lunch meeting and he couldn't linger. Mrs Gaitskell was minding Daniel and needed to be gone. Her husband was waiting for his tea.'

'Al,' Noah said, swallowing hard. 'Are you in effect trying to tell me that you failed to consummate your burning life-long passion for this – this Nigger in the Woodpile; this wretched, black trouble-maker – and all because your cleaning woman's incompetent, sexist male partner *couldn't fix his own snack?*'

'He isn't black,' Ali said. 'I've been telling you that for years. Neither does he "make trouble". He's just a decent social democrat in a country which doesn't recognise that position as a virtue.'

'Okay,' Noah said. 'And then you returned home and you screwed up on the diaphragm, which – if my diary is anything to go by – you didn't need anyway. Al, you know what you deserve right now? You deserve to get knocked up.'

'All right,' Ali said. Fondly and susceptibly, her thoughts flew towards childbirth; towards the midwife's ear trumpet pressed to the full-term abdomen; towards Noah's thoughtfully suppressed yawning, as he passed the night with her in the labour room, quietly swapping urbane, obstetric knowhow with the officiating doctors.

'Are you kidding? Noah said. 'You want me to be collecting toddlers from the playgroup concurrently with collecting on my Old Age Pension? Not on your sweet life, Alison.'

'You are of course perfectly right,' Ali said. Ever since he had taken possession of the Men Against Sexism badge, she had been obliged to hold up the exercise pants, bunched in one hand at the waist, like Jan Arnolfini's wife. 'You could practise premature withdrawal,' she said helpfully. 'Mrs Gaitskell says it's what her husband always did, until she had her change. He used to buy himself a packet of contraceptive sheaths once a year as a Christmas treat.'

'Is that so?' Noah said dryly. 'And how about the lady's Christmas treats?'

'I reckon she had the bath salts and the Cadbury's Milk Tray,' Ali said. 'I didn't like to ask.'

'Well,' Noah said, 'unless you've got any more constructive suggestions –'

'But yes,' Ali said eagerly. 'I have. Noah, I have! If you could possibly cross my palm with a fifty-pence piece, then I'll get you a packet of condoms right away. Just help me to find the car keys. You need not look so horribly stuffed-shirt, you know. I don't plan to get them down the pub from a slot-machine in the Gents.' Noah, though he had come a long way since the day on which he had fixed a gold chain around Shirley's waist, still found – unlike his research associate – that he balked at the idea of having a woman supply him with rubbers.

'I heard you just earned yourself three thousand dollars,' he said evasively. 'How come you can't pay?'

'It's a cheque,' Ali said. 'I don't mind paying by cheque, you understand, but I'd prefer to deal in sterling.' Noah moved with her into the hall and bent cautiously to take up the walking stick.

'I'll go myself,' he said. He kissed her warmly on the mouth. Then he handed back to her the Men Against Sexism badge. 'Here,' he said. 'You're losing your pants.'

Arnie had meanwhile driven to Brighton that same day, in order to bring home Camilla, and had taken Hattie with him for the ride. Upon his return to the Glazers' house, he stayed no longer than it took to deliver Ali's two daughters into the driveway. It was Friday and he meant to put in a good eight-hour stint at the hospital.

'So long, girls,' he said agreeably. 'Somebody drove a truck through the Master's plants, I see.'

'It was Mr Parsons!' Hattie said excitedly. 'It was me who saw him do it and I told Mummy. I was the one who told her. Mr Parsons *mowed* Daddy's plants. Arnie, he *mowed the flowerbeds*!' But neither Arnie nor Camilla was listening to her. They were arranging an outing that evening to a late-night cinema show. Arnie Weinberg was offering her stepsister a double-bill of old

Henry Fonda movies and at the same time entertaining himself with the idea that Camilla was too young to have seen them first time round. The offer piqued Hattie. If youthfulness was the prerequisite for an evening out with Arnie, then what about her? She was so young she hadn't even *heard* of Henry Fonda. It was probably all because Camilla had pierced ears. It wasn't fair. And to think what lengths she had gone to in the car on the way down to make herself agreeable to him! She had kept going all the way with a sheaf of entertaining anecdotes relating to her new cat Susan, whom Arnie had insisted ought really to be called 'Fido'. She had told him all about the headmaster's funny jerseys and the funny way he always talked in assembly, moving his mouth in and out like that, as if they were at lip-reading classes, and about what she had said to Rebecca when the vicar had smelled of whisky that had made Rebecca almost die laughing. She was *sure* that he was always drunk, she said. You could smell it. It had all made Arnie laugh like anything. That was until he had suggested paying her two pence for every mile that she could pass in silence. She had even gone to the lengths of honouring him with a preview of her new school uniform before they had set off, with the lovely blazer and the Panama hat and everything. But on the way back he had insisted that Camilla sit beside him in the front seat and he wouldn't even agree to them taking turns – even after she told him the back always made her feel car sick . . . It was 'safer' for her to be in the back, he said. It was true that Daddy absolutely never let her or Daniel sit in the front seat but that was different. Daddy was much more fussed about safety than Arnie. Arnie liked to take risks. That was what made it the best treat in the world to partner him in the bumper cars at the St Giles Fair. Anyway, he had been inconsistent. If it had been all right for her to sit in the front with him on the way down, why was it suddenly not all right for her on the way back? She stamped off into the house without saying goodbye and went to find Ali. She wanted Ali to know how it was all because of Arnie and Camilla that she felt so sick. Really sick. It was the kind of sick that only proper fizzy lemonade from the shop could make better.

Ali was on the telephone, talking to Julie Horowitz.

'Do you know about Thomas, by the way?' Julie asked. 'About the shots.'

'Shots!' Ali said, leaning weakly against the wall. 'Oh Julie – is he dead?'

'Christ, Ali don't you ever read your newspapers?' Julie said impatiently. 'Thomas is fine. Only someone blew several large holes in his motor car. He wasn't in it at the time.'

'Not this time,' Ali said morbidly. Julie laughed.

'The car is a total write-off. He's having to use mine. Have you seen *Vogue* this month?'

'No,' Ali said. 'Why?'

'Thomas again. He's in it. Do go and buy it. He's looking extremely chic, in his corduroy jacket with Liberty lawn elbow patches. Lorna made the patches, I shouldn't wonder.'

'What do you mean?' Ali said. 'Is he modelling his clothes?'

'No, *no*,' Julie said. 'He's being the up-and-coming theatrical gent. But what a lot of media coverage! To be a political martyr and a man-about-town all in one week! That Bobrow of yours is *eaten up* with envy, but he left town last night, I'm glad to say.'

'I see,' Ali said. 'Gosh.'

'I'll tell you why I 'phoned,' Julie said candidly. 'Though Thomas will tell you himself in due course. His son Andrew wants to leave this bear garden. He wants to fiddle a residence quali- fication and try for Oxford. Can he come and stay with you?'

Ali swallowed hard. 'Does he like curry powder in his scrambled eggs?' she asked.

'Not as far as I know,' Julie said. 'He does chain-smoke and chew peppermints at the same time. But all adolescents have filthy habits.'

'The answer is no,' Ali said firmly. 'He can't come. That's unless he gives up smoking. Smoking isn't allowed in this house.'

'What do you mean, "isn't allowed"?' Julie said. 'Does your old man run a concentration camp there, or what? Let me talk to him.'

'He's resting,' Ali said.

'Resting? In the early afternoon, the poor geriatric. Wake him up for me.'

Ali laughed. 'He came off a night flight this morning, Julie,' she said. 'I wouldn't think of it. Don't be so bossy. What I'm saying is a lung man and a teenage nicotine addict can't coexist. Not in my house.'

'Something's happened to you,' Julie said. 'You used to be so readily exploitable. I assured Thomas that you would be infinitely exploitable.'

'Thanks,' Ali said. 'You make yourselves sound like Rosencrantz and Guildenstern. Why do I like you both so much?'

Noah had not heard the telephone ring. After making love to his wife he had taken the precaution of disconnecting the bedroom extension, and had slept out the course of the afternoon. He woke in the early evening to the smell of frying food and went to take a bath. Then he made his way on bare feet down the carpeted stairs towards the kitchen. He could hear that on the kitchen radio a melodious sixteenth-century Virgin was praising God in Latin for her immaculate conception. It crossed Noah's mind to praise God at that moment that he had taken care not to get Ali pregnant. Daniel would start school that September and he looked forward in consequence to a decade of serene and uninterrupted coffee sessions with her up in his attic study.

Through the kitchen doorway he could see her with that wonderful faraway look which always turned him on. She was in the act of dispensing orangey freezer-food fish cakes to her three children, coaxing them loose from the pan with a spatula, but to him it seemed she looked beyond fish cakes towards plumed helmets and water-lilies. He took the pan from her hand and kissed her on the mouth.

'Sit down, Noah,' she said. 'There is food here, of sorts, but I'm warning you that it's low. There's none of your Szechuan Chinese exotica here as you see. There's no "Live Carp" here; only some very dead fish cakes.'

'I'll eat whatever's on offer,' Noah said.

The girls were greeting him excitedly. Camilla called out to him.

'Noah!' she said. 'Noah, you're home!' Hattie scraped back her chair and flew at him in the leopard-skin disco-suit, unloading a flamboyant rag-bag of traveller's news.

'And in *Juicy Lucy's*,' she said, in conclusion, 'they had green plastic chairs that went round and round! And the lady gave me ice-creams cheaper than anyone else because I went there so often. Mummy let me go there *all the time*!'

'So you had a great time,' Noah said as he embraced her. 'You have some cute new freckles on your nose.'

'I haven't!' Hattie said. Beyond her from the table Daniel was staring at him impassively over a poised spoon. Droplets of milk were falling delicately into the child's lap. It did not pass Noah by that his youngest son was beautiful; nor that he badly needed his hair cut; nor that Ali was allowing him to eat Sugar Puffs for his supper. But what point in raising any objection? Ali would merely conclude that deep down he wanted to eat Sugar Puffs himself. It had to do with jars of Christmas mincemeat and lines of marshmallow fish, he decided. A curious, arrested compensating for pleasures past denied. Noah blamed the Bauhaus. He concluded to his own satisfaction that her abortive and somewhat farcical assignation with Thomas Adderley had been a symptom of the same phenomenon.

'How are you, son?' he said. Daniel made him no immediate reply. He was busy reflecting that, with his father's return, the long nights in his mother's bed had regrettably come to an end.

'Your hair is wet,' Daniel said finally, feeling that speech was necessary.

'You're right,' Noah said. 'I just washed it.'

Camilla was meanwhile patiently waiting her turn. She wore a feather dyed purple hanging from one ear, and purple-tinted ballet slippers on her fine narrow feet. Her skirt, which was short and crenellate, she wore over a ruched nineteen-forties bathing suit with a halter neck. In her lap, Noah observed with some surprise, she held a small marmalade cat. As he bent to kiss her the feather gently brushed his cheek.

'Hi, Camilla,' he said. 'How you doing? I take it that the cat is a part of your costume.' The kitten at that moment, perhaps with fatally bad timing, chose to mount the table where – with the claws of one exquisite, velvet paw – it dragged the fish cake clean off Camilla's plate and began to chew imperturbably at the edges. Hattie and Daniel shrieked with delight at the kitten's deft and barefaced cheek, but Noah stiffened fastidiously.

'Get that animal off the table, Camilla,' he said. 'Come on now and make it quick.'

'Him's a her,' Camilla said, as she lifted the small culprit down. 'Oh go on, Noah, admit that she's just too beautiful. Admit that you love her to bits. You can't not think that she's gorgeous.'

'Dammit, Camilla,' Noah said, being wholly unmoved by the kitten's saccharine graces. 'I have always made myself perfectly clear about domestic pets. I do not want them in my house. I would take it as a great favour if on your next visit home you would leave that feline in Cambridge.'

'Sorry, sir,' Camilla said. 'Diddums won't sniff the grub, not ever again. Not never stick her nosie-pies into the num-nums. Bad girl, Diddums-pussie!'

'Camilla,' Noah said. 'Will you cut the garbage and get that animal out of my kitchen? At least while we eat. Put him outside. Afterwards you and I will discuss his territorial rights here.' Hattie flared in agitation.

'Susan *can't* go out!' she said. 'She'll get lost. Anyway, she's *not* Camilla's. She's mine. I brought her specially – all the way from Johannesburg!' The ensuing silence was terrible. As the implications of her outburst began very slowly to dawn upon poor Hattie she took on the look of a person struck dumb with terror before a firing squad.

'Mummy knew nothing about it,' Camilla said eventually. 'Hattie hid her in some hand-luggage. But Hattie didn't know it was illegal. Look, Noah. Dear Noah, please be nice about it. Please don't do your nut.'

' "Nice",' Noah said through his teeth. ' "Nice", Camilla? I'm always nice. My daughter deceives her mother and smuggles a high-risk animal from a rabies area for which the maximum sentence is a year in prison or a fine of five hundred pounds. She disregards her parents, breaks the law and – just incidentally – puts my vivisection licence in serious jeopardy, and I must be "nice", you say? Sure I'll be nice. Confine that animal securely in the toolshed till I take it to the laboratory and shoot its abdomen full of barbiturate. Then afterwards I'll act like it never happened.' Camilla rose without a word and walked towards the outer door. Her feet in the silence sounded lightly on the brick-tiled floor. The door opened as she approached it. Arnie was stamping slightly on the doorstep, the sun low behind his head. He had appeared with magical timing to offer her his charm, like a pedlar with a box of shiny trinkets. Camilla, as if hypnotised, walked straight into his arms.

'Cam,' he said. 'I'm early but shall we go?' For Ali to watch him place his hands on her daughter's bare and lovely shoulders came as a sudden and disturbing revelation. She knew, of course, why he had come so early. Croak, croak. Arnie had always been there, utterly charming, utterly selfish; enduring like a predestined frog-prince on the edges of Camilla's evolving female consciousness. Arnie would be so much, much more deadly than any hennaed undergraduate playing the piano among dandelions; than any pretty-faced vicar's son with his pockets full of Housman. Arnie would be the person who would break Camilla's heart. Then he would leave for California. Arnie looked up over Camilla's shoulder.

'Noah,' he said affably. 'You're back; you're awake. How do you feel?'

'Fine,' Noah said grimly. 'Just fine.' Camilla pushed the kitten quickly into Arnie's hands.

'Arnie,' she said. 'Lock her in the toolshed and shut the window tight. Noah wants her shut in the shed.' A tear spilled from her eye which she brushed away with the back of her hand. 'I'll get my jacket,' she said.

Arnie took the cat. He looked around the room and straightway read the cues. Hattie was sobbing tears like golf-balls into her fish cake. Daniel sat open-mouthed and curiously impassive, wide-eyed and delicate like a Piero angel; unmoved. Ali's familiar, tell-tale red blotches had sprung up about the throat and cheek bones. It called to mind for him the general smothering error of familial commitment and breeding. Here was Noah's family of tender-hearted carnivores lining up in sorrow and rage over the fate of one small cat, and Noah standing among them like Bluebeard.

'See you later!' he said. 'Come on, Cam, let's hit the road.'

TWENTY-FIVE

NOAH, WHO WAS last to sleep that night, rose earliest next morning. He rose at six and found himself faintly haunted by the presence of William Lister's ghost. William's cut-price instant coffee granules stood on the kitchen workboard. William's newspapers fell through the letter slot. Pointedly Noah pulled on his clothes and walked the distance to the village newsagent to exchange these for *The Times*. He tried hard not to think about his garden which had been violated by one of that breed of hard-luck charlatans whose representatives still wove their way from time to time into Ali's life. Some dubious old chancer, wandering westward from the Social Services Department. A powerful need for caffeine began to overwhelm his system. It reminded him that he had not actually troubled to quiz his wife on the two French railway cups in the garage, but their presence there had by then lost its menace. It was perfectly clear to him from what Ali had said that Thomas Adderley had not been near his garage. And for a person such as Ali – who was capable of cutting cheese with her credit card on summer picnics – all manner of domestic improbabilities were after all made possible.

Homecoming had been a decidedly mixed blessing, he considered, but his whole frame rejoiced at being back again with Ali. Being a loyal and generous man, it had not crossed his mind to blame her for the wretched affair of the marmalade kitten;

even though it had been her absurd indulgence towards the children which had now forced him into the role of villainous patriarch. Over the fate of the kitten he had been resolute, and had driven promptly to the research unit where he had – as he said – 'dealt with' the animal. Ali, on a sound instinct, had begged him to return with the corpse. In this she had turned out to be quite right.

Hattie at first was not to be coaxed from the darkness of her bedroom where she sobbed under a Holly Hobbie quilt, making wet corkscrews of her wild hair, but she had finally sat up and had thereafter thrown herself with gusto into the macabre ritual of the burial. She had gone on stridently to dictate the kitten's needs for the after-life with her usual strength of character. Susan needed rose petals, Hattie said, pink rose petals, and a whole box of her favourite Swiss baby cereal. She needed the small fur-fabric mouse impregnated with catmint herb and the singing of 'All Things Bright and Beautiful'. Then, with a final placing of one tin of Whiskas kitten food in the grave, Hattie had turned the sod over the kitten's lifeless form and had returned to bed with her mind satisfactorily composed.

It was Ali who had seemed most distressed by the animal's death. She had gone to bed so quiet and white and listless that Noah, in attempting to comfort her until she slept, had rendered himself wide awake. He had then retired to his study for some hours, where Camilla found him after the late-night film, plugged into his earphones and drinking whisky with his feet on his desk. Having been deaf to her entry, he jumped a little when she touched him.

'Sorry, Noah,' she said. She smiled at him so exactly as her mother did, appeasingly. 'I gave you a fright,' she said. Noah took off the headphones and laid them in his lap. Then he took his feet off the desk.

'Sit down,' he said.

'Are you all right?' she asked.

'Sure, I can't sleep, that's all. How was the movie?'

'Where's the cat?' Camilla said. 'Did you take it, or has it escaped? It's not in the shed.'

'I took it,' Noah said. 'It's dead. Listen, Camilla, don't imagine that the episode has left me feeling good. I'll get the child another kitten if necessary, just exactly like the last. There was no way I could have allowed her to keep that animal – not without compromising all of us. No person of sense imposes a burden of secrecy on a nine-year-old child. The truth will always out.' Camilla shuddered then, but whether from distress or sudden cold he could not determine.

'Female ginger tabbies are hard to find,' she said. 'And Susan had the smallest speckle of white on the end of her tail. Did you notice? Just like the tiniest spatter of milk. Anyway, won't a kitten give you asthma?'

'The drugs get better all the time,' Noah said dryly. 'All of them tested on live animals, of course, like our lamented friend.' Camilla chewed on her lower lip and found it hard to speak.

'You *did* put her down, didn't you?' she said, hating to ask.

'You tell me what you imagine I did,' Noah said coldly. 'You think I nailed it live to a board, or what?'

'I think you put it down,' she said.

'Thank you, Camilla,' he said. She reached out apologetically and touched his arm.

'Dear Noah,' she said. 'Are you sure that you're all right? You look so thoughtful. Are you worried about Hattie?'

'Some,' Noah said. 'Hattie has behaved outrageously. I believe that she wants rather serious taking in hand.'

'Oh go on!' Camilla said. 'You were never so headmasterish with me; so puritanical. Mummy tells me you've signed up the poor child for that god-awful dump with the prison uniforms. That place where Mr Bobrow sends his child to school. Are you buying her a course in "character building"?'

'In literacy,' Noah said. 'Hopefully in numeracy too. That's all. But I do happen to believe that Hattie will be less of a nuisance when her abilities are usefully employed and directed.'

'"Habits of industry",' Camilla said. 'You're sweet, Noah. You are old-fashioned. I do love you. I love you most dearly. I have always known you to be the best thing since sliced bread – right from that very first day when you kept gritting your teeth and telling Mummy to fasten her seat belt. Do you remember?'

'I do not remember gritting my teeth,' Noah said. 'But I remember thinking you and your mother were two very beautiful women.'

'Is Mummy all right?' Camilla said.

'I guess,' Noah said.

'You don't give much away, do you?' she said. 'Mummy has been a bit funny lately, I've noticed. Ever since you went to Bologna. She's not menopausal or anything, is she?'

'No,' he said. 'That's as regards your first proposition. I can't answer for the "or anythings".'

'God save us all from brainy men,' Camilla said. 'You're telling me I don't speak properly. I'm sorry. But seriously, what's the matter with her? Why did she go rushing off to South Africa like that?'

Noah shrugged. 'Why not? It's where she comes from.'

'So?' Camilla said. 'We don't all go running back to where we come from. Only if we're a bit dotty, like Mr Bobrow. You know. Like the way he embraces Judaism once in every ten years or so. I believe she's having a crisis; a reversion of some sort.'

'Sometimes it helps to go back,' Noah said. 'She's okay. She's just fine, Camilla. Believe me.'

'This Adderley person she used to know,' Camilla said persistently. 'He's featured in *Vogue* this month wearing paisley elbow patches. God, he isn't half gorgeous, Noah.' Noah smiled evasively.

'He's too old for you,' he said. 'Elbow patches or no.'

'*Me?*' Camilla said. 'For *me?* But you don't really mean that about age, I hope. I'm in love, Noah. That's really what I came in to tell you. I've never been in love before. Until now I've just had strings of men.'

'Congratulations,' Noah said. 'With whom are you in love?'

'With Arnie,' Camilla said.

'You're not serious,' Noah said.

'Don't tell him, will you?' Camilla said. 'It might alarm him. I wanted to tell you that the whole thing has been entirely my responsibility from start to finish. I seduced him, and with great difficulty. He was laboriously honourable about the whole thing.'

'The hell he was!' Noah said.

'No, truly,' Camilla said. 'I threw myself at him most insistently. He kept expressing himself with great propriety on the matter. He seemed to think that you might mind.'

'I see,' Noah said. 'And what did you answer to that overnice and wholly irrelevant qualm?'

'I told him that you thought I was so immoderately promiscuous anyway that you would be most of all indifferent,' Camilla said.

'That's not true,' Noah said. 'I'm never indifferent to your well being.'

'I know,' Camilla said. 'But leaving that aside, it's all quite different when you're in love. What I mean is that I had to have him. I know now with absolute certainty that I want Arnie and nobody else. I wish the hours away when he isn't with me. I have no assurance that he will ever want me anything like as permanently or as exclusively. In fact I think it highly unlikely, but I will struggle not to hold it against him. What else is there for me to do?'

'Nothing,' Noah said, marvelling at her clarity and her courage. At that point he got up from his chair and put his glass down on the desk-top. He planted a kiss on her forehead.

'Go to bed,' he said. 'What is there that I can say to you? If you're wanting coffee for two, in the morning, call room service, that's all.'

'You're nice,' Camilla said. 'I knew you would be nice. Perhaps we could have fried rose petals instead of coffee? I read a recipe last term for fried rose petals, to be eaten by brides at midnight. To tell you the truth, Noah, Arnie says we are not to share beds under your roof. Isn't that decorous? I mean for a promiscuous letch like Arnie. I hope you're going to bed too, because you look exhausted. If you sit here all night knocking back your duty-free, you will damage your liver, you know.'

Hattie was next to wake. She joined her father in the kitchen wearing nothing but her small bikini pants and a violent marigold T-shirt bearing the words 'Sunny South Africa'. Seeing Noah there at the table, she climbed on to his knee and sucked cosily at her thumb.

'Can I get another kitten?' she said.

'Sure, baby,' Noah said with a good grace, because he knew now for absolutely certain that Hattie had won the last battle in the pet war, and that he himself had lost it. 'I *would* have gone to jail for Susan,' Hattie said. 'I would have if I'd had to.'

'I know,' Noah said. 'But they don't actually put small children in jail, Hat. Their parents are held to be responsible for some of the things which they do.' Hattie looked quite shocked.

'Do you mean Mummy would have had to go to jail because of me?' she said.

'Don't worry about it, Hat,' Noah said. 'Nobody's going to jail.'

'Can I really have a kitten?' she said. 'Truly?'

'Yes,' Noah said. 'So long as you keep it out of the bedrooms and out of my study.'

'And can I have my ears pierced as well?' Hattie said, jumping in hopefully while blessings to the bereaved were being dispensed.

'No,' he said firmly.

'When I'm older?' Hattie said. 'Like when I'm ten?'

'Like when you're eighteen maybe,' Noah said. 'Some good things are worth waiting for.'

'Mummy's had her ears pierced,' Hattie said. 'Did you notice?'

'Sure I noticed,' Noah said. 'Do you take me for a blind man?'

'And do you hate it?' Hattie said.

'I love it,' Noah said truthfully, since – to his own surprise – he had discovered Ali's pierced ear lobes to be quite irresistibly sexy. 'I bought you a beautiful book, Hat,' he said and he reached across the table and handed to her a hardback poetry book for children, liberally endowed with shiny pastel illustrations. He had bought it for her on the day he had gone bearing gifts to the Brainbox and his new born sister.

'Thanks,' Hattie said and graciously she leafed through her book, though her heart cried out in disappointment for disco roller-skates like Rebecca's. 'I like the pictures,' she said truthfully, because there *was* a lovely picture of a gypsy lady called 'Old Meg' who was all alone on a scary moonlit moor with crags, and she looked sort of wild and brave. Hattie found the picture an inspiration, but she couldn't quite say why and did not try. 'Why are the pictures called plates?' she said. 'Because they're not plates, are they? They're pictures.'

Ali rose at nine-thirty after a restless night of troubled dreams which, having meandered through bullet holes and lifeless cats, had fixed, as usual, upon Camilla. When Ali was troubled it was safe to say that she always dreamed about Camilla. Camilla at three, pulled away from her at cattle trucks or lost on refugee trains; backdrops of barbed wire as in Käthe Kollwitz; Camilla abducted on her way from school; Camilla, trying through tears to pull at parachute strings while aeroplanes flamed in the air. Camilla, as now, disintegrating horribly into particles and atoms before her eyes. Ali woke in terror and ran to the window wanting evidence of Arnie's hired motor car in the drive, but the car was not there. Shaking, she entered Camilla's room to find the empty bed. Perhaps because she was not yet wholly awake, she threw back the covers out of old habit and checked the bed for urine stains. There was nothing on the sheet but a small speck of menstrual blood.

'Camilla!' she called at the bathroom door, but Camilla was not there. Neither was she in the kitchen where Noah sat reading verse with Hattie.

'Noah,' she said shaking visibly, 'Camilla is not here. Arnie's car has gone. What's happened to them?'

'They're home, Al,' Noah said patiently. 'For heaven sakes I saw them come in last night. They parked by the barn not to wake anyone. It was late. Sit down. Relax.'

'I had a dream,' Ali said. 'Where is she?'

'Search me,' Noah said, a little evasively. 'Taking a bath; taking a walk; asleep maybe. Relax.' Ali stared at him.

'She's in Arnie's bed!' she said with sudden violent illumination. 'That philandering bloody bastard has got her in his bed! I'll kill him.' The outburst was not wise before Hattie – a spurned stepsister who jerked violently in Noah's lap, grinding the bones of her pelvis sharply into his testicles and crashing his teeth together with the upward twitch of her head. Noah winced and responded in kind. He smacked her hard on the tender sunburned flesh of her exposed thigh. Ali drew in her breath and watched transfixed, as the brazen imprint of his hand sprang up fast and telling on the skin. Tears of surprise and shock sprang to Hattie's eyes. She leaped to her feet, snatching up the poetry book, and lifted it in readiness to bang him on the head with it. Then, instead, she flung herself wildly at Ali.

'I HATE HIM! HORRIBLE PIG!' she screamed. 'ANY-WAY, I DIDN'T WANT A STUPID POETRY BOOK! SO! I'LL NEVER TALK TO HIM AGAIN! NEVER! SO!' She ran from the room and up the stairs, slamming doors fit to wake the dead. Ali's reproachful glance was enough to make Noah rise up in his own defence, though she said nothing.

'An honest response, Al,' he said. 'An honest response is sometimes necessary. Did you ever get kicked in the balls?'

'I didn't see,' said Ali. 'But whatever she did you oughtn't to have hit her.'

'Pardon me,' Noah said impatiently, on his four hours' sleep, 'but there is room for only one saint and martyr in this house and, baby, it ain't gonna be me. The child needs constraints. Any child needs constraints. Al, for God's sake sit down. Calm down. You're living on your nerves, do you know that?' Ali was visibly shaking by now, on behalf of her daughter.

'What I'm telling you,' Ali said, 'is don't hit my children. Don't you dare ever hit my children.'

'And how about you not feeding mine on Sugar Puffs?' Noah said. 'I don't "hit children", Al, for Chrissake. Sometimes I defend myself against violent assault, that's all. Hey, listen, can I get you some breakfast?' He made a move to accommodate her at the table, but Ali turned away and began to hack crudely at yesterday's loaf on the workboard.

'Would you like some toast?' she said. 'There's no coffee. I'll shop this morning.'

'I'll shop,' he said. 'I'll take the kids. Have yourself some time off. Finish the painting.'

'It's finished,' Ali said. With the painting finished and along with it the days of creative intensity, Ali felt drained and flat.

'How was the gallery interview?' Noah said. 'You never told me.'

'I stood it up,' she said. 'I forgot. I'm sorry. How I must pain you with my lack of ambition.' It was perfectly true that Noah promptly experienced on her behalf a small undemonstrative agony.

'I don't want for you to be ambitious,' he said, 'only for you to be happy.' Ali was fidgeting with bolts on the grill pan. 'How's the old lady?' he said.

'Lousy,' Ali said. 'She's been put into a home. I went to see her there. It's not a good way to go, believe me. The old aren't very nice, Noah. They grumble and they smell. They fidget with their false teeth. No wonder doctors don't like geriatrics. No wonder lungs and hearts are generally more popular.' Noah ignored the jibe sensing that the moment was not appropriate for taking issue with her.

'Her neighbours said there was a fire,' Ali continued slowly. 'They sent for an ambulance and for the firemen. Margaret suspects the landlord. She says he was trying to prise her out. There was no fire, she says. Only a bit of smoke from singed dog meat.'

'For Chrissake, Al, there was a fire,' Noah said. Even before he had said it, Ali knew that there was no way that Noah would not believe the neighbours and the landlord. Profound and gaping differences in allegiance would appear before them which – though affection and loyalty would help them to be tolerant – would never be resolvable. It made her sad.

Arnie appeared suddenly, shirtless, myopic and rumpled, stretching idly like a waking cat.

'What time do you have, Noah?' he said. 'Darn it. I lost my watch last night.'

'Five after ten,' Noah said. 'It's late. God knows how you sleep so well in a house full of children slamming doors.' Arnie laughed on a careless yawn, and staggered to the kitchen tap.

'Hi, Al,' he said.

Ali turned on him a pent-up and hostile stare which, without his glasses, completely passed him by. She found herself resenting his half-naked indolent intrusion into her kitchen; his yawning ease, his underarm hair, his nasty, grizzling wart. It was then that she noticed, to her further intense annoyance, that he was wearing, in his pierced ear, one of the small roseate clusters given to Camilla by her stepfather.

'You are wearing my daughter's earring, you swine,' she said. 'Take it off!'

'Pardon me?' Arnie said, and he compounded the insult by putting an arm around her shoulders. Ali threw him off.

'I said take it off!' she yelled violently. 'And put your clothes on before you come into my kitchen. Do you mind?'

'Hey, wait a bit,' Arnie said. 'The *earring*, did you say? Are you talking about the earring? Camilla gave it to me. What d'you think? You think I stole it?'

'You bloody well seduced her, Arnie Weinberg,' Ali said. 'And in my house. Go on. Deny it.'

Arnie, having stipulated separate beds the previous night, had woken in the small hours to find Camilla sharing his comforter and weeping quietly in remembrance of a small dead cat with a white speck on the end of its tail. She was dressed inadequately in a thin sleeveless nightgown, her arms goose-pimpled from the cold, her feet like blocks of ice. Arnie, who had gone to sleep in his soft twill shirt, peeled it warm off his back and wrapped her in it. In the bleary haze of a heavy sleeper, he had leaned down and groped on the carpet for his thick, discarded sports socks which he had then pulled on over her feet. After that he had drawn her into the warm zone of his bed before returning, very promptly, to sleep.

'Sure, I'll deny it,' he said, filled with righteous indignation. 'Your daughter came to my bed last night, Al. She was crying over the cat. Nothing happened.'

'Like hell!' Ali said.

'Cut it out, Al,' Noah said warningly. 'Drop it. Drop the whole subject right now.'

'Nothing happened,' Arnie said angrily. 'Al baby, your daughter has her period, as a matter of fact.'

'Oh indeed?' Ali said sarcastically. 'And that would stop you I suppose?' Having said it, the greater awfulness dawned upon her that it quite possibly would.

'Oh my God!' she said in disgust. 'Now I see it all. You can screw everything in skirts between here and Middletown just so long as there's no bleeding. Is that right? Oh my God, I almost believe you.'

'I said *drop* it!' Noah said. 'Behave properly, Al, or get out of the kitchen. Go get a shirt on, Arnie. Al's upset. Can't you see that? She's emotional. She's upset about the cat. She's readjusting. She's protective of her children.'

'One of her goddam children just bit me in the leg,' Arnie said ruefully. 'I offered to help the kid tear up a poetry book since the project was giving her some trouble. Meanwhile, she's taking up most of the bathroom. Do you mind if I pee in what your wife's gardener has left of your flowerbeds?' He made a timely exit through the kitchen door.

'And while we're on the subject,' Ali said, turning to Noah with a wish to dredge up grievance, 'can you tell me why you brought the child a poetry book? How often do you read poetry?'

'Al,' Noah said wearily, 'the grill pan is on fire.'

'Poetry is for women, I suppose?' she said. ' "Created by men with women in mind". Like Crimplene. I hope you brought a poetry book for Daniel?'

'Daniel can't read,' Noah said. 'Al, the grill pan is on fire.'

He leaped from his chair as a column of black smoke rose to the ceiling. Stretching over her, he grabbed the flaming pan by the handle, but as Ali turned to face it, they came into collision. An accumulation of William's bacon grease, melted and bubbling treacherously, slopped over both of them, down on to Noah's left forearm and on to Ali's right. Both of them yelled in pain.

'Jesus Christ!' Noah said, crashing the pan down on to the workboard where the flames subdued and died. He took her by the hand to the sink where he held first her arm and then his own under cold running water.

'Sorry, Al,' he said, moved beyond conflict towards inexpressible pity by the injury to her flesh. Ali, undone by pain and by pent-up emotion, sat at the table and cried. Noah sat down beside her, while between them they watched the white blisters rise from the red.

'Mine's bigger,' Ali said. 'Much bigger. Say, doesn't it stink of old dripping in here? A touch of the old streaky rashers, what? I may not be *cordon bleu*, but I don't leave other people's grill pans full of stinking pig fat, do I?' Chastely, Noah kissed her cheek.

'I love you more than my life, Al,' he said. 'I always have. I always will. Can we go out for breakfast? I need coffee.'

'All right,' she said. 'But I have driven out your esteemed, half-naked colleague. Why do you think I care? Is it that

Camilla's sexuality disturbs me? Does it make me jealous? I surely don't want that ever-so-slightly bent Middletown hip for myself, do I?'

'Let's just say you're worried about your daughter,' Noah said. 'That's fair enough – I'll make you a deal. You worry about Camilla and I'll worry about Hattie.'

'Hattie's all right,' Ali said. 'Hattie will go far.'

'Only if the country discovers a sudden need for a good hanging judge,' Noah said. 'How's your arm feel now?'

'Not bad,' Ali said. 'It feels all right.'

Camilla came wafting through the kitchen, trance-like and breathing sleep. Yesterday's eye make-up smudged her cheeks, but could do nothing to sully the remarkable purity of her extraordinary looks. She had on Arnie's socks and Arnie's shirt, the latter flapping loose at the cuffs. She moved right through the kitchen and on into the garden where she embraced Arnie from behind, leaning her cheek on his spine between his bare shoulder blades and rocking him slightly to and fro. Ali, in spite of herself, was profoundly moved. It was while she watched them that the telephone rang. Noah took the call, reaching for the receiver with his unblistered right arm.

'Glazer,' he said abruptly, not wanting the intrusion. Mervyn Bobrow, just back the previous morning, was talking fast and furious with his mouth full of news.

'Hello stranger!' he said. 'It's Mervyn. I didn't expect to find you at home.'

'I come home once in a while to have Al launder my shirts,' Noah said. 'Also to ensure that I stay on the payroll. But I understand that you've done some travelling yourself of late?' Ali could hear Mervyn's laugh, touched with a hint of obsequious malice.

'By profession you travel in time, of course,' Noah said. 'But it seems that you have also travelled in space.'

Ali turned aside from the precarious idyll in the garden to consider admiringly that when it came to the cut and thrust of articulate malice, her husband was no mean slouch.

'Thomas Adderley has had his car blown up,' Mervyn said. 'I 'phoned to tell Ali. Is she there?'

'She knows that already,' Noah said. 'Listen Mervyn, I'll tell her that you called.'

'Congratulate her for me,' Mervyn said. 'I've heard that a West End gallery is buying her paintings these days. Eva and I would also like to buy something of hers as a matter of fact. Have meant to for quite some time.'

'I'll tell her,' Noah said. 'But she ain't cheap. She's selling around three thousand dollars.'

'*Dollars!*' Mervyn said. 'If she's selling in the States, then I suppose we have missed the boat. Incidentally, we have William Lister staying with us at the moment. Eva wondered about a nice, impromptu get-together for dinner tonight. Say seven-thirty for eight?'

'Regrettably,' Noah said, 'it's out of the question for us. Al is suffering from severe burns right now. She got entangled with an unwashed grill pan. You might tell William Lister.'

'Will do,' Mervyn said. 'And give her my sympathies.' Ali was looking up at him admiringly as he replaced the receiver. 'Severe burns?' she said. 'God, Noah. When you really want to you can lie like a pro.'

In the garden Ali made her peace with Arnie, holding out her hand to him self-consciously.

'Arnie,' she said. 'I'm sorry. I think that it is true to say I have had a rather bad time of late. Things have been difficult for me.'

Arnie drew her affectionately towards him, within the shadow of the garage, and kissed the fingers of both her hands.

'You know something, Mrs Glazer?' he said wickedly. 'You still got damn nice pins.' She made a gesture with her hand. A gesture as of casting off or of sowing; as of throwing magic beans into the air. For she saw the whole of her past life firmly behind her as a riotous black comedy upon which the curtain could now fall. And were she to have woken the next morning to find a beanstalk sprung to heaven outside the window, it would have given her no surprise; no terror. Nor any need to climb.

In the bathroom Hattie had stopped shredding her poetry book. Swinging violently from anger to regret, she gathered up the tell-tale pieces and threw them into the lavatory bowl. Then she tried to flush the evidence away, but the pieces clogged the U-bend. In panic she watched the waters rise and rise. Then she slammed down the lid and stood on it. Fervently she counted to a hundred to make time pass before she dared to flush again and peer into the bowl. Mercifully, the water level had sunk.

'Phew!' she said. 'Thank goodness!' Daniel was thumping on the bathroom door needing urgent access. Quickly she took up the book in its reduced condition and retired with it to her bedroom, where she locked the door on intruders and settled cross-legged into a chair. Seduced by the limpid, fairytale illustrations, Hattie leafed on until she came to where, among crags and larch trees, Old Meg was gathering faggots. The poem was written by a man called John Keats whom she had heard her mother talk about and she began to read it. It reminded her of her mother's friend who was an old lady called Margaret, and who lived all by herself and didn't eat properly. Crying her private tears into the text and wiping her nose on her T-shirt, Hattie discovered herself in the web of its rhythms and in the mazes of its fine, stoical agonies.

THE END

A NOTE ON THE TYPE

The text of this book is set in Baskerville, and is named after John
Baskerville of Birmingham (1706–1775). The original punches cut
by him still survive. His widow sold them to Beaumarchais, from where
they passed through several French foundries to Deberney & Peignot
in Paris, before finding their way to Cambridge University Press.

Baskerville was the first of the 'transitional romans' between the
softer and rounder calligraphic Old Face and the 'Modern' sharp-
tooled Bodoni. It does not look very different from the Old Faces,
but the thick and thin strokes are more crisply defined, and the
serifs on lowercase letters are closer to the horizontal with
the stress nearer the vertical. The R in some sizes has the
eighteenth-century curled tail, the lowercase w has no middle
serif, and the lowercase g has an open tail and a curled ear.

Pick a Powerpuff Path

brand-new blossom

by Paul Siefken

Scholastic Inc.
New York • Toronto • London • Auckland • Sydney
Mexico City • New Delhi • Hong Kong • Buenos Aires

ISBN 0-439-33227-3

Cover and interior illustrations by Bill Alger

Designed by Mark Neston

12 11 10 9 8 7 6 5 4 3 2 1   2 3 4 5 6 7/0

Printed in the U.S.A.

First Scholastic printing, January 2002

⭐ Read This First!⭐

Sugar...Spice...and Everything Nice...

These were the ingredients chosen to create the perfect little girl. But Professor Utonium accidentally added an extra ingredient to the concoction—Chemical X!

And thus, The Powerpuff Girls were born! Using their ultra superpowers, Blossom, Bubbles, and Buttercup have dedicated their lives to fighting crime and the forces of evil!

But now, The Powerpuff Girls need your help! In every *Pick a Powerpuff Path,* you will take on the role of one of the characters and help save the day.

In this adventure, you will be Blossom, the brainy leader of The Powerpuff Girls. Blossom's tired of being nice, helpful, and responsible. And following the rules, as she always does, makes it too easy for the villains she fights to predict her actions. So, in this book, she will try to become a "brand-new Blossom"—an un-nice person and a rebel, in fact! You will choose what Blossom will do as her new behavior takes her into some sticky situations! The story will be different depending on the choices you make. After you choose a path, follow along to continue the story.

When you're done, you can start over, make new choices, and read a completely different story.

So what are you waiting for? Rebels aren't very patient!

The city of Townsville! Home of The Powerpuff Girls! Although the Girls are stuffed with super-powers, they're also made of the same stuff as ordinary little girls. Bubbles has the sugar, Buttercup brings the spice, and everybody knows that Blossom is everything nice! But when it comes to bad guys, Blossom's all business. And it looks like she'll be busy soon, because the evil monkey genius, Mojo Jojo, is up to something sneaky at the jewelry store!

Mojo Jojo stood outside of Townsville Jewelry Store looking much too innocent.

"Pay no attention to me, people of Townsville," Mojo said loudly. "I am just an innocent bystander like you. You can see that I am innocent because I am not committing any crimes." To himself, the villain muttered, "But you cannot see my invisible robot thief, who *is* committing crimes!"

Inside the jewelry store, the Mayor was looking for a new watch with his assistant, Ms. Bellum. The Mayor of Townsville was a sweet man who loved being Mayor, and Townsville loved him. But everyone knew that the Mayor was not smart enough and was far too forgetful to have any real political power in Townsville. It was the brilliant Ms. Bellum who truly ran Townsville.

"What time is it, Ms. Bellum?" asked the Mayor.

"It's ten-fifteen," answered Ms. Bellum.

"No, it's not," said the Mayor. "It's time to get a new watch! Get it?"

"Yes, Mayor, I get it," said Ms. Bellum. "You've told that joke four times already."

"I have?" asked the Mayor. "Oh, well. Do you like that watch over there, Ms. Bellum?"

Ms. Bellum looked where the Mayor was pointing.

"What watch?" she asked.

"That's funny," said the Mayor. "It was there a second ago. Now it's gone. In fact, all the watches are gone!"

"If watches are disappearing, someone might be stealing them. Maybe you should make the call," said Ms. Bellum.

"You mean, to the store manager? To tell him to put out more watches?" asked the Mayor.

"No, Mayor, the *other* call. To The Powerpuff Girls," Ms. Bellum suggested impatiently.

So, the Mayor hurried to his limousine to call The Powerpuff Girls on the hotline.

Seconds after he finished saying, "Powerpuff Girls, hurry! Trouble at the jewelry store," the superhero sisters zoomed on to the scene, ready to solve Townsville's latest crisis.

"What's the problem, Mayor?" asked Blossom.

"Someone is robbing the store," said the Mayor.

The Powerpuff Girls looked around.

"I don't see any crooks," said Blossom. "Unless they're...aha!" Blossom noticed Mojo Jojo standing outside.

"It's Mojo Jojo!" shouted Bubbles.

"Let's get him," said Buttercup. In far too much of a hurry to use the door, she crashed through the store's front window and grabbed Mojo.

"Wait, Buttercup," said Blossom. "We can't beat up Mojo just because he's standing there. We know he's always up to no good, but we've got no proof that he robbed the jewelry store."

"What are you talking about?" asked Buttercup.

"I know it looks bad, but we need evidence that Mojo took the watches and the other jewelry before we can toss him in jail," Blossom explained.

"That is correct," said Mojo Jojo. "You have no evidence against me, so I am free to go."

The Girls could see that Mojo Jojo wasn't holding any stolen property. But they *couldn't* see the invisible robot at his side, which was carrying all of the jewelry from the store.

"Can't I just give him one good punch?" asked Buttercup.

"I'm afraid not," said Blossom.

Mojo laughed an evil laugh. "I knew that Blossom would follow the rules. She is always so nice and so predictable. But I am not nice. I am evil. So I laugh at Blossom's niceness."

Blossom was embarrassed.

"Does that mean we have to let him go?" asked Bubbles.

"Yes!" shouted Mojo. "And you can thank your sweet sister Blossom for letting me go free!"

Mojo Jojo walked down the street, laughing at Blossom. His invisible robot floated behind him.

Blossom let Mojo Jojo go free! How could being nice and following the rules cause so much trouble? Maybe it's time for Blossom to make a few changes.

That night, Blossom couldn't sleep. She was embarrassed. Her niceness was too easy to predict.

She made up her mind that, from then on, the world would see a new Blossom. A rebel! And the best way to rebel was to break the rules.

The next morning, Blossom thought about which rule she wanted to break first. She could conduct an experiment in the Professor's lab—the Professor had always forbidden the Girls to enter his lab when he wasn't there. Or she could go fight the Professor's new super-tough robot, a robot so powerful that none of the Girls was allowed to fight it alone.

If Blossom conducts an experiment in the Professor's lab, turn to page 28.

If Blossom fights the Professor's new robot, turn to page 40.

Princess took Blossom to every inch of the mall. Blossom watched Princess buy shoes and dresses and toys and jewelry. Soon, Princess had bought everything in the entire mall!

Blossom even helped Princess carry everything back to the Morbucks Mansion. By the time they got there, Blossom was so tired she could barely stand!

Then, Princess got an evil grin on her face. "Ha! You fell for it!" she shouted. "Thanks to you, I now control all of Townsville's stuff! No one can buy anything unless they buy it from me!"

"Hey! You can't do that!" cried Blossom. But there was nothing she could do. Princess had bought everything fair and square.

Being a rebel didn't seem worth it anymore, not if it meant helping Princess with her villainous plans to control Townsville. It was time to get back to what Blossom did best: being nice...and fighting the forces of evil! So she flew back to Pokey Oaks to tell her sisters what Princess had done, and how she, Blossom, had helped Princess without meaning to.

"What are we going to do?" asked Buttercup.

"Let's go to the mall and see if we can help," suggested Blossom.

When The Powerpuff Girls got to the mall, there was a party going on!

"Why is everybody so happy?" Bubbles asked.

"Because Princess bought all of our old merchandise," said the mall manager. "Now we can get newer, better stuff! The mall will be better than ever!"

"Princess spent all that money, and now she'll be stuck with everything," said Blossom.

"She deserves it for hoarding all of Townsville's stuff," said Buttercup. "Why were you hanging out with Princess, anyway?"

"I don't know. I was being a rebel, remember? I thought that's what a rebel would do. I never would have gone shopping with that nasty Princess otherwise," said Blossom.

Continue on page 64.

11

The noise woke the Professor and Bubbles and Buttercup. When they got to the lab, they couldn't believe their eyes!

"What are you doing in my lab?" asked the Professor. "You know you're not supposed to be in here by yourself. That's my number one rule!"

"Rules are meant to be broken," said Blossom, trying on her new role, and she floated right past the Professor and her two sisters. The Professor was so surprised, he was speechless. So Blossom didn't even get punished!

Later, on the way to school, Buttercup spoke up. "What's going on, Blossom?" she asked. "Why are you acting so weird?"

"What's the matter, Buttercup, haven't you ever seen someone break the rules?" Blossom responded. "Well, get used to it. Because I'm not a nice person anymore! I'm a rebel!"

"But I thought you *liked* following the rules," said Bubbles.

"Rules are boring," said Blossom. "And so is school. I think I'll go somewhere else today."

If Blossom goes downtown, turn to page 16.

If Blossom goes to the arcade, turn to page 18.

Blossom just couldn't beat this super-tough robot all by herself. She hit the emergency power switch, and the robot stopped moving.

Exhausted, Blossom collapsed on the floor.

The noise from the battle had woken the rest of the house, and Bubbles, Buttercup, and the Professor all came to the battle room to see what was happening.

"Blossom, you know you're not supposed to play with that robot all by yourself. It's against the rules," said the Professor.

"From now on, I follow my own rules," said Blossom. And she flew to the Girls' bedroom. The Professor was so surprised by what Blossom had said that he didn't even punish her!

Later, on the way to school, Blossom started bragging. "The Professor's battle robot sure is tough!" she said. "But I almost defeated him."

"You're lucky he didn't smash you into a million pieces," said Buttercup.

Continue on page 14.

"You're just jealous because I got to fight him all by myself," said Blossom.

"Why are you acting so weird?" asked Bubbles.

"I'm not acting weird," said Blossom. "I'm just being a rebel. And rebels don't go to school. I'm going somewhere else today. Good-bye."

If Blossom goes swimming in Townsville Lake, turn to page 24.

If Blossom goes to the candy store, turn to page 22.

Blossom thought that hanging out with the Amoeba Boys would be more fun. And, while they might break the rules, at least the single-celled trio wouldn't be committing any crimes—they weren't smart enough for that.

"What should we do first?" asked Blossom.

"I don't know," said Bossman. "We've never had our own turf before."

"Why don't we go for a walk?" Blossom suggested.

Blossom and the Amoeba Boys wandered all over Townsville. Everywhere they went, they broke the rules. They crossed the street without using the crosswalk. They went in through all the EXIT ONLY doors. They even talked loudly in the library!

But pretty soon, Blossom got bored. Breaking the rules was kind of fun, but the Amoeba Boys were really *dull*. Should she stay with the Amoeba Boys, she wondered, or go find something more interesting to do?

If Blossom stays with the Amoeba Boys, turn to page 36.

If Blossom goes to the mall, turn to page 35.

15

When Blossom got downtown, she saw the Gangreen Gang, a bunch of green-skinned punks, and the Amoeba Boys, a trio of single-celled criminals who were the most harmless villains in Townsville, arguing in Townsville Square.

Ace, the leader of the Gangreen Gang, was standing face-to-face with Bossman, the leader of the Amoeba Boys.

"Listen, you big blob," Ace warned Bossman. "Townsville Square is our turf. We don't want no overgrown science project wiggling all over it!"

"Oh, yeah?" Bossman answered. "Well, you stink! How do you like that?"

That was not a very good reply, but then, the Amoeba Boys weren't very good at arguing.

"I'll show you how I like it," said Ace and he gave Bossman a big shove.

Blossom had seen enough. She swooped down and stood between Bossman and Ace.

"Hold it right there, Ace," Blossom said. "I'm the only one around here who gets to beat up bad guys. Who wants to be beat up first?"

"What are you doing here, Blossom?" asked Bossman.

"Ain't you supposed to be in school?" wondered Ace.

Blossom wasn't sure what to do next. As a Powerpuff Girl, it was her job to fight villains. On the other hand, she was being rebellious today. Were rebels supposed to fight the forces of evil?

If Blossom decides to fight the Gangreen Gang and the Amoeba Boys, turn to page 49.

If Blossom decides not to fight, turn to page 62.

Blossom flew straight into Townsville Arcade. It was always open!

The only person in the arcade was Lenny Baxter, the creepy fan collector. He was playing Robot Wars. It was the coolest game in the whole arcade.

Blossom wanted to play. But Lenny had a pocket full of quarters. He might be there all day!

"Hey, Lenny," said Blossom.

"Don't distract me," said Lenny. "I'm ten robots away from beating my high score!"

That gave Blossom an idea. She flew to the window and looked outside.

"It sure is pretty today," she said. "Look! Up in the sky, it's Major Man!"

Lenny ran to the window and looked outside. (Before The Powerpuff Girls put him out of business, Major Man had been Lenny's favorite superhero.)

While Lenny was at the window being tricked, Blossom took over the controls to Robot Wars. She fired shots at super-speed, blasting every robot to smithereens. By the time Lenny figured out Blossom's trick, she had already won the game and entered her name in the high scores list.

"No fair," said Lenny. "You're not supposed to fool people like that. You're a Powerpuff Girl!"

"From now on, I'm not being nice—I'm doing exactly what I want to do," said Blossom. "And I wanted to play Robot Wars. See you later, Lenny!"

When Blossom left the arcade, she wasn't sure where to go next. She could go to school after all—but this time only to break some of Ms. Keane's rules. Or she thought that having some candy would be a nice reward for her Robot Wars victory.

If Blossom goes to Pokey Oaks, turn to page 38.

If Blossom goes to the candy store, turn to page 22.

Blossom flew straight to Townsville Park and relaxed under a big shady tree. The park was always full of people, and today was no different. All around her, people were jogging and throwing footballs and having picnics.

Blossom closed her eyes and enjoyed playing hooky and being a rebel.

Meanwhile, in his observatory high above the park, Mojo Jojo was looking through a giant telescope.

"Look at Blossom, so innocent and unsuspecting. Look at everyone having fun," said Mojo. "My invisible robot will disrupt their fun. And, just like yesterday, Blossom will let me get away with it!"

Steering his invisible robot (the same one that took the jewelry store watches) by remote control, Mojo began ruining everyone's good time! He tripped the joggers! He intercepted the footballs! He even stomped on the picnics!

Blossom opened her eyes to see what was causing all the ruckus. But she didn't see any suspects.

With all of the trouble going on around her, the park didn't seem like a fun place anymore. A rebel wouldn't be nice and would leave the park and go in search of more fun somewhere else—Townsville Lake, maybe. But a Powerpuff Girl would try to find out who was ruining everyone's day at the park.

If Blossom leaves the park and goes for a swim, turn to page 24.

If Blossom tries to fix the problem at the park, then turn to page 43.

21

Like any little girl, Blossom loved candy! So, she hurried over to the candy store for something sweet. But when she got there, three of the hillbilly villain Fuzzy Lumpkins's relatives—Furry, Fluffy, and Harry Lumpkins—were causing trouble.

"We wants all yer candy," Harry yelled at the store owner.

"Cousin Fuzzy is downright hungry fer somethin' sweet," said Fluffy.

"Take anything you want. Just don't destroy my store," said the owner. He was upset about losing all his candy, but knew that he wasn't strong enough to fight Harry, Fluffy, and Furry.

The backcountry creatures each took an armful of candy and stormed out of the door...where Blossom was waiting for them!

"All right, Lumpkins clan, put down that candy!" said Blossom.

Fluffy, Furry, and Harry looked at Blossom and started to laugh. Unlike their cousin Fuzzy, they had never fought The Powerpuff Girls before.

"How's a purty little thing like you gonna stop us?" asked Furry.

"Like this!" Blossom cried, and she socked him, sending his candy flying into the air.

Then all three Lumpkins cousins jumped on Blossom. There was a cloud of dust and candy, swirled with the bright pink of Blossom's dress! When the air cleared, the Lumpkins clan was piled in a heap on the sidewalk.

Blossom was feeling pretty good. She had defeated the Lumpkins clan all by herself! What should she do next?

If Blossom takes some of the candy as a reward, turn to page 54.

If Blossom teases Fuzzy's cousins, turn to page 25.

Even though it was against the Professor's rules to swim by herself, Blossom flew over to Townsville Lake to take a quick, refreshing dip. After all, she was being a rule-breaker today.

Blossom plunged into the lake with a big splash. But the water was so cold that her teeth began to chatter!

"B-r-r-rr, th-the w-w-water's freezing," Blossom muttered.

Blossom wanted to change the way she did things, but turning into a Powerpuff-cicle wasn't part of her plan. Maybe if she kept swimming, she'd get warmer. Or would it be a better idea to dry off and go someplace else, like the mall?

If Blossom keeps swimming, turn to page 42.

If Blossom goes to the mall, turn to page 35.

24

"Hey, you Lumpkins bumpkins," Blossom teased. "You must be pretty dumb to think you can beat a Powerpuff Girl! Don't you know I'm a superhero?"

Then Blossom showed off much more of her superpowers for the exhausted Lumpkins clan.

"I'm super-strong," she exclaimed, and she threw Harry, Furry, and Fluffy in the air and juggled them like oranges!

"I'm super-fast," Blossom said, and she flew in circles so fast that she created a small tornado that lifted the Lumpkins into the air!

"And I have ice breath," she explained, and she created an ice sculpture of the three Lumpkins using her ice breath.

But as Blossom worked on her sculpture, Fluffy managed to run off.

If Blossom chases Fluffy, turn to page 57.

If Blossom ignores Fluffy, turn to page 58.

Blossom chose the Gangreen Gang because they were so cool.

"Sorry, Amoeba Boys, maybe next time," said Blossom.

"You heard her! Get lost, you wiggly freaks!" Ace yelled at the Amoeba Boys. Rejected, the Amoeba Boys slid off to find another place to hang out.

"So what do we do now?" Blossom asked.

"Duh, we usually just stand here and look tough," said Big Billy.

"Not today," said Ace. "Today we're going on a little field trip."

"We're not going to do anything illegal, are we?" asked Blossom.

"No, we're just gonna spray paint our names on some buildings," said Ace.

"Umm, Ace, that's against the law," said Blossom.

"It is?" asked Ace. "Well, then, we'll break a few windows and dent a few cars."

"That's against the law, too," said Blossom.

"Oh," said Ace, and he tried to think of something that wasn't illegal. Finally, Ace had an idea.

"I know," he said. "We can go to the bank and ask for a tour!"

"That's not illegal, but I don't know if that's such a good idea," Blossom said. She was worried that the Gangreen Gang might try to trick her.

If Blossom goes to the bank with the Gangreen Gang, turn to page 30.

If Blossom decides to join the Amoeba Boys instead, turn to page 15.

Blossom decided to break one of the Professor's most important rules: not to enter the lab by herself!

Blossom slipped out of bed and floated down to the Professor's lab.

"I've got an idea. I'll create a formula to make me unpredictable. That way I won't always be nice," Blossom said. Then she started mixing chemicals.

KAPOW!

A huge explosion filled the room with smoke.

"Uh-oh," said Blossom. The Professor would surely hear the noise. What would he do when he found her in his lab without permission and he saw the mess? Would he punish her? Maybe if Blossom sneaked out of the house and went somewhere— the lake, maybe—before the Professor came into the lab, she could avoid getting in trouble.

If Blossom leaves the mess in the lab and goes to the lake, turn to page 24.

If Blossom stays in the lab to face the consequences, turn to page 12.

Blossom wasn't sure if there was anything wrong with taking a tour of the bank, so she agreed.

When they got there, the bank manager was worried about what the Gangreen Gang might do, but since Blossom was with them, he showed them around.

The last stop of the tour was the safe. Just as the bank manager opened it up, Ace pulled Blossom aside.

"Hey, Blossom, I need to show you the gang's secret handshake," said Ace. "Let's go to the other side of the room where there's more space."

"Okay," said Blossom. She had never learned a
secret handshake before.

When Ace and Blossom left, Big Billy sat on the
bank manager! Then Little Arturo, Grubber, and
Snake stuffed their pockets with money!

By the time Ace and Blossom returned, the
Gangreen Gang had closed the safe with the bank
manager inside.

"Where's the bank manager?" asked Blossom.

Continue on page 32.

"Duh, he went home," said Big Billy.

"But it's only ten o'clock in the morning!" said Blossom.

"Bankers don't work long hours," said Ace. "Anyways, don't you want to see our hideout?"

"I sure do!" exclaimed Blossom.

So, Blossom and the Gangreen Gang headed to the gang's hideout.

Back at the bank, the manager pulled the alarm inside the safe, and the police showed up in no time.

The bank security camera had videotaped Ace and Blossom shaking hands! The policemen couldn't believe their eyes! They called the Mayor, and he called Bubbles and Buttercup on the Powerpuff hotline to give them the bad news.

Bubbles and Buttercup zoomed over to the bank to watch the videotape. The Mayor was waiting for the Girls there. The three of them watched the videotape, stunned.

"Why would Blossom rob the bank?" Bubbles asked Buttercup after they had finished watching the tape.

"I don't know," said Buttercup. "But if it's true, we'll find the Gang at their hideout in the junkyard. Let's go!"

Bubbles and Buttercup hurried to the Gangreen Gang's hideout and blasted through the doors.

"Hi, guys!" said Blossom. "What are you doing here?"

"You know why, Blossom," said Buttercup. "To take you and the rest of these punks to jail!"

"What are you talking about?" asked Blossom.

"The bank cameras saw you shaking hands with Ace when you robbed the bank," said Bubbles.

"Hey, you tricked me!" Blossom said to Ace, and she sent him crashing through the wall of the hideout.

"I didn't know they were robbing the bank," Blossom told her sisters. "I promise!"

"Then why don't you help us clean up the rest of this mess?" said Buttercup.

So, together again, The Powerpuff Girls defeated the Gangreen Gang and carried them off to jail.

Continue on page 64.

Blossom figured that hanging out at the mall would be a cool thing to do, so she flew straight there.

While Blossom looked at the newest *TV Puppet Pals* toys, Princess Morbucks walked up next to her. Princess was a spoiled, sneaky little girl who had once tried to buy her way into The Powerpuff Girls, but the Girls wouldn't let her.

"What are you doing here, Princess?" asked Blossom. "Aren't you supposed to be in school?"

"I'm skipping school today," replied Princess. "I've got more important things to do—like shopping. But what about you? Skipping school, too?"

"I'm just hanging out," said Blossom. "That's what rebels like me do."

"Hanging out? Well, for me, shopping is hard work!" said Princess. "Especially since I can buy anything I want!"

"I never thought of it like that," said Blossom.

"Come with me, and I'll show you what shopping is all about!" said Princess.

Blossom was enjoying hanging out at the mall, but she worried that Princess might try to trick her. Also, she was starting to get hungry. *Some candy would taste great right now*, Blossom thought.

If Blossom goes shopping with Princess, turn to page 10.

If Blossom decides to go get something to eat at the candy store, turn to page 22.

"Why don't we go play in the park?" Blossom suggested.

"But the park is no place for master criminals like us," said Bossman.

"I'm sure we'll find something bad to do," said Blossom.

At the park, there were KEEP OFF THE GRASS signs everywhere.

The Amoeba Boys got excited.

"We can commit the biggest crime of our lives!" exclaimed Bossman. "Come on, boys!"

The Amoeba Boys wiggled onto the grass and jiggled their squishy bodies up and down on the grass right next to a KEEP OFF THE GRASS sign.

Suddenly, the ground started to rumble! Then, a giant earthworm exploded from beneath the ground, tossing the Amoeba Boys high into the air!

Blossom sprang into action. First, she carried the Amoeba Boys safely to the ground. Then, she slammed into the big worm at full speed! But she bounced off the worm's rubbery skin. She tried to grab the worm by its tail, but its skin was too slippery! Blossom needed help! The giant worm was headed for downtown!

Luckily, Ms. Bellum spotted the worm, which was slithering toward City Hall. The Mayor called Bubbles and Buttercup, who showed up in no time. Together, The Powerpuff Girls lifted the giant worm into the air and tossed it all the way into the countryside, where it quickly burrowed into the ground, out of sight.

Continue on page 64.

Blossom headed over to Pokey Oaks to break some of Ms. Keane's rules. But when she got there, a giant slug was munching on the playground! Bubbles and Buttercup were doing their best to stop it, but they kept slipping and sliding on the slug's slimy skin! They needed help!

Blossom blasted the giant slug with her ice breath and froze it in its silvery tracks!

"It's about time you got here," said Buttercup. "The whole school was almost destroyed!"

"What difference does it make?" said Blossom. "We still stopped the monster in time."

"But I'm all gooey!" whined Bubbles.

"I don't care," said Blossom.

"Blossom, that's not a very nice thing to say to your sister," said Ms. Keane.

"I know," said Blossom. "I'm not being nice today."

"We'd better clean up this mess," said Buttercup.

"I have a better idea," said Blossom. "Since I stopped the slug, I think you and Bubbles should clean up the mess."

"No fair!" shouted Bubbles and Buttercup together.

"I'm tired of being fair, too," replied Blossom. "So I'm going to a place where I can just look out for me, and not think about anyone else!"

If Blossom goes to the mall, turn to page 35.

If she goes to the park, turn to page 21.

Blossom chose to break the most important rule of The Powerpuff Girls: teamwork. She was going to fight the Professor's new training robot all by herself!

Before anyone else was awake in the house, she went to the battle room and turned on the robot. She set the controls for COMPLETE DESTRUCTION and pressed the START button.

The robot sprang into action! It had the powers of all three of The Powerpuff Girls combined! Blossom put up a good fight at first. She dodged laser blasts and avoided the robot's lightning-fast kicks. She even got in a few punches of her own!

But soon, she started to get tired. Her power punches began losing their pizzazz, and the zip went out of her eye beam zaps. The robot, being a machine, didn't get tired, and only increased the strength of its attacks.

The robot was winning, and Blossom was pooped. If she tried one more all-out attack, perhaps she could defeat the battle robot. On the other hand, maybe it was time to call it quits and shut the robot off, using its emergency power switch.

If Blossom decides to keep fighting, turn to page 61.

If Blossom shuts off the robot with the emergency power switch, turn to page 13.

Blossom ignored the cold and kept swimming.

But Blossom didn't know that there was something else swimming in the lake that morning: a giant lake monster with ten eyes and twelve tentacles!

Suddenly, the monster grabbed Blossom! Blossom was taken completely by surprise!

Before the monster could swallow her whole, Blossom broke free of his grip. Then, she attacked the monster!

If Blossom ties the monster's tentacles in a knot, turn to page 46.

If Blossom uses the tentacles to swing the monster around and around, turn to page 50.

Blossom decided to stay at the park and figure out who or what was ruining everyone's good time. She flew from person to person asking them if they knew what had happened. But no one had seen anything.

Blossom decided she couldn't solve the problem by herself. So, she zipped over to Pokey Oaks to get her sisters.

"Blossom, where have you been?" asked Ms. Keane.

"I was skipping school," said Blossom. "I know I'll be in trouble for that, but for now, I need Bubbles and Buttercup right away. It's an emergency!"

"Well, okay, but you have some explaining to do when you get back," said Ms. Keane.

"I thought you were too busy breaking rules to come to school," Buttercup said when Blossom approached.

"I was, but I need your help," said Blossom. "Something's causing trouble at Townsville Park!"

"Let's go check it out," said Bubbles.

The Powerpuff Girls rushed to Townsville Park.

"You weren't kidding," said Buttercup. "This place is a mess!"

"I bet that mean Mojo Jojo is behind this," said Bubbles.

"But he's not even here," said Blossom.

"He wasn't in the jewelry store, either, remember?" said Buttercup. "Let's see if we can figure out what he's up to."

Continue on page 45.

43

The Powerpuff Girls flew up to Mojo Jojo's observatory and peeked in the window. Inside, they saw Mojo with his remote control, watching the confusion in the park and laughing. They had seen enough!

The Powerpuff Girls crashed through the window and shouted, "Hold it right there, Mojo Jojo!"

Mojo Jojo hid the remote control behind his back.

"Hello, Powerpuff Girls," Mojo said with a smile. "What brings you here?"

"You messed up the park!" said Buttercup.

"But without proof, I am innocent, isn't that right, Blossom?" asked Mojo.

"How's this for proof?" shouted Blossom, and she grabbed the remote control from Mojo's hands. It was marked INVISIBLE ROBOT CONTROL.

"Aha!" said Blossom triumphantly, and smashed the robot control to pieces.

As soon as the remote was destroyed, the robot stopped causing trouble and everyone in the park returned to having fun. And *this* time, The Powerpuff Girls took Mojo straight to jail.

Continue on page 64.

Blossom tied the monster's tentacles in a giant knot. Unable to swim, the monster slowly sank down to the bottom of the lake.

"That will teach you to mess with a Powerpuff Girl!" Blossom shouted.

Blossom took a deep breath.

"Pew-wee! That monster stinks!" she said, sniffing. "But he was kind of cute, in an ugly sort of way." Even though Blossom was trying to be a rebel today, she couldn't help being nice.

Blossom looked down at the defeated lake monster and felt sorry for him. After all, he was just minding his own business when she came splashing in. And he really needed a bath—he was all covered with stinky slime.

So, Blossom swam to the bottom and lifted the monster's huge body into the air.

"Don't worry, big fella, we'll get you cleaned up," Blossom said.

But where was there a bath large enough for a slimy, ugly (but still kind of cute) monster? Luckily, the Townsville swimming pool was nearby.

"That will be the perfect place to wash up!" Blossom exclaimed, and she plopped the monster into the pool. Before long, Blossom and the monster became friends, splashing and playing games.

But Blossom didn't know that this monster was only a baby. His mother had only left him alone for a few minutes while she went fishing. Now, the worried mama monster was rampaging through Townsville looking for her baby!

Continue on page 48.

Back at Pokey Oaks, Bubbles and Buttercup got an urgent call from the Mayor about the monster. And the two Powerpuff Girls, minus their sister, Blossom, went in search of the monster. The mama lake monster was easy to find—she was ten stories tall and her tentacles spread as wide as a city block! Although the monster was one tough cookie, she was no match for Bubbles and Buttercup.

As they battled the mama monster, Bubbles and Buttercup looked down and saw Blossom playing in the swimming pool with the baby lake monster.

"No wonder she's upset," said Bubbles. "Blossom took her baby away!"

Bubbles and Buttercup brought the mama monster to the pool. She was so happy that she grabbed her baby with all twelve of her tentacles and gave him a big hug! Then, the two happy monsters wriggled back to the lake.

"I hope you're proud of yourself," said Buttercup.

"Yeah, you took that poor baby monster away from his mommy," said Bubbles.

Blossom realized that if she hadn't broken the rules by going swimming alone, she would never have taken the baby monster away from his mother. Even though she hadn't meant any harm, she'd caused a lot of trouble, both for Townsville *and* her sisters. Would her sisters ever forgive her?

Continue on page 64.

Well, even though Blossom was being rebellious today, that didn't mean that she had to stop fighting villains. Rebels fought, too, didn't they? So she just let her fists do the talking and knocked out all the members of both gangs in seconds.

"It looks like Townsville Square is *my* turf now," Blossom said proudly.

She waited for a while, to see if she would have to defend Townsville Square against anyone else, but no one else showed up. The square remained quiet. Now that she had her own turf, what was she actually supposed to *do* with it? Soon, Blossom was bored.

"Maybe there's something exciting going on at the park," she said.

Continue on page 21.

Blossom took the lake monster by his tentacles and swung him around and around in the air. As the monster spun, stinky slime flew from his body and splattered over everything in town.

Then, Blossom sent the monster plunging back into the lake.

After defeating the monster, Blossom flew around Townsville a few times to dry off. She didn't realize that the monster's slime had made the whole town—and herself—smell like fish!

Soon, all the cats in Townsville were coming outside to find out what the delicious smell was. Cats came from all over the countryside. At Townsville Zoo, the lions and tigers escaped from their cages and went looking for the yummy fish. Before long, all of Townsville was swarming with cats!

At Pokey Oaks, Ms. Keane had to stop class because the school was overflowing with cats.

"Bubbles, you can talk to animals. Why don't you ask the cats what's going on?" Buttercup suggested.

Bubbles leaned over to listen to one of the meowing cats.

"He says that something smells fishy, and the cats won't stop running all over Townsville until they figure out where the smell is coming from!" said Bubbles.

"What are we going to do?" asked Buttercup. "We can't catch all the cats in Townsville."

"I have an idea!" said Bubbles. "Come on!"

Bubbles and Buttercup headed straight for Townsville Animal Shelter. When they got there, the supervisor allowed Bubbles to ask the dogs to help chase all the cats away. But she made the dogs promise to come back as soon as they were finished.

Continue on page 52.

The dogs happily agreed to help. And in no time, the dogs had chased away all the cats in Townsville!

Now, Bubbles and Buttercup had to find out what had caused all the trouble in the first place.

At that moment, Blossom flew up.

"Hey, Girls, what's up?" asked Blossom.

"Phew! Townsville might smell bad, but *you* stink, Blossom!" Bubbles cried.

"Yeah, what have you been doing?" asked Buttercup.

"All I did was twirl the lake monster in the air," said Blossom.

"That must be what covered the town in stinky slime and made all the cats go crazy!" shouted Buttercup.

"Oops, I guess that is a possibility," said Blossom.

"It looks like we have some cleaning up to do," said Bubbles.

Since Blossom caused all the trouble in the first place, she did most of the work. Soon, The Powerpuff Girls had cleaned up all the fishy slime in town.

Continue on page 64.

"I stopped the Lumpkins clan from stealing all of the candy," Blossom said proudly to herself. "So I deserve a reward."

Blossom scooped up an armful of candy and flew off.

When the store owner saw Blossom take off with the candy, he couldn't believe it! Blossom was stealing! He called the Mayor right away.

Ms. Bellum answered the phone and listened to the store owner's story, shocked.

"Mayor, Blossom just robbed the candy store," she said, entering the office.

"What's that? Blossom just mopped a sandy floor?" asked the Mayor, confused as usual.

"No, Mayor, Blossom stole candy from the candy store," Ms. Bellum repeated.

"She did? Why didn't you say that in the first place?" asked the Mayor, and he called Bubbles and Buttercup on the hotline right away.

Bubbles and Buttercup looked all over town, but they couldn't find Blossom anywhere! Finally, they went home to break the bad news to the Professor.

The Professor met them at the door.

"Shhh, your sister is upstairs in bed," he whispered. "She's not feeling well because she ate too much candy."

"That's not all," said Bubbles. "Blossom stole all the candy that she ate!"

"She did?!" cried the Professor. "Well, in that case, Blossom, get down here!"

Blossom wearily floated down the stairs.

"What's this I hear about you stealing candy?" asked the Professor.

Continue on page 56.

55

"I didn't steal it," said Blossom. "I took it as a reward for stopping the Lumpkins clan from stealing it. Anyway, the store owner had already allowed the Lumpkins to take the candy so they wouldn't destroy the store. I thought eating the candy would make me a rebel."

"But it just made you sick!" said Buttercup.

"Did you save any candy for me?" asked Bubbles.

"Now, Girls, let's leave Blossom alone," said the Professor. "She needs to get better so she can go back to the candy store."

"She gets to go *back* to the candy store?" exclaimed Buttercup.

"She's going to help out after school to make up for the candy she took," said the Professor. "That candy should have gone back to the store owner. It was as good as stolen. Blossom, isn't there something you want to say to your sisters?"

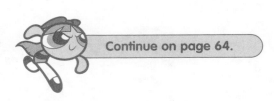

Continue on page 64.

Blossom chased after Fluffy. When she caught the runaway Lumpkins, she threw him so far that he landed all the way across town at the edge of the woods where Fuzzy Lumpkins lived!

By the time Blossom got there herself, Fluffy was nowhere in sight. Blossom figured that Fluffy had learned his lesson, so she decided not to chase him anymore. Besides, it was such a beautiful day! She didn't want to spend such a great day just flinging around bad guys. Instead, Blossom thought it would be nice to go to Townsville Park and enjoy the sunshine.

Continue on page 21.

Blossom was having too much fun building her ice sculpture, so she just let Fluffy Lumpkins go.

Meanwhile, Fluffy ran to the woods and told Fuzzy what happened.

"That Powerpuff brat's got no right to be hasslin' my kin," screamed Fuzzy.

Fuzzy stormed out of his cabin and headed to the Townsville candy store. He was so angry that he destroyed everything in his path! He smashed windows! He stomped cars! He even threw a big rock through the Mayor's office window!

"Ms. Bellum," called the Mayor. "Did I order a giant rock?"

"No, Mayor, not today," replied Ms. Bellum.

"I didn't think so," said the Mayor. "We'd better call The Powerpuff Girls."

Bubbles and Buttercup got the Mayor's call and headed straight to his office. On the way, they saw Fuzzy's path of destruction.

"It looks like Fuzzy Lumpkins!" said Buttercup.

"Let's see where the trail leads," said Bubbles.

The Girls followed the trail right to the Townsville candy store. Below, Blossom was still working on her sculpture. And she didn't see Fuzzy rushing up behind her!

"Look out, Blossom!" called Bubbles.

But it was too late. Fuzzy hit Blossom with a full head of steam and sent her flying into a brick wall.

That's when Bubbles and Buttercup stepped in.

Continue on page 60.

"Shame on you, Fuzzy," said Bubbles. "You shouldn't pick on little girls!"

Bubbles knocked Fuzzy head over heels with a superpowered uppercut!

Next, Buttercup rammed Fuzzy like a wild bull, sending him into the candy store!

"I've had enough of you pesky girls!" Fuzzy complained as he staggered to his feet. "I'm goin' home to eat me some vittles. Tell yer sister to leave my kin alone!"

Fuzzy picked his cousins up off the sidewalk and headed home.

"Are you okay, Blossom?" asked Bubbles.

"I think so," said Blossom.

"Fuzzy Lumpkins won't be bothering us again any time soon," said Buttercup.

Continue on page 64.

Blossom was tired, but she kept fighting!

Suddenly, the robot grabbed her and threw her across the room. Blossom smashed into the wall! Before she could recover, the robot hit her with a laser shot.

Just as the robot was about to stomp her like a bug, Blossom blasted it with her ice breath. It worked! The robot was covered in ice!

The robot turned on its defrosters. But as the ice melted, the robot's circuits got wet. Sparks flew every-where, and the robot lost all its power. Blossom had won!

Blossom figured she would celebrate her victory by going to the arcade to blast a few video game robots. So, she left a note for the Professor and her sisters and *whooshed* off to the arcade.

Continue on page 18.

Blossom decided not to bother fighting the Gangreen Gang and the Amoeba Boys. Instead, she waited to see what would happen next. The Gangreen Gang and the Amoeba Boys just stood there. They were too confused to do anything. Why was Blossom here? They weren't even committing crimes.

"You're in luck today," Blossom said. "I've decided not to fight you. Today, I'm breaking all the rules."

That gave Ace an idea.

"Hey, Blossom, since you're not going to fight us, why don't you join one of our gangs for the day?" he suggested. "We can show you what rule breaking is all about."

"Yeah, what he said," agreed Bossman.

"Whichever gang you choose controls the turf," added Ace.

Blossom joining a gang? This rebel business might get out of control!

Blossom knew she shouldn't join either gang. But it was only for one day, and besides, that's what a *real* rebel would do!

If Blossom joins the Gangreen Gang, turn to page 26.

If Blossom joins the Amoeba Boys, turn to page 15.

62

"I'm sorry I've been acting so unlike me," said Blossom.

"Does that mean you're back to being the old Blossom?" asked Bubbles.

"It sure does," said Blossom. "I don't care if Mojo Jojo *does* laugh at me. I like being nice, and being predictable is a good thing!"

"Why don't you leave being unpredictable to me from now on?" Buttercup suggested.

"That's right," said Bubbles. "We're used to Buttercup acting up!"

"Well, at least I don't play with dumb old dolls all the time, like you do," said Buttercup.

"Girls, stop arguing," said Blossom. "The most important thing is that we're back together again."

You said it, Blossom! Thank goodness for that! And so, once again, the day is saved! Thanks to The Powerpuff Girls!

THE END